Food and Architecture

Food and Architecture

At the Table

EDITED BY SAMANTHA L. MARTIN-MCAULIFFE

Bloomsbury Academic
An imprint of Bloomsbury Publishing Plc

B L O O M S B U R Y
LONDON · OXFORD · NEW YORK · NEW DELHI · SYDNEY

Bloomsbury Academic

An imprint of Bloomsbury Publishing Plc

50 Bedford Square	1385 Broadway
London	New York
WC1B 3DP	NY 10018
UK	USA

www.bloomsbury.com

BLOOMSBURY and the Diana logo are trademarks of Bloomsbury Publishing Plc

First published 2016

© Samantha L. Martin-McAuliffe, 2016

Samantha L. Martin-McAuliffe has asserted her right under the Copyright,
Designs and Patents Act, 1988, to be identified as Author of this work.

British Library Cataloguing-in-Publication Data
A catalogue record for this book is available from the British Library.

ISBN: PB: 978-0-8578-5734-7
HB: 978-0-8578-5685-2
ePDF: 978-1-4725-2022-7
ePub: 978-1-4725-2021-0

Library of Congress Cataloging-in-Publication Data
A catalog record for this book is available from the Library of Congress.

Cover Photograph by Samantha L. Martin-McAuliffe

Typeset by Integra Software Service Pvt. Ltd.
Printed and bound in India

Contents

List of Illustrations

List of Contributors

Ken Albala is Professor of History at the University of the Pacific and Director of the Food Studies MA program in San Francisco. He has authored or edited twenty-three books on food including *Eating Right in the Renaissance*, *Food in Early Modern Europe*, *Cooking in Europe 1250–1650*, *The Banquet*, *Beans* (winner 2008 IACP Jane Grigson Award), *Pancake*, *Grow Food*, *Cook Food*, *Share Food* and *Nuts: A Global History*. He was co-editor of the journal *Food, Culture and Society* and has also co-edited *The Business of Food*, *Human Cuisine*, *Food and Faith* and edited *A Cultural History of Food: The Renaissance* and *The Routledge International Handbook of Food Studies*. He was editor of the Food Cultures around the World series, the 4-volume *Food Cultures of the World Encyclopedia* and the 3-volume *Sage Encyclopedia of Food Issues* published in 2015. He is also series editor of Rowman and Littlefield Studies in Food and Gastronomy for which wrote *Three World Cuisines* (winner of the Gourmand World Cookbook Awards best foreign cuisine book in the world for 2012). He has also co-authored two cookbooks: *The Lost Art of Real Cooking* and *The Lost Arts of Hearth and Home*. His latest works are a *Food History Reader* and a translation of the sixteenth century *Livre fort excellent de cuysine*. His course *Food: A Cultural Culinary History* is available on DVD from the Great Courses. In the spring of 2016 his *At the Table: Food and Family around the World* will be published. He is now working on a book about noodle soups.

Nicola Camerlenghi received art and architectural history degrees from Yale University, MIT and Princeton University. He is an Assistant Professor in the Department of the History of Art at Dartmouth College where he specializes in the study of early Christian and medieval architecture, with particular interest in the city of Rome and the area of the Mediterranean. He is currently preparing a book on the architectural transformations that took place at San Paolo fuori le Mura from its construction in the fourth century to its destruction in the nineteenth century.

Lisa Cooperman is the Curator of Education at the Haggin Museum in Stockton, California. She is responsible for providing interpretation for the museum's late nineteenth century American and European art collection as well as developing and managing all education related aspects of the museum's exhibitions, programs and services. In the past two years she co-curated the exhibitions *Picasso, Miró & Hawaii Five-0: Prints from the Jack Lord Collection Fortunes & Family: The Haggin McKee Legacy* and *Dark Garden: The Sculpture of Carla Malone*. She is a lead artist in *DeltaFusion* a community arts and culture collaboration, now entering its sixth year. She has provided illustrations for a number of projects with Ken Albala. Ms. Cooperman holds a BA in English Literature from Bowdoin College, and an MFA in Sculpture and Metalsmithing from Montana State University. She taught studio art at the University of the Pacific and is a member of the A.I.R. Gallery in New York. She maintains an active national and international exhibition schedule.

Kevin Donovan is an architect who has worked for award-winning Irish design practices. He teaches at the University College Dublin School of Architecture, Planning and Environment Policy, as well as at the Dublin School of Architecture, Dublin Institute of Technology. He holds a Centennial PhD Scholarship at UCD where he is researching crossovers in cultures of making, writing and architecture in mid-twentieth century France. Recent publications include chapters in *Infra-Éireann: Infrastructures and the Architectures of Modernity in Ireland, 1916–2016* (Ashgate, 2015) and *Industries of Architecture* (Routledge, 2015).

Jamie Horwitz, PhD, was professor of architecture and industrial design at Iowa State University between 1986 and 2015, and visiting faculty at MIT, The School of the Art Institute of Chicago, UC Berkeley, and was the University of Louisville's Morgan Chair of Sustainable Architecture during 2007–2008. Best known for her pioneering collection, *Eating Architecture* (MIT Press, 2004/2006), her publications on the role of product design in eating habits appear in *Gastronomica, Places, AD* and *the Chronicle of Higher Education*. Today, she cooks, paints and writes in Louisville KY and is an editor of the new *International Journal of Food Design*.

Tom Hudgens is the author of *The Commonsense Kitchen: 500 Recipes + Lessons for a Hand-Crafted Life*, published by Chronicle Books in 2010. He lives, works and cooks in Marin County, California.

Aglaia Kremezi was born in Athens and now writes and teaches cooking to travellers at Kea Artisanal on the Cycladic Island of Kea, Greece. She is currently researching and testing recipes for her sixth book. She won the Julia Child award for her first book *The Foods of Greece* (Stewart, Tabori & Chang, 1993). *Mediterranean Hot and Spicy* (Broadway) is her latest book, while *The Cooking of the Greek Islands* (Houghton Mifflin, 2000) is her best-seller. She blogs at *The Atlantic Monthly* Food/Health site, and writes regularly in Greek, European and American publications, including *Saveur*, the *LA Times* and *Gourmet*.

Ruth Lo is a PhD candidate in the Department of the History of Art and Architecture at Brown University. She was the Donald and Maria Cox Rome Prize Fellow in Modern Italian Studies at the American Academy in Rome from 2013 to 2015. Her contribution to this volume is adapted from part of her dissertation titled 'Feeding Rome: Food, Architecture, and Urbanism during Fascist Italy'.

Máirtín Mac Con Iomaire is a lecturer in The School of Culinary Arts and Food Technology in the Dublin Institute of Technology. Máirtín is well known as an award winning chef, culinary historian, food writer, broadcaster and ballad singer. In 2009 he became the first Irish chef to be awarded a PhD for his thesis 'The Emergence, Development and Influence of French Haute Cuisine on public dining in Dublin Restaurants 1900–2000: An Oral History.' He is a regular contributor at the Oxford Symposium on Food and Cookery, and is chair of the Dublin Gastronomy Symposium, a biennial gathering of food scholars and enthusiasts alike. He is currently building a research cluster around Ireland's culinary past and heritage.

Samantha L. Martin-McAuliffe is on the faculty in the School of Architecture, Planning and Environmental Policy at University College Dublin, where she directs a post-graduate seminar course on the intersection of food and architecture. She has published studies of Dublin's Victorian market halls and is presently researching the influence of maize on America's architectural identity. Since 2012 Samantha has also been an architectural historian on the Methone Archaeological Project in Greece. Her research and writing has been supported by several awards, including a Fulbright and the Royal Institute of British Architects (RIBA) Historical Research Prize. She completed her PhD in Architecture from the University of Cambridge in 2007, and is a graduate of Smith College.

Heather Paxson is William R. Kenan, Jr. Professor of Anthropology at the Massachusetts Institute of Technology, where she teaches courses on the anthropology of craft and the politics of food. She is the author of two books, most recently *The Life of Cheese: Crafting Food and Value in America* (University of California Press, 2013), 2014 winner of the Diana Forsythe Prize.

William Rubel is a writer living in Santa Cruz. He is the author of *The Magic of Fire: Hearth Cooking: One Hundred Recipes for the Fireplace or Campfire* and *Bread: A Global History*. He is now writing a history of bread for University of California Press. A longtime mushroom collector, William's article in *Economic Botany* on the historic esculent uses of Amantia muscaria, the iconic mushroom in children's books and cartoons, has inspired a reappraisal of that mushroom's edibility. William writes for *Mother Earth News*, most recently an article on distilling alcohol at home. He has a research project with the Kenyan

Samburu tribe documenting their smoke cured and fermented milk. William is the founder and co-editor of *Stone Soup*, the magazine by children.

Fanny Singer is an American art historian, critic, curator and illustrator based between Cornwall and London. In 2013 she completed a PhD on the late work of Richard Hamilton at the University of Cambridge, following which she worked on the Hamilton retrospective that toured from Tate Modern to the Reina Sofia in 2014, as well as contributing an essay to the catalogue. She is a regular contributor to a number of publications, including *Art Papers*, *The Burlington Magazine* and *Print Quarterly*, and has taught and lectured extensively in the UK. Fanny is currently co-curating a two-person survey of the work of David Ireland and J. B. Blunk, and is developing a book on the intersections between social practice and food politics.

Henriette Steiner is Associate Professor at the Section for Landscape Architecture and Planning at the University of Copenhagen in Denmark. She holds a PhD from the University of Cambridge and held a position as Research Associate at the ETH Zurich in Switzerland for five years prior to coming to Copenhagen. Her research investigates the cultural role and meaning of architecture, cities and landscapes. She is author of the book *The Emergence of a Modern City: Golden Age Copenhagen 1800–1850* (Ashgate, 2014) and is co-editor of six academic collected volumes of which the most recently published book is *Phenomenologies of the City – Studies in the History and Philosophy of Architecture* (Ashgate, 2015).

Amy B. Trubek is the Faculty Director for the Food Systems program and an associate professor in the Nutrition and Food Science department at the University of Vermont. Trained as a cultural anthropologist and chef, her research interests include the history of the culinary profession, globalization of the food supply, the relationship between taste and place, and cooking as a cultural practice. She is the author of *Haute Cuisine: How the French Invented the Culinary Profession* (University of Pennsylvania Press, 2000) and *The Taste of Place: A Cultural Journey into Terroir* (University of California Press, 2008) as well as numerous articles and book chapters.

John Tuomey teaches in the School of Architecture, Planning and Environmental Policy at University College Dublin, where he is the inaugural Professor of Architectural Design. He is a member of Aosdána, an affiliation of creative artists in Ireland. He has worked in practice with Sheila O'Donnell for more than twenty-five years. O'Donnell + Tuomey are engaged in the design of cultural and educational buildings at home and abroad. They have exhibited three times at the Venice Biennale. They were awarded the Royal Institute of British Architects Royal Gold Medal in 2015.

Acknowledgements

Fittingly, the idea for this volume emerged through a chance conversation during a meal at the Oxford Symposium on Food and Cookery. Every year the Symposium organizes and presents a series of talks around a particular theme, but 'Symposiasts' will often single out the communal meals – lunches and dinners served in the hall at St Catherine's College – as the highlights of the gathering. During one lunchtime, the conversation evolved into a discussion about the ways that food contributes to notions of regionalism and craft. That spirited exchange also proved to be a sort of epiphany for me: being an architectural historian by training, I can distinctly recall the revelation of hearing so many familiar 'architectural' terms being employed and scrutinized within a conference dedicated to food.

I have had the good fortune to develop and hone ideas about the interconnections between food and architecture through my 'Building Dwelling Eating' postgraduate seminar at University College Dublin. Many of my students have gone on to write dissertations on themes and questions that were first posited in our seminar. In addition, over the years, our discussions have been enriched by the generosity of visitors such as Kaethe Burt-O'Dea and Gerry Andrews.

Several audiences have allowed me to present and receive critical feedback on a number of themes present in this book: Maximilian Sternberg kindly invited me to discuss my work in a seminar at the University of Cambridge, and important conversations about the role of ethics in both food and architecture influenced papers presented at 'Portrait of the City' (Dublin, 2010), 'Emerging Landscapes' (London, 2010) as well as 'Food and Markets' at the Oxford Symposium (2014). A session on gastronomy and architecture at the Society of Architectural Historians annual meeting in 2011 enabled me to see, for the first time, not only the relevance of but also the enthusiasm for this topic within current debate.

Thanks are due to Louise Butler, the commissioning editor who was supportive and encouraging about this project from the very beginning, and to Jennifer Schmidt and the staff at Bloomsbury for their continued professionalism. The staff at the Richview Library, UCD, especially Catherine Bailey, provided valuable assistance. Livia Hurley and Dikran J. Martin graciously proofread portions of the volume in its last stages.

Finally, I am deeply grateful to my contributors, all of whom have brought to the table a rich conversation that will undoubtedly continue to evolve well into the future.

Preface

Samantha L. Martin-McAuliffe

Food and architecture have long held analogies. Both can be described and characterized by words such as 'tasteful', 'bland' and, most prominently in recent years, 'organic'.[1] The synergy between eating and building is embodied by the Latin verb *colere* (to till, tend), which is also the root of our modern term 'to cultivate'. Importantly, cultivation is understood as a stratified enterprise, extending from the pragmatic and mundane to the metaphorical and symbolic. In a very basic sense it is primarily agricultural, such as tilling soil and tending crops. Yet, as Martin Heidegger observed, the term also carries social meanings relating to human inhabitation and dwelling, in particular the idea of settling and taking care of something.[2] Cicero was one of the first to fuse the agrarian and figurative inflections of the term, proposing that the human mind must be cultivated in order 'to fruit'.[3] During the Enlightenment, this analogy was widened into architectural theory when J. F. Blondel defined 'taste' as the 'fruit of reasoning'.[4] Just as chefs designed recipes for fine cuisine, architectural theorists began to devise rules for good architecture.

Food studies and architecture both espouse fundamental principles, yet neither can be wholly controlled by absolute prescriptions or rigid formulae. They rely on a combination of intuition, inventiveness and even wonder. Paradoxically, however, while both fields undeniably espouse similar values, they seldom come into dialogue with one another, much less consider or integrate their approaches in pursuit of common endeavours. *Food and Architecture: At the Table* is a direct response to this situation. As such, this is the first book that explores, interrogates and illuminates the reciprocity between the vocabularies of these two fields in the present day. Fundamentally, this volume has a twofold objective: to clarify the commonalities between eating and building at the same time as it demonstrates how those working within the fields of food studies and architecture can learn from each other.

The starting point for this book was the realization that academics and practitioners from both food studies and architecture employ similar lexica to describe and characterize their work. While a great number of words are shared by both fields, this volume focuses on four key terms that surface repeatedly in current debates and discourse: 'regionalism', 'sustainability', 'craft' and 'authenticity'. These terms have been selected not solely because of their prevalence but also – and especially – because they are malleable and often ambiguous; as such, they accommodate several interpretations. They therefore tend to be misunderstood or, worse, used so casually that they become nearly empty of genuine meaning. Their etymology and root meanings as well as wider relevance often remain overlooked. The principal aim of the book is to flesh out the underlying significance and interpretative qualities of such vocabularies across the fields of food and architecture. It is essential to mention that this volume does not aim to find the lowest common denominator or absolute meaning of a given term – an impossible task. Rather, it brings together many voices that in sum clarify points of connection, analogies and also, importantly, questions of difference.

Food and Architecture is structured as an edited volume, yet it also departs from the standard anthology or collection of independent essays. Significantly, it is designed as a series of dialogues on the most pressing and relevant topics in food and architecture today. Each section of this book is devoted to a key term and contains contributions from individuals working within and across food studies and the built environment: chefs, architects and designers, as well as historians and anthropologists. The individual chapters thus represent a diversity of topics and vantage points. Additional editorial commentaries, which complement and widen the relevant points and arguments of the individual contributions, accompany each of the four main sections. It is envisaged that this methodological approach, which is rooted in critical reflection and observation, will ultimately foster more precise investigations about food and the built world. Put simply, we can make better use of these terms if we acknowledge, interrogate and consider their full spectrum of meanings.

Notes

1   While the practice of qualifying food as organic is now so prevalent that it is considered mainstream – complete with its own standards and certification process – 'architecture' maintains a more fluid, ambiguous and metaphorical relationship with this term. In the United States, organic food is certified by the Department of Agriculture, whereas in Europe the EU Regulation on Organic Farming covers the production, processing and labelling of organic foodstuffs. At this time, there is, of course, no equivalent process for architecture, the closest things being LEED certification for green building or the Passive House concept. A conference at the Pratt Institute School of Architecture led to a volume considering and exploring the interplay between the value of the organic and the built environment: D. Gans and Z. Kuz, *The Organic Approach to Architecture* (Chichester, England: Wiley, 2003). For an examination of the organic metaphor in architecture, see M. Hvattum,

'"Unfolding from Within": Modern Architecture and the Dream of Organic Totality', *The Journal of Architecture* 11 (2006): 497–509.

2   Martin Heidegger, 'Building Dwelling Thinking', in *Poetry, Language, Thought*, trans. A. Hofstader (New York: Harper and Row, 1971), 147.

3   Cicero *Tusculan Disputations* 2.5.

4   Jacques-François Blondel as cited in M. Frascari, '"Semiotica ab Edendo", Taste in Architecture', *Journal of Architectural Education* 40 (1986): 6. For a wider discussion of Blondel's interpretation of taste in architecture, see F. H. Schmidt, 'Expose Ignorance and Revive the *Bon Goût*. Foreign Architects at Jacque-François Blondel's École des Arts', *Journal of the Society of Architectural Historians* 61 (2002): 4–29. An English translation of Blondels' definition of taste is provided by L. Lefaivre and A. Tzonis, eds., *The Emergence of Modern Architecture: A Documentary History, from 1000–1810* (London: Routledge, 2004), 393–395.

1

Introduction

Cuisine and Architecture: Beams and Bones – Exposure and Concealment of Raw Ingredients, Structure and Processing Techniques in Two Sister Arts

Ken Albala and Lisa Cooperman

The most familiar and enduring example comparing architecture and cuisine hails from the nineteenth century and the magnificent edible fantasies of Marie-Antonin Carême, king of chefs and chef of kings. Carême is credited with having said, 'The Fine Arts are five in number: Painting, Music, Poetry, Sculpture, and Architecture – whereof the principle branch is Confectionery', and indeed his cakes were discernible only in scale from their non-edible counterparts. Other examples also come to mind: the towering stacks of food faddish in the 1980s, not to mention structures which themselves recall wedding cakes like the monument to King Victor Emmanuel that hovers over the Roman Forum, or the Brighton Pavilion.

But these examples obscure some of the deeper aesthetic affinities between these sister arts. Their origins follow a directly parallel development: at a vital juncture in our evolution, hominids came to depend not only on fire but also upon mechanical means of processing raw materials, rendering them edible through cutting, pounding, soaking, drying and fermentation. Thus cuisine was born. At a comparable stage, humans employed natural materials such as wood, stone and hides to fashion shelter for protection from the elements and predators. While early forms of architecture may predate the invention of cooking, both these arts have since become indispensable for human existence; both are resolutely functional, as a building one cannot enter becomes sculpture, likewise an inedible meal.

Architecture and gastronomy employ, in much the same way, compositional principles of balance, contrast, proportion, scale and emphasis. Visual and structural elements find parallels in the organization of flavours and the schema of their presentation. Not surprisingly, they also share a similar aesthetic vocabulary that describes the complex relationship to their raw materials, at times seeking to emphasize and lay bare the 'natural' or organic origin of ingredients, as well as the basic means of construction, while at other times seeking to hide through artifice the creative process to highlight the inventiveness of the artist as a moulder of unformed matter.

We might then describe two fundamentally opposed approaches to raw material as a function of the prevailing aesthetic trends. Roughly speaking, these trends divide into oppositional pairs familiar from the language of art history: classicizing and romanticizing, 'Poussinists' and 'Rubenists', *disegno ou colour* (line and colour), Picasso and Matisse. Of course, while aesthetic developments represent the continual process of synthesis, absorption and rejection of competing ideologies and practices, one persuasion usually dominates. For example, during one phase of a period artists may intentionally lay bare the beams that conceptually and physically hold a structure together, emphasizing the comprehensibility of its organization and character of materials. Likewise some cookbooks expose the structural 'bones' of a meal, not only as in actual bones on a plate but also in emphasizing the origin and straightforward honesty of the ingredients, prepared without fuss or extravagance.

Gastronomically, we are in the middle of exactly such a period and one could argue likewise architecture is undergoing an organic, sustainable phase, literally and figuratively speaking the same language as cooking. Witness the current popularity of home gardening and butchery, and the premium placed on locally sourced materials. The do-it-yourself approach to home renovation stems from the same basic impetus. The impulse to present natural unaffected ingredients stretches from the home cook and builder right up to the most expensive restaurant and professionally designed architecture.

Such periods stand in contrast to those in which the ingredients and the process are less important than the artistic statement, when the creative genius of the artist turns raw matter into something novel, intellectually stimulating, and occasionally intentionally obscure and difficult to read. In cuisine, the most contemporaneous example would be the disguised and scientifically transformed inventions of molecular gastronomy, the Ferran Adriàesque colloidal suspensions and foams. Adrià's late twentieth-century architectural parallel is Frank Gehry, in particular his geometrically gymnastic exteriors of the Disney Concert Hall and Guggenheim Museum Bilbao. It is not to say this approach cannot exist at the same time as more 'natural' artists are working, but one approach tends to prevail at a particular time.

What triggers such alternating currents of approach is a matter for speculation. In periods of austerity it is likely that people tend to forgo expensive, fussy white tablecloth meals and return to simple ingredients and traditional preparations. Contrariwise, a wildly speculative economy with fortunes quickly made leads to stiff competition for restaurants to attract ever-wealthier clients, which they do with hyper-designed food fantasies. The same process is of course involved in physical structures, going over the top when patrons want to display their wealth and sophistication and coming more 'down to earth' when tight budgets focus concerns on conservation and efficiency or a return to 'traditional' values.

An ancient example will illustrate the perennial juxtaposition of these two basic approaches to ingredients and techniques and their relation to status. In the mid-fourth-century BC the ancient Greek connoisseur Archestratus composed a verse book of recipes (*Hedypatheia* or Life of Luxury) at Gela on the south coast of Sicily. It survives in fragments in the compilation of Athenaeus written several centuries later. There is no doubt that Archestratus was responding to what he considered excessively fussy cooking using brash combinations of contrasting flavours. In one recipe for amia, a small bonito, he warns not to use too much oregano, no cheese, no fancy nonsense. Instead he focuses on the finest ingredients, sourced from places only the well-heeled traveller could expect to access and recognize. His gastronomic approach favours simple direct presentations in which the techniques are straightforward and highlight quality and freshness. This is a kind of sophistication that reflects not mere profligate wealth or abundance, but the cultural capital of knowledge, experience and *savoir faire*.

The architectural equivalent of Archestratus is a Doric temple about forty-five miles to the west in Agrigento. The Temple of Concord is among the best preserved of all ancient Greek temples, and not a single structural element of its perfect geometric balance is hidden. Bold fluted columns comprise the peristyle. The abiding aesthetic is perfectly analogous to Archestratus' cooking. It is practical, solid, earthbound and resolutely functional. Its boldness comes from scale, balance and compositional integrity. The ingredients and techniques are allowed to speak for themselves through purity without artifice.

One might argue that the opposite approach is apparent in the next great cookbook of ancient times, usually known as *De re coquinaria*, attributed to the first-century AD Roman gourmand Apicius, though probably a compilation made several centuries later judging from the language. In any case, Apicius' cookbook employs a wide array of exotic ingredients: flamingo tongues; dormice; ostrich; and sow's womb, with flavours dramatically juxtaposed through the use of salty fish sauce called garum or liquamen, the sweetness of honey, the bitterness of herbs like rue, the sourness of vinegar and the piquancy of imported pepper. Moreover, the texture of these dishes often pounded fine (like the rose patina, a smooth mixture of brains and rose petals) or cooked into a jumble of ingredients suggests that the basic elements are intentionally obscured. One would have to guess the welter of ingredients that enter into most of the dishes. Why, one may wonder, the distantly sourced flavourings, the curiously named dishes (a la Apicius or Vitellius)? These are meant to create distance from the aspiring nouveau riches. They are over-the-top inventions possible only within a massive empire of unbounded social mobility, and in particular one in which the old landed wealth feels threatened by social upstarts. The impression one gets from the cookbook is that it may well have been written for exactly this sort of person, one who is trying hard to impress, and 'pass' among social superiors.

The general tone of late Imperial architecture follows in the same spirit. A shifting axis of influences brings motifs and flavours from the east as well as a revision of ancient sources. Combined with the technical innovations afforded by the use of tile-covered concrete and brick, architecture experiences a leap to free-flowing interior spaces and decorative impulses delighted with doodads: swags, putti, balustrades, medallions in relief and stairs leading nowhere. Straightforward structural columns are replaced with marble pilasters and faux colonnades that line façades for decorative effect. The structures themselves become imbalanced, top heavy and strewn with frou-frou. Consequently, they become hard to read; the form outweighs the function and at times even defies it. The Arch of Constantine (AD 312–15) is perhaps the most analogous structure to Apicius' cookbook, not only because it too is a mishmash of earlier borrowed elements but also because the elements are tossed together in such frenetic profusion. It is almost impossible to read and the entire mass is squat and ungainly, especially compared to the much earlier and classically balanced Arch of Titus (ca. AD 81), which stands nearby to the northwest. Additionally, its purpose is purely propagandistic: it serves to declare the greatness of its subject, his conquests and the extent of his massive empire. It is meant to overawe in much the same way Apicius' recipes are often merely for shock value.

However, the switch from one approach to another need not be simply a matter of resources, political clout or patronage. A style may, on its own accord, evolve in excessively self-referential and sophisticated ways due to theoretical elaboration or because it is driven by the processes of social emulation. For example, once direct trade routes opened up to Asia in the sixteenth century, spices arrived in Europe in much greater volume and common people had greater access to them. The wealthiest of customers therefore gradually abandoned spices in most dishes or marginalized them to dessert. Thus, when fashions – culinary as well as architectural – can be imitated by social aspirants (i.e. nouveau riches), the style no longer serves as a mark of distinction, and something new must be invented to re-establish that distance in taste and discernment. At this juncture style may look backward again to reinvigorate traditional forms.

Such is the case in Renaissance Italy beginning with one of the perfect examples of humanistic architecture, the Tempietto of Donato Bramante within San Pietro in Montorio, on the Janiculum Hill in Rome. Built in 1502, it is mathematically proportioned, and perfectly balanced, showing restrained surface ornament. Most importantly, this small martyrium, a miniature house of worship, is on a human scale, not attempting to overawe, but meant for quiet reflection and the kind of direct spirituality that would so heavily influence the Reformation just a decade later. Its harmonious unity is a product of resolute belief in the values of Classical antiquity synthesized with Christianity. Without pretension or erudite reference, the small domed temple symbolizes the pinnacle of High Renaissance style.

The cookbook and health manual of Bartolomeo Sacchi, known as Platina (*De honesta volupate*), is a few decades older but comparable in its use of Classical references to describe the properties of individual ingredients. Like the Tempietto, it is balanced, sober and self-assured. It goes so far as to combine health advice with a cookbook by Martino of Como, which is a slightly older work, at least stylistically. At times his recipes are a little too extravagant or certain ingredients a little too dangerous in Platina's mind and he does not hesitate to respond to these with comments like 'I would only feed this to my enemies'. But as a whole the text is equally an expression of Renaissance taste: health is balanced with pleasure, meals should be rational, flavours balanced so as to generate the best humours and flavourings used judiciously. That is, the logic of Platina's diet is easy to understand – the strange, extravagant and exotic make way for well-tempered meals.

If we move into the next century to the age of Mannerism, the spirit of the arts has shifted entirely. Mannerist art and architecture are both intentionally obscure, crowded, even dizzying. The clarity of proportion and human scale of the Renaissance give way to surprises, marvels and sheer technical proficiency. Exoticism prevails. Arnold Hauser called this an age of anxiety, the result of recurring invasion by Spain and France. But it seems here too the engine of social mobility may once again have been at play. The sixteenth century was a period of rapid inflation and population growth. Even if one was fortunate not to have been among the lower social strata, both land and basic foodstuffs still held a high premium. In such periods, social mobility runs rampant, and the 'old' nobility naturally try to protect their position, which is reflected directly in the hyper-sophisticated palaces they built for themselves. They are meant to be 'artificial', again a positive value for them. Take, for example, the Palazzo del Te outside Mantua designed by Giulio Romano in the 1520s–1530s. On the elongated courtyard façades, triglyphs on the frieze appear to have slipped out of position, threatening to fall on the heads of observers. The joke is of course apparent only to those who know where these should be, only to the aesthetically savvy. The inside joke is brought to seeming reality once one enters the Hall of Giants, where the ceiling literally comes hurtling down from above, the walls disappearing beneath the cascade of tumbling giants and boulders. The structure is intentionally hidden, not merely through trompe l'oeil effects, but literally transforming into sculpture above one's head. The function of the room, beyond funhouse, is not apparent. But it does serve to distinguish the Gonzaga patrons as connoisseurs of the most titillating and bizarre art imaginable.

Operating on the same level is the exactly contemporaneous Mannerist cookbook of Christoforo di Messisbugo written at the Este court of Ferrara, which was closely related to the Gonzaga court through marriage. Here we find pearls and coral ground into food, not for any medicinal or gastronomic reason, but merely to flaunt wealth. In the meals described, courses proceed in staggering profusion, each laden with sweets and savouries, soups and pastries, roast fowl, fish and meat in defiance of any recognizable order or progression. Some ingredients are presented in every single course, though prepared differently in each, to showcase the genius and inventiveness of the cook (exactly as in Guilio Romano's work). Most importantly, the flavours are wildly erratic, food is disguised and sugar and cinnamon are strewn liberally on practically every dish. Foreign recipes abound – from Turkey, Hungary, France, even a Hebraic dish – the more exotic the better. Where the ingredients come from, whether they are discernible in the final meal, is not important, but rather the technical sophistication of how they are prepared, transformed, even if they ultimately confuse and repel the diner. How else can one account for a pie filled to the brim with eyeballs of tuna? The taste, if not the function, is sacrificed to the creative spirit of the chef.

It may be that every style ultimately evolves into a kind of Mannerist phase before being completely abandoned to something new. The Mannerists of the sixteenth century saw what they were doing as the perfection of Renaissance style until their works became so busy, fussy, difficult to read and filled with bizarre and obscure references that eventually they were replaced by the very straightforward, direct style of the early Baroque.

In France, where the power of its monarchy extended to most issues of aesthetic thinking, this process appeared in the cookbook of La Varenne and those that followed in the mid-seventeenth century. This generation sought to reinvent cooking with a new kind of sophistication unobtainable by ordinary people, one that depended not on any particular ingredient, expense or quantity of food, but upon meticulous technique which only years of professional training and experience could provide. It also involved the creation of canons of taste, codified by experts. The garden designs of Le Notre, and the palace of Versailles by Levau, Mansart and Le Brun, function in exactly the same way. Their rational, controlled and stoic Baroque programmes codify standards of orthodox correctness, which only the educated consumer could hope to comprehend and the thoroughly trained artisan hope to replicate. The shift from material to technique as creative signifier suggests a new kind creative possibility inherent in traditional solutions.

These canons of taste dominated European gastronomy and architecture everywhere in Europe for nearly a century. The perpetual search for novelty saw the monarchy eventually move to occupy the more intimate and functional architectural forms of the early Rococo. The direct 'authentic' and natural approach applied to food as well as buildings; food should now 'taste like itself' rather than be disguised. Buildings should exhibit integrity of materials with function as the primary consideration. It is apparent in the so-called nouvelle cuisine of the eighteenth century, when simpler preparations, explicit reference to common, ordinary and wholesome food served with less pomp and elaboration became fashionable. François Marin is perhaps the best example and his populist attitude is evident in his designing recipes not only for the court but also for bourgeois households. This reversal of approach to ingredients is nowhere more apparent than in Jean-Jacques Rousseau's educational treatise *Émile*, wherein the philosopher's young pupil is kept away from dainty fripperies and fed honest wholesome bread, cheese and vegetables. Rousseau quipped that only the French know nothing about eating because so refined an art is necessary to make food palatable for them. This taste for rusticity might of course be seen as an elaborate and highly artificial pose. There is no other way to interpret Marie Antoinette dressing up as a milkmaid and playing shepherdess in her little country dairy at the Petit Trianon and later at the Chateau de Rambouillet. With the French Revolution, aristocratic taste for asymmetry and ornamentation dead-ended in the Rococo, and the ascendancy of the First French Empire resulted once again in architecture of unadorned columns, straight lines and bold symmetry. The late eighteenth-century Neoclassical style functions much as Rousseau's natural aesthetic; in both, the structure of the ingredients is exposed to full view, the food and the buildings are easy to interpret and function prevails over style for its own sake. Thomas Jefferson's Monticello is designed exactly in this spirit.

At the risk of overschematizing these two contrasting approaches to art, and noting that in all periods there are architects and chefs who fit under either rubric, nonetheless, there are two opposing aesthetic urges that apply with equal logic to cooking and building. Just as a concern for local ingredients, chosen in season and grown with organic methods, may be a guiding principle for a home cook or in a restaurant, a building too may employ local materials, sustainably harvested and designed to work within the elements of its environment. Opposed to this 'natural' aesthetic are 'artificial' approaches, in the original positive sense of that term, that seek out exotic materials, used year-round in defiance of nature, that are transformed with scientific processes and requiring great technical sophistication. In a way that the former approach seeks directness and authenticity, the latter is elitist, obscure and intellectual. The former often draws on indigenous or vernacular sources for inspiration, while the latter employs historicizing elements removed from context, and often applied in novel profusion, indeed sometimes with a horror vacui. These two approaches may also be contrasted by their political leanings and by implication intended audience or source of patronage. The former are populist and turn to local affordable traditions. The latter is elitist, often produced in imperial contexts for wealthy patrons anxious to display the products of their colonial dominions, incorporating motifs and techniques that speak of power and far-flung connections. However, it is unsurprising that at junctures these urges intersect and overlap. At $10 a pound the heirloom tomatoes found in today's urban farmer's markets are priced for the elite shopper, while faux Tudor mansions and chateaux jostle for driveway space in the land of suburban McMansions.

The predecessors of these artificial and multi-referent landscapes, the gardens at Ramboulliet, for example, with their *anglo-chinois* vistas, are even more evident in nineteenth-century examples of the Victorians. The aesthetic sensibilities of this era are dominated by multiple revival styles: the Neo-Baroque of Garnier's Opera House and the Gothic style of Westminster Palace as well as borrowed motifs from the far-flung corners of the British Empire. Regardless of their propriety or even consistent contextual logic, Indian elements were juxtaposed with African or Chinese, in an eclectic mix. These ingredients are usually only superficially pasted onto structures whose basic frames are thoroughly English. The patrons are meant to be visually and intellectually reminded of British possessions abroad or now at home as with the relocation of the Elgin Marbles. Appropriating these motifs, as well as their people, of course, expresses sophistication and knowledge of the exotic that is still relatively inaccessible to the middle classes. In other words, they denote distinction of the same sort that first inspired the discipline of anthropology – a fleeting taste of the exotic and primitive, which most consumers would not have been expected to appreciate.

The same impulse governs taste in food of this era. Pineapples proliferate, especially with the advent of canning. Bananas and coconuts evoke tropical locales that only the wealthy could visit as tourists (i.e. not as civil servants). Mass-produced curry powders and pickles are used liberally. Freshness is not a consideration, nor is authenticity of dishes prepared as they would be in their original locales. Adaptation to suit one's own taste is perfectly legitimate. In fact, exotic ingredients are usually merely tossed onto European dishes, atop cakes or as a bit of condiment to flavour a roast chicken or to lace a fricassee. This was meant to be an international style that could be replicated anywhere and at any time, given the proper training. Naturally the style did trickle down thanks to mass production and advertising, the proliferation of popular cookbooks, and most importantly through conscious social emulation of the middle classes seeking to try the latest fashions and impress their peers with their aesthetic sophistication. Restaurant culture actively contributed to these social forces; at the Ritz Hotel in London one might, for a price, eat like one's superiors in elegant surroundings sampling the dishes prepared in the kitchens of Escoffier, which eventually found their way to more humble establishments.

A typical cookbook of this era is *Mrs. A.B. Marshall's Cookery Book*, published in 1888, which recommends dishes for their 'daintiness' and elegant presentation. They are named for nobles like the Rothschilds or labelled 'royale'. As Nicola Humble puts it, 'Mrs. Marshall mercilessly tweaks and decorates her individually portioned food, and includes many recipes for food disguised as other food.'[1] She uses fancy aspic moulds to form swans, fussy dishes meant to be admired rather than taste good. Every dish is primped with little coloured piped rosettes, mousselines or gold leaf as decoration. She even invented new dishes, perverse concoctions with bizarre combinations of flavour. It is food not only as show but also as something that will especially appeal to social aspirants. Most interestingly, Mrs. Marshall also sold equipment and colourings, and her own brand of curry powder, so people could purchase class and then impress their guests at dinner parties.

The Arts and Crafts movement, which drew much of its stringency from Gothic Revivalism, was a reaction to the Victorian aesthetic, not merely in turning to handcrafted products rather than industrial but in seeking to revive indigenous forms, using authentic materials and local ingredients that might appeal directly and honestly to the senses without intellectual obfuscation or esoteric references. The most telling description of what food might be like in the era comes from William Morris' *News from Nowhere*, where he imagines the transformation of London as a time traveller, years after a revolution in the 1970s. Along the banks of the Thames, now devoid of hideous factories, the protagonist notices salmon nets, well-tended gardens and attractive houses. The breakfast he enjoys in one of them includes fresh unadorned strawberries and 'bread [which] was particularly good, and was of several different kinds, from the big, rather close, dark-coloured, sweet tasting farmhouse loaf, which was most to my liking, to the thin pipe stems of wheaten crust' by which he means bread sticks.[2] Fresh food appears in market scenes, where baskets of fresh fruit are offered. And naturally the people are healthy, robust and attractive on such a simple wholesome diet. Elsewhere in the book he describes the setting of a dinner, but no further details than that 'there was no excess either of quantity or of gourmandise; everything was simple, though so excellent of its kind'[3] – in other words, truth in material, presentation and utility.

The change of style is evident in other cookbooks of the era. The preface of the second edition of Arthur Kenney-Herbert's *Common-sense Cookery for English Households* reads as follows:

> During the period that has elapsed since the first edition of this book was published, the Art of Cookery has advanced, and Fashion, which always influences administration of the table, has changed. People of taste now expect a short but carefully thought-out menu, simplicity in the treatment of the dishes of which it is composed, soups and sauces neither overpowered with loaded wines nor adulterated with ready-made specialties, and entrées without the colorings and frippery which in the earlier nineties gained favor with many who knew no better.[4]

That is, the nouveau riche of the gilded era who had money but no real taste had by 1905 come to tone down their vulgarity, and forced the author to practically rewrite the book, as he himself claims. On the topic of garnishing the author is adamant that there is a difference between ornamentation and garnishing, the former to be condemned as a useless 'high-class device squeezed out of a bag in diverse colours, to be scraped off the thing that it adorns, and left on the side of the plate untasted'.[5] His use of the term *high-class* obviously points to social aspiration; no one as a member of this class would describe food this way. But his larger point is that garnishes are an integral part of the dish; they are functional, but should not be excessive. And the quality of the ingredients they are made of is just as important as the main ingredient of the dish. The aesthetic, as in the Arts and Crafts buildings, is for integrity of material, utility and practicality.

The irony of this style, despite its populist, and sometimes socialist, overtones, is that only the wealthy could afford handmade furniture, artisanally crafted books, open beamed ceilings, not to mention food picked at the peak of freshness and prepared with unaffected grace. Yet this truth fits squarely within the theme of elite reinvention. When exoticism of the Victorian era could be imitated, the upper-most invented a new style which was in fact a new species of sophistication, albeit cast in terms that are ostensibly organic, native, traditional, but really entirely novel and sometimes affordable only to the wealthiest of consumers. The Greene and Greene houses of California,

Gustav Stickley chairs and Dirk van Erp hammered copper and mica lamps, all speak the same aesthetic language of cookbooks in the early twentieth century and in effect are still a means of distinction. It is not by chance that Chez Panisse, the flagship restaurant of an elite cuisine, is housed in a California iteration of this style. Widely popularized, and in turn mass-produced, these versions of aesthetic elitism were later rejected for new styles as Modernism firmly changed the aesthetic landscape.

Though the responsibility for the origins of Modernism is claimed by aesthetic, philosophical, technological, economic and social, among other, forces, the reality is likely the confluence of these impulses as well as a reaction to the eclecticism of the Victorians. The cast iron and glass marvels of Les Halles (Victor Baltard, 1851–66) and the Crystal Palace (Joseph Paxton, 1851–7) had by the early 1900s given way to architecture using improved technology – steel for lightness and strength, and concrete as a significant visual element. The bones of buildings, previously hidden under marble and brick, became exposed. Frank Lloyd Wright in the United States, Le Corbusier in France, Mies van der Rohe and Walter Gropius in Germany evolved an uncluttered, minimalist design ethos that focused on function, transparency and simplicity. Using the language of science and progress, Modernist architects created a style that sought to embody universal ideals of the future. What came to be known as the International style was all angles, glass curtain walls and the illusion of efficiency and ease.

Gastronomy likewise took a turn for the technological. In the United States, the post–Second World War boom saw home cooks enchanted by gadgets and appliances that beckoned their prim mistresses with promises of multi-course meals prepared at the touch of a button, thus ensuring a chilled martini and ample time for entertaining in the rec room. Interestingly, at the same time, the ex-pat Julia Child rigorously sought the authenticity of French cuisine, and convinced legions of American cooks that it could be theirs too with sufficient aplomb and a glass of sherry.

By the 1960s and 1970s, however, the children of the home cooks who prepared groaning buffets featuring (perhaps all at once) 'Lasagne, Fancy chicken a la king, Turkey Parisian, Chicken-rice bake, Salmon Tetrazzini, Jiffy turkey paella, Veal parmesan with spaghetti, Burgundy beef stew, Swedish meatballs, Pizza supper pie, hamburger pie, Church-supper tuna bake, Pork chop suey bake' revolted.[6] This new generation's back-to-the-land diet relied heavily on yogurt, brown rice, tofu and wild greens. And many of them lived in yurts. Modernist design had taken a swing at the organic during one of its more fanciful stages when biomorphic shapes and curvilinear forms were found in domestic architecture. But the search for authentic forms that answered the call to nature among this latest generation was better realized in redwood tree houses, carpeted tents and caravans of customized VW vans. Rootlessness did not deter these seekers; rather it conferred on them the validity of their mission. Children of the universe, they were inspired by the global scene in all its flavours, shapes and guises. Their parents were horrified.

When the pendulum swung again Postmodernism arose. This architectural style might be thought of as a commercial, large-scale and populist rendition of the hippie's multi-referent world. With its plethora of historical reference and jumbled, de-contextualized ornamental quotations, this style found favour in principled urban environments. There the ideals of the past were plucked willy-nilly in a profusion of historical reference, meaningful to elites who could 'read' the coded messages. Gastronomically this resulted in the stacked towers of obsessively garnished food of the 1980s and 1990s with exotic fusion combinations, witty references and of course the molecular gastronomy movement.

Hyper-stylization has of late given way to a more direct, fresh, local and organic aesthetic focusing on integrity of ingredients and simplicity of presentation, including the current trend towards local sustainable materials, environmental consciousness and affordability. The downturn in the current economy seems to be the most logical catalyst to this shift, though it may well be, as suggested earlier, that the Postmodern style, like the cooking of the past few decades, has finally run its course and patrons are now in search of a more refined aesthetic vocabulary that ironically values simplicity and traditional methods. No doubt current architecture and gastronomy will respond to the zeitgeist, searching anew to invent novelty from tradition, merging cultural aspiration with design solutions perhaps as yet unknown.

Notes

1   Nicola Humble, *Culinary Pleasures: Cookbooks and the Transformation of British Food* (London: Faber and Faber, 2006), 21.

2   William Morris, *News from Nowhere*, ed. D Leopold (1890; Oxford: Oxford University Press, 2009), Chapter 3.

3   William Morris, *News from Nowhere*, Chapter 16.

4   A. R. Kenney-Herbert, *Common-sense Cookery for English Households: With Twenty Menus Worked Out in Detail* (London: E. Arnold, 1913), v.

5   Arthur Kenney-Herbert's *Common-sense Cookery for English Households*, 87.

6   *Better Homes and Gardens Casserole Cook Book*, 2nd ed. (New York: Meredith Books, 1968).

Bibliography

Crouch, Christopher. *Modernism in Art Design and Architecture*. New York: St. Martin's Press, 2000.

de Botton, Alain. *The Architecture of Happiness*. New York: Pantheon Books, Random House, 2006.

Fletcher, Banister and D. Cruickshank, ed. *Sir Banister Fletcher's a History of Architecture*, 20th ed. 1896; repr., Oxford: Architectural Press, 1996.

Rykwert, Joseph. *The Dancing Column: On Order in Architecture*. Cambridge, MA: MIT Press, 1996.

Schwartz, Selma. 'The "Etruscan" Style at Sèvres: A Bowl from Marie Antoinette's Dairy at Rambouillet'. *Metropolitan Museum Journal* 37 (2002): 259–66.

Scully, Vincent. *Modern Architecture: The Architecture of Democracy*. New York: George Braziller, 1961.

Trachtenberg, Marvin and Isabelle Hyman. *Architecture, from Prehistory to Post-Modernism*. New York: Harry N. Abrams, 1986.

Wilson, Nigel. *Encyclopedia of Ancient Greece*. London: Routledge, 2005.

Wilson-Jones, Mark. *Principles of Roman Architecture*. New Haven: Yale University Press, 2000.

PART ONE

Regionalism

Commentary for Part One: Regionalism

Over the River and through the Wood: Nomenclatures of Regionalism

Samantha L. Martin-McAuliffe

The architect, curator and designer Bernard Rudofsky (1905–1988) is perhaps most famously known for his exhibition *Architecture without Architects* (Museum of Modern Art (MoMA), New York, 1964), which set a benchmark for the study of traditional building design in a global context. Its accompanying catalogue remains to this day an important reference for vernacular architecture and community-focused or collective design.[1] However, it is not widely known that one of Rudofsky's later exhibitions concerned food. *Now I Lay Me Down to Eat* (Cooper Hewitt, 1980–81) explored the material culture of everyday life, including eating utensils.[2] Never easily pigeonholed into one specific discipline, Rudofsky maintained a lifelong engagement with, and sympathy for, the habits, traditions, native materials and climate of a given locality. As such, he is still considered an important voice in the study of regionalism.

Like many terms that are commonly used to describe a locale or site, the word 'region' typically embodies a duality: while its physical limits may be ambiguous, malleable and marked by a sense of permeability, a region is just as likely to express a distinct and deep-rooted set of characteristics. Because of their sensory and highly visual natures, both food and architecture are protagonists in the contemporary debate surrounding regionalism.

In recent years both chefs and architects have reignited an enthusiasm for the local: a prioritization of materials, approaches and techniques that originate close to the point of production and consumption. In both fields an emphasis is placed on time-honoured practices as well as a connectedness to place, that is, an acute awareness and consideration of the wider context of a finished product, principally the given landscape and its attendant culture. This first section of *Food and Architecture* examines how both food studies and the discipline of architecture describe this orientation to context. Importantly, the contributions presented here widen the conventional, discipline-focused discussions of regionalism. For example, they demonstrate how architecture – understood to encompass buildings, planning and designed landscapes – can have a significant bearing on the ways that a meal is prepared, consumed and even appreciated. Similarly, they also evince how the social and cultural dynamics of preparing and consuming food are often the overriding determinants in the construction of space.

A central theme threading through the chapters in this section on regionalism is landscape. Sometimes latent, yet always at hand, both given and designed landscapes provide the raw ingredients with which we construct homes, prepare meals and build communities. Nicola Camerlenghi's contribution (Chapter 2), '*Terroir* and Architecture', productively extends the concept of *terroir* into the realm of the built environment, paying particular attention to how factors such as soil, terrain and climate inform not only food production but also building practices. His analysis of the stone walls scattered across the productive landscapes of New England illuminates the reciprocity between given environmental conditions and the specific building techniques of an agrarian culture. Built due to practical necessity out of stones from local fields, over time these walls have come to characterize the region. Indeed, their attributes and construction techniques can be imitated and even replicated on a global scale, but like many mass-produced or standardized foodstuffs, the final results do not embody or reflect the characteristics of any particular landscape.

In Chapter 3, 'Sweetness and Taste: Mapping Maple Syrup in Vermont', Amy Trubek revisits and explores the topic *terroir* – 'the taste of place' – within a distinct topographical and cultural context: maple sugar production. This contribution looks at the remarkable social and material culture that has grown out of the long-standing practice of 'sugaring' in North America. Like the New England stone walls described by Nicola Camerlenghi, maple syrup is inextricably rooted within a specific landscape, in this case the northern forests of the New World that run from the north-east United States to south-east Canada. In theory the raw ingredient of syrup, the sap, could be harvested and then processed elsewhere beyond its original provenance. But in reality this is plainly impossible because maple syrup is not merely a tangible commodity but also a set of regional conditions that encompasses traditional harvesting techniques and a deep-seated social culture. What also deserves to be highlighted here is that the syrup does not conform to formal boundaries but instead reflects natural, pregiven criteria of the landscape: soil, mountain slope and climate. In fact, food rarely observes political borders. This is something that the late, great Marcella Hazan strove to clarify in her own descriptions of the food of her homeland. In the preface to her inaugural book, *The Classic Italian Cookbook*, she overturns the common presumption of a comprehensive 'Italian' cuisine. Instead, she argues, 'the cooking of Italy is really a cooking of its regions'.[3] What follows is an eloquent portrait of Italy's landscape, especially its rugged mountains and extraordinary coastline, but also of course its fertile plains and productive river valleys. For Hazan the content as well as meaning of food could only be perceived through regional conditions. It is, moreover, not surprising that the etymology of the word 'region' stems from the Latin *regio*, which in a basic sense is defined as a boundary-line or limit, but which also encompasses indefinite meanings, such as a portion of the country or heavens, neighbourhood, or even 'the field'.[4] To a large degree, landscape *generates* both food and architecture, and yet we now increasingly turn our backs on it, both in a metaphorical and literal sense.

One of the most enduring images of Amy Trubek's chapter is the description of the sugarhouses in Vermont. These simple wooden structures directly respond to the process of turning sap into syrup, and yet they are also so much more: for sugarmakers, they confirm a connectedness to place. Generally speaking, the phenomenon of regional architecture being inextricably linked to the production and preparation of food is certainly not uncommon, but it tends to be understudied.[5] Aglaia Kremezi's contribution (Chapter 4), 'Slaughtering the Pig in Kéa', provides an important glimpse of an analogous situation in Greece.

On the Cycladic island of Kéa, the tradition of pig slaughtering remains an important annual winter festival for local inhabitants. Similar to how the sugarhouses of Vermont become gathering places for the community during sugaring season, the vernacular farmhouses on Kéa, called *kathikies*, for generations have accommodated the habits and associated festivities of the post-slaughtering process. The interior spaces of the house as well as the porch – a room half inside, half outside – were originally designed to reflect the need to hang, butcher and ultimately cook the slaughtered pig. It is crucial to acknowledge, however, that while some of these dwellings may well be regarded and studied as historic structures, they by no means are ossified specimens of an architectural history. Highly functional and utilitarian, they have been adapted over time to suit the changing needs of the island inhabitants. Like most architecture, *kathikies* are not as forthcoming as we would like them to be; yet they nonetheless are a lens through which we can observe the relationship between the landscape of the island and the social conventions that it engenders. It is perhaps no coincidence that the impetus for Bernard Rudofsky's lifelong enthusiasm for regional architecture was his fieldwork as a young student on Santorini (Thira), another island in the Greek Cyclades.

This section on regionalism culminates by asking how food can shape not only the identity but also the physical topography of towns and cities. Máirtín Mac Con Iomaire's contribution (Chapter 5), 'The Gastro-Topography and Built Heritage of Dublin, Ireland', explores the etymology of food-related place-names in Ireland, focusing particularly on the greater Dublin region. There are a great many streets, neighbourhoods and even whole towns that have their origin in the culture of food. Historic market grounds, long-established routes for transporting animals and ancient commonage sites are just a few examples of places that forged the shape of communities and have left a tangible impression on the fabric of towns and landscapes.[6] However, in the present day we tend to overlook these conditions and characteristics. Their physical marks may remain but often our memory of them has faded, recalling the situation that the writer Nicola Twilley has described as an 'agricultural unconscious'.[7] What is particularly fascinating about the fabric of Dublin is that some ancient place-names, and even entire districts, have stubbornly persisted throughout waves of urban development. During the eighteenth century, new civic buildings and residential quarters were developed alongside scores of new street names; but food markets still cluster in the present day near the north bank of the River Liffey, as they have since antiquity.

In his early studies of regionalism, well before he developed his argument on *terroir* that is elucidated in this volume by Nicola Camerlenghi, Lewis Mumford also made important connections between food and topography. Decrying the systematic and arbitrary administrative units or types (such as political boundaries) imposed upon the post-Enlightenment city, Mumford argued for a different interpretation of order, one that is based on pregiven conditions of geographical units: 'In each of these natural regions, certain modes of life have arisen in adaptation to the fundamental conditions: these modes have been modified by previous cultural accumulations and by contacts with other peoples ... did not salt, even in the earliest dawn of history, travel thousands of miles and pass through many hands before [it] was finally used?'[8] Mumford's mention of salt is crucial, not necessarily because of its inherent value as a commodity but rather because it historically was a product that connected so many people and their respective communities and cultures. As Carolyn Steel has demonstrated, food miles have been around for millennia, but the alarming disconnection between cities and the productive landscapes that feed them is quite a recent phenomenon.[9] Our capacity to bridge this rift requires a fundamental shift in how we eat, and part of this is changing the way we understand and interpret regionalism. The scale of many cities now renders the ideal of a verdant, fertile greenbelt an impossible fantasy. As such, in prioritizing what is local we must search within – not solely beyond – our cities for a new paradigm of regionalism, one which will reassess how the urban landscape itself can nourish and sustain us.

Notes

1   Bernard Rudofsky, *Architecture without Architects: A Short Introduction to Non-pedigreed Architecture* (Albuquerque: University of New Mexico Press, 1964). Rudofsky was also, interestingly, a winner in the 1941 'Organic Design Competition', which was sponsored by MoMA. For this, see 'Biographical Notes on Bernard Rudofsky', MoMA, November 1964.

2   The full title of the show was *Now I Lay Me Down to Eat, A Salute to the Unknown Art of Living*. 18 November 1980–22 February 1981 at the Cooper Hewitt, Smithsonian Design Museum. A separate book of essays was published to accompany the exhibit: *Now I Lay Me Down to Eat: Notes and Footnotes on the Lost Art of Living* (Garden City, New York: Anchor Press/Doubleday, 1981). The first chapter is entitled 'Table Manners at the Last Supper'.

3   Marcella Hazan, *The Classic Italian Cookbook* (New York: Harper's Magazine Press, 1973), Preface. This discussion reappears in nearly identical form in later editions of the text as well as other publications, including the introduction to *The Essentials of Italian Cooking* (London: Pan Macmillan, 2012).

4   S.v. *Lewis and Short, A Latin Dictionary,* 1879.

5   One recent exception to this status quo was the Bahrain Pavilion at the 12th International Venice Architecture Biennale in 2010. The curators of the exhibition *Reclaim* dismantled a series of fishermen's huts from their original sites on the coast of Bahrain and reinstalled them in the Arsenale in Venice. Conceived as an appraisal and critical commentary on the conditions facing the fishermen in the present day, the exhibition was awarded the Golden Lion, the Biennale's highest accolade for a national exhibit.

6   A growing number of studies examine cities from this perspective. Carolyn Steel's examination of London is a key example. Steel, *Hungry City: How Food Shapes Our Lives* (London: Chatto and Windus, 2008), 118–120. Rebecca Solnit's innovative reinterpretation of an atlas for San Francisco, *Infinite City*, also considers surviving place-names. R. Solnit, *Infinite City: A San Francisco Atlas* (Berkeley: University of California Press, 2010), see especially 'The Names before the Names', 10–12, and L. Conrad, 'A Map the Size of the Land', 12–17. For a study of Dublin through this perspective, see Samantha L. Martin-McAuliffe, 'Feeding Dublin: The City Fruit and Vegetable Market', in ed. M. McWilliams, *Food and Markets. Proceedings from the Oxford Food Symposium on Food and Cookery 2014* (Totnes: Prospect Books, 2015), 241–253.

7   Nicola Twilley, 'Cow Tunnels', in *Edible Geography* (blog), 10 April 2010, http://www.ediblegeography.com/cow-tunnels/ (accessed 23 March 2015).

8   Lewis Mumford, 'Regional Planning'. July 8, 1931 Address to Round Table on Regionalism, Institute of Public Affairs, University of Virginia, Avery Library, Columbia University, reprinted in V. Canizaro, *Architectural Regionalism: Collected Writings on Place, Identity, Modernity, and Tradition* (Princeton: Princeton Architectural Press, 2007), 236–243.

9   Steel, *Hungry City,* 72–76.

2

Terroir and Architecture

Nicola Camerlenghi

Building, food and time

Since primordial times, food and shelter have been of the utmost priorities
for humans. Our ancestors selected the locations of their settlements
based on the availability of food, and in at least one case the by-products
of nourishment served the needs of building. Some of the earliest human
settlements in North America – the 'coastal shell rings' along the southeastern
seaboard of the United States – were constructed with shucked oyster shells
and occasionally included animal or fish bones. Some of the more famous
of these circular enclosures are dated to about 4,700 years ago and located
on Sapelo Island, Georgia. They feature diameters of up to 250 feet and wall
heights of about 20 feet that would have constituted considerable circuits of
defence. And yet it is unclear to what extent the enclosures were defensive
or ceremonial, convenient waste heaps or some combination of these likely
factors.[1] These structures serve as a prehistoric instance of the direct and
reciprocal rapport between food and shelter.

Even after the arrival of European settlers, oysters continued to play a role in
the architecture (and gastronomy) of the region. From Florida to South Carolina,
a number of colonial and postcolonial buildings were constructed with tabby –
a concrete mixture comprised of sand, water, ash, lime and oyster shells
that functioned as aggregate (Figure 2.1).[2] To make tabby, builders employed
quarries of discarded oyster shells, which had been generated by Native
American populations with an obvious appetite for local bivalves. The origins of
tabby are unclear. Some scholars consider it as an import from North Africa, via
Spain, while others relate it to Totonac architectural practices originally centred
near present-day Vera Cruz, Mexico.[3] There one finds remnants of structures

FIGURE 2.1 *R.S. Schuyler, 'Tabby House,' Fernandina Beach, Florida, c. 1885. Courtesy of Judson McCranie, Creative Commons.*

from as early as AD 600 built with concrete that includes a seashell aggregate. Whether its origins are transatlantic or trans-Caribbean, tabby was most likely imported. Yet, over time, it became a traditional building material with ties to the southeastern American seaboard. This process of acculturation sheds light on the problems inherent to categorizing regional architecture. Regional aspects of a building – or of a food for that matter – are not solely a matter of place but also of time. The role of both place and time in the development of techniques such as tabby has counterparts in the realm of food and its regional products.

Because tabby is a unique building material that relates to both food and architecture, it offers a fitting starting point for this contribution, which is aimed at examining the nexus of these two disciplines.[4] Despite scattered instances of food used for construction, in this study, I am less interested in that direct, reciprocal physical connection between food and building practices. Instead, I begin by examining the definitions of *terroir* – a term that originated in gastronomical studies. I then explore a parallel development devised by legislators of the European Union, who deployed a triad of factors – environmental, technical and historic – to regulate and distinguish gastronomic products. Following these preliminary observations, I employ both the notion of *terroir* and European food legislation as powerful paradigms by which to understand not only gastronomy but also architecture. Indeed, the nature/

culture dialogue encapsulated by notions like *terroir* bears insights into the relationship between nature and architecture. In an effort to draw analogies between these disciplines and to ground my comparison in hard evidence, in the second half of the chapter, I turn to stone walls as emblematic case studies. Ultimately, the aim of this chapter is to identify a few basic points of comparison between food and architecture in order to enrich the theorization, design, construction and critique of the built world.

That this chapter's closing observations address architecture, and not gastronomy, is a reflection of the fact that multifaceted conclusions would require lengthier treatment. To date, comparisons between food and architecture have rarely risen above mere analogy (witness McDonald's and McMansions), in part due to gastronomy's still precarious foothold in academia. Yet, it is a testament to the strides made by pioneering food scholars that, in this chapter, gastronomy is employed to enliven the more established discipline of architecture.

Terroir and its definitions

At its core, *terroir* is an all-encompassing term for those factors that determine the qualities of a wine. The most commonly cited factors it encompasses are soil, terrain, exposure and climate. Though the French term *terroir* has been linked to a broad range of agricultural products since the Middle Ages, only from the start of the twentieth century has it been used to distinguish and legislate wines.[5] Despite this notable history, French agents who regulate wine production and nomenclature do not agree on its precise meaning. As recently as 1998, a survey found that approximately half of those agents interviewed defined *terroir* as comprised uniquely of environmental qualities, while the other half believed it was a blend of these natural factors with human factors.[6] In more recent years, the latter definition has gained traction and *terroir* has been applied to a variety of gastronomic products and expanded to include human know-how and production techniques.[7] This broader definition reflects our times and denotes the interdependence of natural and manmade factors espoused by contemporary environmental theorists. The tenets of 'deep ecology' postulate that it is false and counterproductive to isolate manmade factors from natural factors, when these are clearly linked and interrelated.[8] If the notion of *terroir* is to remain topical, its definition ought to reflect the values of this more holistic ecological notion.

A fitting definition of *terroir* might be the amalgam of environment, technique and tradition that confers unique qualities to products tied to the land – be they wines, cheeses or, as proposed here, buildings. Such an inclusive definition, which enfolds the complexities of 'deep ecology', should resonate among theoreticians and practitioners of architecture engaged in critically questioning the rapport between the environment and buildings. Likewise, given both these affinities between regional or even sustainable builders and advocates of *terroir* in gastronomy, it seems fitting to broaden the use of *terroir* beyond gastronomy.[9] Theoretically, at least, *terroir*-driven architecture is responsive to and expressive of environments, techniques and traditions. Such characteristics are often espoused by architects interested in regional and sustainable design.[10] But what patterns would such 'terroirchitecture' display and what potential might it hold?

The connection between gastronomy and architecture is neither far-fetched nor novel. Already in 1941, in his *The South in Architecture*, the historian Lewis Mumford noted that the principles of a *terroir*-driven farmer or winemaker were exemplary for builders aspiring to foster regional architecture:

> It is only after hundreds of years of planting grape vines and making wine, that the people of Burgundy, say, developed the grapes that were specially fit for their soil; and it needed much further sampling before one patch of soil could be distinguished from another … That kind of co-operation and re-adaptation and development is what is necessary to produce a truly regional character. The very last refinement of regional culture in wine-making is limited perhaps to an acre or two of ground: and centuries were needed before the grape, the soil, the skill in wine-making and the sensitivity in wine-tasting were brought into a harmonious partnership … It takes generations before a regional product can be achieved.[11]

Mumford highlighted the importance of techniques that fine-tuned qualities pre-existing in nature. In this respect, he was advocating for centuries-old tenets already familiar and practiced by landscape architects like Lancelot 'Capability' Brown.[12] Mumford described the combination of hard effort, trial-and-error and slow technological innovation that eventually yield a regional product. As in the case of tabby construction, it is important to acknowledge the temporal and the environmental components of a regional product. The complex relationship between environment, technology and tradition, which can only arise over time, can be investigated further by questioning the techniques we humans adopt in our interaction with the environment and by considering the traditions – or lack thereof – that inform these specific techniques. Indeed, these two questions are at the core of a contentious schism in the wine world.

One faction of producers – which we might refer to as alchemists – aims to produce wine that is pleasant, recognizable and responsive to commercial expectations. Also referred to as 'branded wine', their product is often created from blends of must shipped from remote and disparate places before being heavily worked, altered, bottled and labelled.[13] Alchemical wine has qualities that are both imitable and often imitated. A desired outcome has been specified in advance – often in response to marketing surveys or popular tendencies – and the means to achieve it is prescribed, standardized and industrialized. I use the term 'alchemical' because it captures this heavy-handed type of winemaking, wherein technology obfuscates any traceable semblance of specific environmental qualities. In alchemical wine, the potential to display characteristics of a place of origin or to express qualities inherent to a grape varietal is stunted by aggressive production techniques that transmute any innate – often base – qualities.[14]

Another faction – the 'terroirists' – believes its role in wine production is to perfect qualities pre-existing in nature. In this case, they intervene with techniques that subtly tweak or highlight qualities that are inherent to a varietal of grape growing in a specific place during a particular time (for example, its year of production, or vintage). The resulting wines reflect their environment, express a grape varietal (or varietals) and display vintage variations attributable to climate. In sum, *terroir*-driven wines are generally inimitable and less predictable than their alchemical counterparts. Every vintage, indeed, every bottle, is a surprise – hopefully a pleasant one (but not always).

Of the two approaches, that of the terroirist is the more traditional and long-standing – despite the fact that in some places it is deemed 'progressive'. It is what Mumford alluded to in his discussion of American regional architecture. To be sure, the polarity just described is a simplification, and many wine producers lie somewhere in the middle of these extremes. If quantifiable at all, their position on the terroirist/alchemist spectrum depends on how the techniques they adopt relate to both winemaking traditions and the environment. The complexity that emerges from these enological examples points to the fact that *terroir* is hardly a straightforward concept. Perhaps because of its encompassing breadth and resulting slipperiness, the term has been co-opted and recast – particularly by marketers – to stand in for wholesome attitudes and traditional techniques adopted in respect for the environment.[15] It is important to decipher the possibilities this terminology embodies and enables.

European gastronomical legislation

While the complexity of *terroir* makes it a useful term for interdisciplinary studies, it is problematic in other contexts. In fact, a perusal of European regulations reveals that it is seldom used in food legislation, for little would be gained by such an amorphous term. Unsatisfied with the broad scope of *terroir*, legislators of the European Union have focused their attention more specifically on the environmental, technical and traditional facets of food production. Together these factors are used to distinguish, regulate and develop gastronomic products. These centrally codified regulations – akin to those guiding architectural heritage and preservation – are by nature restrictive and thus potentially problematic.[16] That said, for the purposes of this chapter, I focus on the factors used to distinguish, regulate and develop gastronomic products.

Since 1992, the European Commission on Agriculture and Rural Development has settled on legislation that designates and protects food products – in a manner akin to trademarks – on the basis of such factors as '(i) a unique geographic region, (ii) establishment of a collective know-how, and (iii) demonstration of a cultural tradition'.[17] The distinct legal designations devised on these bases are: Protected Designation of Origin, or PDO; Protected Geographical Indication, or PGI; and Traditional Speciality Guaranteed, or TSG. The appearance of these labels on selected food products strengthens the market for these goods, assures their quality and elevates them to the status of cultural artefacts.

A brief synopsis of the differences among the three designations will elucidate how they are categorized – a fundamental step before relating them to architecture.[18] Only an alignment of environment, technique and tradition secures the strictest designation – PDO. Among such products the European Commission recognizes Gorgonzola, Parmigiano Reggiano and Mozzarella di Bufala Campana, to take just three well-known examples from the category of Italian cheese. In order to receive a PDO, a Mozzarella di Bufala Campana must come from whole milk of buffalo cattle of the Italian Mediterranean breed raised in defined regions, and it must be processed in situ according to specified traditional practices. The end product has organoleptic qualities – that is, discernible by the senses – that have been directly linked to the locations where it is made, to the techniques used and, finally, to the historic traditions that arise from those techniques and locations. While heavily regulated, more universal and global forces are inevitably at play, too. The cheesemaking machine could be German, the consuming public American, for example. Importantly, this collusion of forces is neither rejected nor regulated.

To receive the second designation, PGI, the connection to a specific region need not be essential or exclusive, but it has to be causal. Not all aspects of production must take place in a specified geographic area, but location must determine some discernible organoleptic quality. The first two categories (PDO and PGI) are location based, albeit in varying degrees; the third category – TSG – is uniquely technique based.[19] For a product to be labelled TSG, it must be produced in accordance to a stringent codification of tradition-based techniques.[20] The end result is that one can eat a TSG-certified Pizza Napoletana as far away from Naples, Italy, as Eugene, Oregon. As with alchemical wines, a desired outcome has been specified in advance and the means to achieve it is prescribed, standardized and untethered from a specific place, but – unlike those wines – a TSG Pizza Napoletana cannot be industrially produced. In sum, the three types of products can be described through varying and specified attention to environmental, technical and traditional factors. This triad permits far more nuanced approaches to food production than would be permitted by an overarching term like *terroir*.

In addition to regulating the manufacture and quality of these select foods, the EU designation has elevated their price and status. It is estimated that as much as 30 per cent of European food expenditures fall within these three designations. In 2008 alone, 14.5 billion euros were spent on these products, and in February 2011, the EU Commission certified its one-thousandth product.[21] A designation also fixes quality standards. Innovation and progress of a particular food type is wilfully stifled in exchange for a protected identity and elevated quality. In other words, Gorgonzola is Gorgonzola and can only be Gorgonzola, until legislation changes or a producer drops out of line with regard to environment, technique or tradition. I will return to this controversial aspect of stifling the evolution of a food type – or an architectural form – in my closing observations. To be sure, singling out certain food products for their attachment to a place, to production techniques or to historic traditions elevates those products along with the status of their producers. Behind each PDO, PGI and TSG is a squadron of lawyers and a strong lobby of farmers or food producers. While protectionist and lucrative, the alliance between politicians and food producers necessary to achieve certification is also driven by a deep philosophical principle: gastronomic products are cultural artefacts. For many historians and critics, foods have long had deep connections with the cultures that produce and consume them. The idea that what a person eats says a lot about her – to paraphrase Brillat-Savarin – is testament to the deep connection between food and identity.[22] So the European legislation is, like the notion of *terroir*, witness to the bond between food, place and people. Accordingly, it can deepen the relation between specific environments and human production.

To summarize, the enological roots of the notion of *terroir*, its recent, more holistic redefinition and even the European Commission's triad of legal factors, all seek to link products to a place, a time and a production technique. In so doing, standards are guaranteed and the product in question acquires a cultural value it previously lacked. The elevated cultural associations as well as the attachment to place, time and technique echo the aspirations of a number of contemporary architects.

Terroir in architecture

Food producers who reject blanket industrialization understand the value of direct contact with and responsiveness to nature along the lines celebrated by Mumford. It therefore is no surprise if these food practices might inspire progressive architecture schools likewise disillusioned with approaches that promised to grant control over the environment. At this pivotal moment, when design schools are beginning to substitute tired declarations of independence from nature for covenants of interdependence with nature, the time seems ripe to explore how the tenets of *terroir*-driven gastronomy might apply to architecture.

In *The South in Architecture*, Mumford wrote: 'Since the adaptation of culture to a particular environment is a long, complicated process, a full-blown regional character is the last to emerge.'[23] As with wines, he argued, so too with buildings. For Mumford, then, attitudes towards food had pedagogical potential for the discipline of architecture. His emphasis on place and time in determining a regional character recalls early definitions of *terroir* and foreshadows the environmental, technical and traditional factors later singled out by European food regulators. Despite the apparent timelessness of his comments, Mumford was very much a man of his time. His study, published in 1941, was intended to counter German blood and soil (*Blut und Boden*) ideologies, which held that ethnicity was determined by ancestry and homeland. It was essential, in Mumford's opinion, to rid regional architecture of the racial overtones ascribed to it by the Nazis. In contrast to Nazi policies that favoured *Heimatsarchitektur* and wilfully rejected the rationality and the universality of Modernism, the regionalism expounded by Mumford was founded on a give and take between 'the universal imprint of the machine' and the 'local imprint of the region and the community'.[24] While Modernism and machines per se are no longer a priority, other universal and global tendencies remain a powerful counterpoint to local forces. Upholding uniquely one extreme, if unchecked and unbalanced, has profound consequences for the built world: we risk homogenized human landscapes if only global values are pushed, factionalism and provincialism if only local values are prioritized.

Mumford's quotations may seem old fashioned, but to contemporary scholars he still provides a solid theoretical foundation for all varieties of regionalism. Gary Coates's bio-regionalism, Anthony Alofsin's constructive regionalism and, of course, critical regionalism – defined and redefined over the last thirty years by Alexander Tzonis, Liane Lefaivre and Kenneth Frampton – all have roots in Mumford's work.[25] But what lessons can be drawn from Mumford's analogy to winemaking – and from the study of *terroir*, more generally – for the current pedagogy and practice of architecture?

To formulate an answer to that question, I turn to an example – that of farmers who were also builders, albeit begrudgingly. Stone walls began crisscrossing New England landscapes after only a century or so of colonial settlement.[26] The initial impetus for their construction was not picturesque but practical. In order to farm the land, colonists engaged in a campaign of rampant deforestation, which in turn caused topsoil erosion and with it the emergence of a previously submerged underworld of rocky rubble. Each stone is a testament to New England's rich geologic past; but to farmers, they were nuisances. Affectionately known as 'New England potatoes', these stones were no laughing matter: these hazards caused ploughs to be dented, scythes shattered and backs bent out of shape. For New England farmers, 'spring cleaning' meant clearing a path for the plough. Presumably stones were collected into piles and, like coffee dregs drying at the bottom of a mug, they accrued around the edges of arable land. Eventually the piles were carefully shaped into sturdy walls that came to define fields – the whole became a handmade landscape with a long and still evolving history.

Now, let us borrow a framework and terminology from gastronomy to interpret these stone walls. In the course of their development, heavy-handed farming techniques severely altered the environment in just a few generations and set in motion the slow, incidental development of stone walls as an architectural type. The size, colour and type of stone and even the dominant lichen population dotting a wall's surface were prescribed by the environment. In other words, soil, geology and climate determine certain essential and unique qualities of a wall. But – as with the coastal shell rings of Georgia – it is human techniques and traditions linked to the environment that determine a wall's form. The stones that emerged from those fields complicated farming techniques, and as stone piles rose, so did the need for new techniques – not agricultural but architectural. In time, building techniques and traditions developed to suit new needs and new sorts of patrons. Over the course of centuries, New England stone walls were transformed from dumps of unwanted stone to separations between fields, then property markers, expressions of social status and – most recently – evocations of quaintness, tradition and even wealth. By the time stone walls became more than just a by-product of farming, the importance of well-developed construction techniques and local traditions was already becoming apparent. Professional builders took over where begrudging farmers left off.

One of the most noted architects to pick up on the formal and spatial qualities of New England stone walls was Henry Hobson Richardson. This is most evident in his 1881 Ames Gate Lodge in North Easton, Massachusetts, built on grounds landscaped by Fredrick Law Olmstead (Figure 2.2).[27] Vincent Scully has memorably referred to its 'plum-pudding boulders' as 'earthly

FIGURE 2.2 *Henry Hobsen Richarson, 'Ames Gate Lodge', North Easton, Massachusetts, ca.1881. Courtesy of Creative Commons.*

and rooted in place'.[28] Elsewhere, Scully has celebrated the structure as 'a cyclopean statement of human permanence on the American earth'.[29] While there is no denying the building's heroic quality, it ought not overshadow the simple concept of the Gate Lodge – it was, in essence, a riff on the ubiquitous New England stone wall, which Richardson essentially turned about itself and gloriously roofed. It is no surprise that Mumford and others have regarded Richardson as 'the first truly American regional architect'.[30] Both the Gate Lodge's exterior and interior are so intimately tied to the landscape and so evocative of the region's glacial remains and (once prevalent) dark-wood forests that one might refer to Richardson's work as a full-blown instance of terroirchitecture.

If Richardson responded to local stones and traditional building techniques, the same cannot be said for many examples of stone walls found in contemporary suburbs around the world (Figure 2.3). This photograph is a startling case in point. As of May 2013, a Google image search reveals that this very image appears on the websites of sixteen independently owned stonemason companies located in such places as Maryland, New Jersey, Oklahoma, Georgia, North Dakota and even in Scotland, Sweden, Ireland and England. This is a truly global stone wall! On these websites, it functions as an indicator of the sort of work the contractors in question can and will carry out,

FIGURE 2.3 *Stone wall, somewhere – perhaps anywhere – on planet earth.*

if hired. But – *caveat emptor* – it is not an example of work they have done. Though I can no longer determine where this wall is located and who actually built it, evidently it is desirable the world over! As a result, the wall offers a quintessential example of non-place-based building traditions. Without the linchpin of local building traditions, techniques are likely to be standardized and unresponsive or indeed opposed to *terroir*.[31] From an architectural point of view, the result of that disconnect is an overall loss of diversity and the triumph of generic, industrial production: all but assuring a creeping homogeneity across vast swaths of our built landscape. The standardized wall promised around the world via the image in question is the architectural equivalent of alchemical wines.

A comparable distinction exists in gastronomy. Consider the two major types of mozzarella commonly available in stores. Alongside the PDO Mozzarella di Bufala Campana – or other fresh, but uncertified, mozzarella cheese – there exists the dehydrated block, string cheese or shredded versions. The latter are the result of production techniques in no way inflected by tradition tied to place. If anything, they respond to market demands for products with a longer shelf-life, or to the limitations of household ovens that – unlike wood-fired brick ovens – cannot cook pizza at a hot-enough temperature to keep fresh mozzarella from leaking and creating a soggy dough. Indeed, the dehydrated version is the salvation of many homemade pizzas. In contrast, for southern Italian cheese makers as for New England farmers, techniques and traditions are informed by slow, at times generational, mutations. It is important to note that the actual product – cheese ball or stone wall – need not take long to make; that said, centuries and sometimes eons of history are contained within each bite and boulder.[32] This slowness was recognized by Mumford: 'We are only beginning to know enough about ourselves and about our environment', he wrote, 'to create a regional architecture'.[33] The introspection that he deemed necessary reflects the central position of regional buildings – and *terroir*-driven gastronomic products – in a culture. They stand in contrast to standardized, universal construction or food production.

A final case through which to consider the affinities between *terroir* and architecture is an example of a stone wall that – like the Ames Gate Lodge – encompasses an entire building. Since the 1960s Christian Mouieux – proprietor of some of the most esteemed vineyards in Bordeaux, including Château Petrus – has been collaborating with winemakers in Napa Valley. When Mouieux decided to build his own Napa winery, he hired the architectural firm of Jacques Herzog and Pierre de Meuron to design Dominus Winery in Yountville. Completed in 1997, it was the Swiss architects' first American commission. The winery is a long low building that consists on all sides of galvanized steel cages, called gabions, which are filled with dark-green basalt stones from nearby American Canyon.[34] The local basalt blends seamlessly with the surroundings so the building sits in the landscape with a subtlety and sensibility absent in more manorial and bombastic wine châteaux of France, or elsewhere. The stone is loosely fit in the gabions to let air and light seep through. The designers carefully studied the winds that prevail at this location beneath the Mayacamas Range to determine not only the siting but also the thicknesses of the permeable wall, factors that help to secure the thermal balance between night and day – essential to the wine aged within. Offices and interior spaces are enclosed by panes of glass largely undetectable from the exterior, but for a few parts of the elevation marked by windows. From the road, where most people experience it, the building is svelte and stealth. Up close, the raw materials and straightforward building techniques command attention. Though the gabions are meshed together with steal wire wrapped like the tendrils of a vine (Figure 2.4), they are essentially glorified versions of the retaining walls built along many of the world's highways. In the end, the Dominus winery is the result of a French winemaker hiring an international firm based in Switzerland to build in Napa with Californian stones set into an industrially engineered steel framework. Such a fusion of factors and origins evinces the complexity of our contemporary built environment and the frequent collusion of local and global forces present also in gastronomical products. Like the wine produced there, the Dominus winery exudes global pedigree

FIGURE 2.4 *Herzog and De Meuron, stone wall at Dominus Winery, Yountville, California, 1997. Photo courtesy of Sarah Ackerman.*

while embodying local *terroir*. This is precisely the give and take between local and universal forces that comprises the regionalism championed by Mumford and by the field of gastronomy.

Closing observations

More often than not, *terroir*-driven products – whether gastronomic or architectural – display qualities that respond to and reflect local factors. The geographic and topographic borders that bound such products and distinguish them from neighbouring ones can be permeable, ever-shifting and hard to define. As a result, it is difficult to assess whether, more than seventy years after Mumford's publication, we are any closer to creating regional architectures. Where the answer is no – as in the case of many suburban stone walls – it is important to confront the threat of homogenous, industrially produced structures that ignore local contingencies. Where there is a hint of a *terroir*-driven architecture or where it is full-blown – as in the case of the Ames Gate Lodge or the Dominus Winery – it is important to recognize, nurture and develop the tendency further.

From the broadest, planetary perspective, we are advancing dangerously towards homogenous, industrially produced solutions. The vast majority of new constructions in southern and eastern Asia – like many commercial and residential developments in the West – belong to this variety. Often these rapidly built structures rise on the former sites of traditional cityscapes. There are practical and financial motivations behind this tragic homogenization of the landscape, but I will limit myself here to addressing a more circumscribed set of challenges with wider implications.

If *terroir*-driven foods and buildings are worth producing, as I believe they are, then certain principles need to be addressed at the level of instruction. Is it better for schools to teach globally applicable skills, locally relevant ones or – if possible – both? Since most professional schools – culinary or architectural – teach students to be competitive in an increasingly diverse and global job market, local skills, when taught, tend to be presented as universally applicable principles. But that notion of overarching applicability comes suspiciously close to the standardized, alchemical, top-down model that exists in the food industry and in sprawling developments. At some point, students have to get their hands dirty. They have to dig into the characteristics of a particular *terroir*, learn its traditions and master its techniques. That process is, as Mumford intuited, a slow one. Aspiring chefs travel, undergo stages at various restaurants or intern with colleagues, all the while eating voraciously to learn from one another. Such a journeyman tradition has value in architecture as well. Given that in North America such experiences tend to happen on a case-by-case basis and with a degree in hand, perhaps the burden of favouring such diverse training could pass to professional associations?

One possible solution comes, again, from gastronomy. Every two years, in Turin, Italy, thousands of famers, livestock owners, gastronomes as well as social and political activists from around the world converge at a conference called *Terra Madre*. These individuals are prominent players within their food communities, 'involved in the production, transformation, and distribution of a particular food, [and...] closely linked to a geographic area either historically, socially, or culturally'.[35] Though participants are naturally immersed in their own local techniques and traditions, 'they share the problems caused by industrial intensive agriculture and the standardization imposed by a food industry aimed at mass markets'.[36] Participants are at once empowered and empowering, educated and educating. Thanks to the dialogue that takes place at *Terra Madre*, local pragmatism is united with universal experience. In North America, regional and national professional design associations might foster comparable dialogues across building communities in order to devise strategies, formulate pedagogical methods and, possibly, consider legislative opportunities.

Indeed, one is left wondering if there might be an advantage to categorizing *terroir*-driven buildings like gastronomical products. Might certifying a material, a building or a firm as exemplary of a *terroir* help to strengthen it? Of course, this raises many questions that cannot be answered here. Who, for example, would distinguish the characteristics of one *terroir* from another? Also, we have seen how innovation tends to cease once a food type comes under a certain protected designation. Were similar designations to be applied to the built world, would the enhanced cultural identity and guaranteed quality compensate for that loss in innovation? Might it be possible to gain those advantages while also fostering innovation? This is a balance that designers and critics must gauge. I leave these questions open, but hope they only expand the dialogue I have begun here by investigating the intersection between gastronomy and architecture. *Terroir*, in its complex assimilation of environment, technique and tradition, is a useful paradigm for investigating worthy alternatives to a hauntingly homogenized built landscape.[37]

Notes

1   Michael Russo, 'Measuring Shell Rings for Social Inequality', in *Signs of Power: The Rise of Cultural Complexity in the Southeast*, eds. Jon L. Gibson and Philip J. Carr (Tuscaloosa: University of Alabama Press, 2004), 26–70. Drew Smith, *Oyster, A World History* (Stroud: The History Press, 2010), see especially Chapter 8.

2   Etymologically, the term 'tabby' derives from *tapia*, Spanish for mud wall.

3   Robert Thornton, 'What Is Tabby Architecture?', April, 2011, http://www.examiner.com/article/what-is-tabby-architecture (accessed 20 May 2013).

4   Other spectacular overlaps between food and architecture include the Wieliczka salt mines near Krakow and the Corn Palace in Mitchell, South Dakota.

5   Émile Littré's *Dictionnaire de la langue française* (1872–77) noted that already in the thirteenth century *terroir* was related to wine. In the first edition of the *Dictionnaire de l'Académie française* (1694), *terroir* was defined as 'terre considerée par rapport à l'agriculture (soil as related to agriculture)'.

6   S. Scheffer and B. Sylvander, 'The Effects of Institutional Changes on Qualification Processes: A Survey at the French Institute for Denomination of Origins (INAO)', in *Typical and Traditional Products: Rural Effects and Agro-Industrial Problems*. 52nd EAAE Seminar (Istituto di Economia Agraria e Forestale, Facoltà di Economia, Università di Parma, Italy, 1998), 463–482.

7   On *terroir* see James E. Wilson, *Terroir* (Berkeley: University of California Press, 1998); Amy B. Trubek, *The Taste of Place: A Cultural Journey into Terroir* (Berkeley: University of California Press, 2008); Rowan Jacobsen, *American Terroir: Savoring the Flavors of Our Woods, Waters and Fields* (New York: Bloomsbury, 2010).

8   The work of Arne Næss is foundational to deep ecology. See, for example, Alan Drengson and Bill Devall, eds., *Ecology of Wisdom: Writings by Arne Naess* (Berkeley, CA: Counterpoint, 2008). Also, Bill Devall and George Sessions, *Deep Ecology* (Salt Lake City: G.M. Smith, 1985).

9   The terms 'regional' and 'sustainable' are constantly debated and defined by scholars and practitioners. I use them with some hesitation here.

10 Brian MacKay-Lyons and Robert McCarter, *Local Architecture: Building Place, Craft, and Community* (Princeton: Princeton Architectural Press, 2015).

11 Lewis Mumford, *The South in Architecture* (New York: Harcourt, Brace and Co., 1941), 29–30.

12 John Dixon Hunt, *Greater Perfections, The Practice of Garden Theory* (Philadelphia: University of Pennsylvania Press, 2000), 11 and the entirety of Chapter 3.

13 Cornelis van Leeuwen, 'Soils and Terroir Expression in Wine', in *Soil and Culture*, eds. Edward Landa and Christian Feller (London: Springer, 2010), 453–465.

14 The feature-length documentary *Mondovino* captures the tension.

15 The commodification of *terroir* – like that of 'local', 'natural', 'heritage' or 'heirloom' – is part of a wider trend in the reproduction and invention of heritage (tangible and intangible). The work of David Lowenthal is seminal here, particularly his *Possessed by the Past* (New York: The Free Press, 1996). I am grateful to an anonymous reader for this suggestion.

16 For a critique of the food designation system, see Rachel Lauden, 'Too Many Designations in the Kitchen Editorial', *The Los Angeles Times*, 1 November 2010, http://articles.latimes.com/2010/nov/01/opinion/la-oe-laudan-unesco-20101101 (accessed 20 May 2013).

17 For an early exploration of this legislation see Amy B. Trubek and Jean-Pierre Lemasson, eds., *Cuizine: The Journal of Canadian Food Cultures*, 2 (2010).

18 A concise summary is provided in: London Economics, 'Evaluation of the CAP policy on protected designations of origin (PDO) and protected geographical indications (PGI), Short Summary', November 2008. http://ec.europa.eu/agriculture/eval/reports/pdopgi/short_sum_en.pdf.

19 Only the first two (PDO and PGI) match geographic factors (i.e. the strict definition of *terroir*) with traditional know-how, while TSG is strictly know-how based with no component of geography (i.e. an aspect of the broader definition of *terroir*).

20 http://eur-lex.europa.eu/LexUriServ/LexUriServ.do?uri=OJ:L:2010:034:0007 :0016:EN:PDF (accessed 20 May 2013).

21 http://ec.europa.eu/agriculture/quality/schemes/index_en.htm (accessed 20 May 2013).

22 In the aphorisms section of his *The Physiology of Taste* first published in 1825, Jean Anthelme Brillat-Savarin's famously proclaimed: 'Tell me what you eat: I will tell you what you are.'

23 Mumford, *The South in Architecture*, 29.

24 Ibid., 111–119, especially 114.

25 For a synopsis of these varieties of regionalisms see Vincent B. Canizaro, *Architectural Regionalism: Collected Writings on Place, Identity, Modernity and Tradition* (New York: Princeton Architectural Press, 2007).

26 Susan Allport, *Sermons in Stone: The Stone Walls of New England and New York* (New York: W.W. Norton, 1990); Kevin Gardner, *The Granite Kiss: Traditions and Techniques of Building New England Stone Walls* (Woodstock, VT: Countryman Press, 2001).

27 Francis R. Kowsky, 'H. H. Richardson's Ames Gate Lodge and the Romantic Landscape Tradition', *Journal of the Society of Architectural Historians* 50 (1991): 181–188.

28 Vincent Scully, *American Architecture and Urbanism* (New York: Henry Holt and Company, 1988 (new revised edition)), 115.

29 Vincent Scully, *Modern Architecture* (New York: George Braziller, 1994 (revised edition)), 18.

30 Anthony Alofsin, 'Constructive Regionalism', in *Architectural Regionalism*, ed. V. Canizaro (Princeton: Princeton Architectural Press, 2007), 369.

31 An analogous landscape divided by stone walls is found on the Aran Islands, Ireland. For an enlightening study, see Mary Laheen, *Drystone Walls of the Aran Islands* (Wilton: Collins Press, 2010).

32 One seldom thinks it, but every sprinkling of Parmigiano Reggiano is a mélange of the recent present and the distant past. The former because the cheese is never aged longer than thirty-six months, the latter because it is part of a tradition already in place in 1348, when Giovanni Boccaccio mentioned it in his *The Decameron* (VIII, 3).

33 Mumford, *The South in Architecture*, 30.

34 The winery measures 136 m × 24 m × 8 m.

35 Glossary definition for 'Food Communities', http://www.slowfoodib.org/en/slowfood-ib-glosario.php (accessed 20 May 2013).

36 Ibid.

37 My gratitude to Daniel Rosenberg, Samantha Martin-McAuliffe, Albert Narath and Amy Gaddis for their suggestions and help with this study.

Bibliography

Allport, S. *Sermons in Stone: The Stone Walls of New England and New York*, New York. W.W. Norton, 1990.

Alofsin, A. 'Constructive Regionalism' revised and republished. In *Architectural Regionalism: Collected Writings on Place, Identity, Modernity and Tradition*, edited by V. Canizaro. New York: Princeton Architectural Press, 2007.

Boccaccio, G. *The Decameron*. Bari: G. Laterza, 1955.

Brillat-Savarin, J. A. *The Physiology of Taste or Meditations on Transcendental Gastronomy*. New York: Dover Publications, 1960.

Devall, B. and G. Sessions. *Deep Ecology*. Salt Lake City: G.M. Smith, 1985.

Drengson, A. and B. Devall, eds. *Ecology of Wisdom: Writings by Arne Naess*. Berkeley, CA: Counterpoint, 2008.

Gardner, K. *The Granite Kiss: Traditions and Techniques of Building New England Stone Walls*. Woodstock, VT: Countryman Press, 2001.

Kowsky, F. R. 'H. H. Richardson's Ames Gate Lodge and the Romantic Landscape Tradition'. *Journal of the Society of Architectural Historians* 50 (1991): 181–88.

Laheen, M. *Drystone Walls of the Aran Islands*. Wilton: Collins Press, (2010).

Lauden, R. 'Too Many Designations in the Kitchen Editorial'. *The Los Angeles Times*, November 1, 2010. Accessed May 20, 2013. http://articles.latimes.com/2010/nov/01/opinion/la-oe-laudan-unesco-20101101.

van Leeuwen, C. 'Soils and Terroir Expression in Wine'. In *Soil and Culture*, edited by E. Landa and C. Feller. London: Springer, 2010.

Littré, E. *Dictionnaire de la langue française*. Paris: Hachette, 1877.

London Economics. *Evaluation of the CAP policy on protected designations of origin (PDO) and protected geographical indications (PGI), Short Summary*, 2008. Accessed May 20, 2013. http://ec.europa.eu/agriculture/eval/reports/pdopgi/short_sum_en.pdf.

Lowenthal, D. *Possessed by the Past*. New York: The Free Press, 1996.

Mumford, L. *The South in Architecture; The Dancy Lectures, Alabama College*. New York: Harcourt, Brace and Co., 1941.

Russo, M. 'Measuring Shell Rings for Social Inequality'. In *Signs of Power: The Rise of Cultural Complexity in the Southeast*, edited by J. L. Gibson and P. J. Carr. Tuscaloosa: University of Alabama Press, 2004.

Scheffer, S. and B. Sylvander. 'The Effect of Institutional Changes on Qualification Processes: A Survey at the French Institute of Denomination of Origins (INAO)', 52nd Seminar: EU Typical and Traditional Productions: Rural Effect and Agro-industrial Problems, Parma, June 19–22, 1997. La Haye: EAAE, European Association of Agricultural Economists, 1997.

Scully, V. *American Architecture and Urbanism*. New York: Henry Holt and Company, 1988.

Scully, V. *Modern Architecture*. New York: George Braziller, 1994.

Slow Food, Glossary. Accessed May 20, 2013. http://www.slowfoodib.org/en/slowfood-ib-glosario.php.

Smith, D. *Oyster, A World History*. Stroud: The History Press, 2010.

Thornton, R. *What Is Tabby Architecture?* 2011. Accessed May 20, 2013. http://www.examiner.com/article/what-is-tabby-architecture.

Trubek, A. *The Taste of Place, a Cultural Journey into Terroir*. Berkeley: University of California Press, 2008.

Trubek, A. and J. P. Lemasson, eds. *Terroir*. A special volume of *Cuizine: The Journal of Canadian Food Cultures* 2 (2010).

Various Authors. *Dictionnaire de l'Académie française*, 1694. Accessed May 20, 2013. http://artfl-project.uchicago.edu/node/17.

3

Sweetness and Taste: Mapping Maple Syrup in Vermont

Amy B. Trubek

We asked the living wood to give us something sweet and good.[1]

Introduction

Critics of the modern global food system are seekers, embarking on long journeys (following the supply chain, tracing political policies) to discover foods possessing clear virtues (or not). Such exercises illuminate the complexity of how we make and eat food, but do they tell the whole story? Another type of trip involves looking for stories about food at the intersection of moral, sensory *and* social values. These stories reveal the interdependence of multiple values, or as anthropologist Heather Paxson calls it, an ecology of values.[2] Binary thinking will limit any honest understanding of the sheer vastness, chaos and complexity of what constitutes our modes of production, transformation, distribution and consumption of food.

What if we looked more closely at a food that easily meets the contemporary checklist for a virtuous food – local, sustainable, natural, wild – but look at material conditions rather than claims for moral virtue? In the case of an ongoing interdisciplinary research project on Vermont maple syrup, we found values about food that emerge from everyday production and consumption practices. These values, however, were chiefly informed by a larger ethic about the relationship of human beings to the natural environment. Interestingly, the moment of coalescence for everyone involved *tasting* maple syrup, and figuring out the parameters for maple syrup that tastes *good*. Of particular note are the sensory preoccupations of people who transform the tree sap into sweet, sticky syrup along with the sensory evaluations of people who choose between a delicate light or robust dark syrup. Good tasting syrup involves an ethos which integrates sensory quality into an ecology of values.

How do we *know* the tastes of food? How are tastes related to judgements? What makes us think that some tastes are desirable? Problematic? When humans taste food or drink, when the bite or sip rests in the mouth and then moves into our bodies, culture, biology and nature are integrated; this is a universal process. At the same time, taste is ultimately subjective, a sense that can never truly be physiologically shared. The body (or at least the mouth, nose and brain) always mediates between food and drink as an external social object and an internal sensory subject. Thus, once the food or drink enters the human body, sensing taste also requires talking taste. Sharing this particular sensory experience requires oral communication, a shared dialogue with others. The complexity of discerning taste, therefore, lies in how that dialogue develops and what factors shape both the conversation and the final sensory evaluation. Taste can not only be understood or explained at the individual level; our *cultural* tastes ultimately shape our physiological taste experiences. Physiology, context, perception and experience constantly interact as we chew, sip and swallow.

The quest for good maple syrup requires a constant mediation between natural and cultural worlds. To explore sensory tastes requires an engagement with natural and cultural environments in order to 'ground' any abstraction in a lived experience. The sensory experience of tasting food is a pivotal moment when meaning is generated *and* when meaning is confirmed. Sensory studies of food require a phenomenological perspective: not what *should be*, but *what is*.[3] We need to illuminate taste by 'bringing [taste experiences] into the daylight of ordinary understanding'.[4] In the case of maple syrup, focusing on *sensation* and sensory values brings the lived experience of food to front and centre. You cannot remain at the level of moral abstraction or moral absolutism when making a marinade with dark maple syrup and balsamic vinegar or pouring fancy grade Vermont maple syrup on your pancakes.

Focusing on the taste experience as a dialogue between physiological taste and cultural tastes, an interaction between the natural world and social relations, addresses limitations, both in form and content, of much of the contemporary research on food. There is a tendency to marginalize or dismiss the sensory moment, when inner and outer worlds intersect; implicit or explicit critiques of sensory evaluation and discernment reduce the total sensory experiences and meanings to the 'performance' of status and identity. This is reductionism that fails to take account of the multilayered meanings that reside in any given sensory object (maple syrup), the sensory context (the Northern Forest, the sugar houses) and the making or receiving subject (Vermonter).

Mapping the senses: The case of maple syrup

Terroir, or the taste of place, values the ways in which foods can reflect the natural environment, the intersection of that nature with human production practices and the cultural context in which production decisions are made, often carrying on the practices of generations. *Terroir* has long been valued in France as a mode of sensory evaluation while also helping to frame engagements with the agrarian landscape.[5] An interdisciplinary collective of faculty and graduate students at the University of Vermont is involved in exploring such a relationship between food (and drink), place and taste in Vermont. Activities are based on the shared conceptual framework that the tastes of food and drink are mutually constituted by the natural environment and the cultural context. The collective is called the Taste of Place Working Group.[6] All of the research done by working group members considers the experience of tasting and evaluating artisan products from Vermont, with the goal of helping producers, consumers and policymakers better understand sensory qualities and quality.[7] The working group began in 2007 as a collaboration between scholars at the University of Vermont and Middlebury College to better understand the sensory qualities of Vermont maple syrup.[8] The early work involved attempts to link geology, geography and practice to the final sensory experience of tasting maple syrup. By 2008 the Taste of Place Working Group was actively involved in collaborations with the Vermont Agency of Agriculture, Food and Markets, seeking to share the insights of *terroir* (or the taste of place) as a way of understanding maple syrup to sugarmakers in Vermont.[9]

In our research on the contemporary tastes of maple syrup, the importance of the environmental and cultural contexts was clearly central to everyday practice, and thus we determined *must* be considered in order to 'do justice to the lived complexity of experience'.[10] The research programme assumed that *neither* the physical nor social qualities of maple syrup were reducible. In our research collaboration with Vermont sugarmakers, a sensory scientist, the maple expert at the Vermont Agency of Agriculture, Food and Markets and others, we quickly realized that we were not going to find a simple mechanistic understanding for the unique tastes of Vermont maple syrup. Like most researchers, we were tempted to design our research in order to figure out that the answer lay in some simple solution: the soil, the evaporators and timeless tradition. After a long debate, we decided to heed anthropologist Michael Jackson's call that scholars should 'avoi[d] those selective redescriptions, reductions, and generalizations which claim to capture the essence of the lived'.[11] We decided to organize our research with the understanding that the taste of maple syrup was crucial to both producers and consumers and we sought to capture and communicate this importance.

What can the taste of maple syrup tell us about the lived experience of people living in the Northern Forest of Vermont? At the same time, how do the everyday practices of people making maple syrup in the Northern Forest of Vermont shape the taste of maple syrup? These questions framed our research involving ethnographic interviews, participant-observation and sensory panels to document the complex flavours, aromas and tastes of Vermont maple syrup. Placing taste at the centre of the research, considering the sensual moment to be when culture and nature coalesce, was our most important assumption. However, such an approach went counter to the contemporary discussion of maple syrup. In this region, everyone *knows* about this unique food that comes from the sap of trees, most people *see* the trees, but does everyone really *taste* the syrup? An important realization that emerged over the course of the research involved the power of *paying attention* to the sensual moment. We had to figure out how to pay attention as researchers. But we also realized that paying attention to the taste of maple syrup was not a given to those residing in the region. Among maple researchers and sugarmakers, much of the emphasis was on increasing the yield of sap and syrup of the maple trees. Among Vermonters, the long-time convention of selling maple syrup according to colour grades dominated their choices of what maple syrup to buy and use. So the sensory richness of maple syrup was a bit hidden: the centrality of taste suppressed by seemingly more important discussions of traditions, technologies and markets.

Ecology and culture of Vermont maple syrup

Sugar maple trees (*acer saccharum*) grow almost exclusively in the north-east region of Canada and the United States (Figure 3.1). Some stands are found as far south as Georgia, but the larger tracts needed for sugaring are found primarily in the Northern Forest.

As Gregory Bateson would say, 'every schoolchild knows' that sap is the lifeblood of a tree, bringing nourishment (water, sugar, nutrients) from the soil up to the branches, leaves and fruit. Somehow people living in the densely wooded areas now named New York, Vermont, New Hampshire, Maine, New Brunswick, Quebec and Ontario discovered the hidden gift of sugar maples. The uniqueness of the species *acer saccharum* is the high percentage of sucrose: these are sweet trees found only in the northern forests of the New World. Only in this place exist forests of trees full of running sweet sap, and only for one or two months a year, in a time of warm days and cool nights. Now a practice known to many, sugaring has long been a visible part of communities and landscapes in the northern region.

Maple sugaring long predates the establishment of strong national borders between the United States and Canada; fur trappers and traders were aware of and possibly trading syrup by the early 1700s. In Vermont, there is evidence that the Abenaki taught the colonists how to gauge the sugar maple tree with an axe and then use bark buckets to collect the sap. By 1749, other settlers were writing about harvesting sap and boiling it down to maple syrup in large ironware kettles. The methods of procuring sap and making syrup used by the Native Americans and early settlers relied completely on natural conditions. Reed, bark or wood spouts were used to draw off the sap into clay or bark vessels. The sap was boiled into syrup in large kettles, usually suspended by a metal rope hanging from a pole, hanging over a constantly stoked wood fire. The pole was held up by two forked stakes. By the mid-1800s, much of the process was brought indoors. As an early twentieth-century bulletin of the Vermont Department of Agriculture describes, 'The old method of boiling in an open kettle out of doors has been changed. At first a sort of open shed was built and the kettles were placed in an arch. Next the iron pan was substituted for the kettle. Another improvement was the heater, which heated the sap before it entered the pans.'[12] Most rural families owned lands with a 'sugar bush' or a stand of sugar maple trees.

Owning a sugar bush and a sugarhouse, and annually harvesting sap to make maple syrup persists as a rural family tradition throughout Vermont. Each spring, thousands of people go into the woods to tap the maple trees, harvest the sap and move the sap into the many small sugarhouses that dot Vermont's heavily wooded landscape. These sugarhouses are the descendants of the earlier open sheds. They vary in size and appearance, but are generally one main room with a side room or two for wood, propane and other materials needed to help the sap evaporate into syrup. Almost exclusively made of wood, sugarhouses tend to have a steeply pitched roof to prevent pileups of snow and a few windows to help let out the steam generated from the evaporator. Spending time in the sugarhouse with friends and family is commonplace, a rite of spring. John Elder, an environmental writer whose family owns Maggie Brook Sugarworks, writes eloquently of this moment:

Not only does sugaring help us remember that spring is coming, it also gives us a reason for desiring that it not progress any *faster*…This time for standing in the warm, sticky sugarhouse, witnessing the alchemy of air and water into gold. For talking through the night with family beside the shimmering evaporator. Or for drinking a beer with friends who step into the sugarhouse and out of their usual routines.[13]

Unlike other functional buildings populating Vermont's still primarily agrarian and wild landscape, sugarhouses are seen to be centres of both instrumental and social activity. Many, if not most, sugarmakers sell their maple syrup. But when it is time to boil, by bringing people around to talk, share food and drink, and help with the sugaring, the sugarhouse is transformed. This might be due to the snow all around, or the secluded sites of most houses, or the time when sap is most often boiled: 'The sugarhouse was a beautiful sight when we arrived in the dusk. Steam was billowing out of the louvers we had so laboriously built, and a golden light from the Coleman lantern within was shining out of the open door... illuminating both the steam and the smoke from our chimney.'[14] It is in the sugarhouse that all the new season's maple syrup is first tasted and crucial decisions are made: the grade of each run, the possibilities for blending, the markets for selling and the gifts to give to friends.

By the late nineteenth-century metal evaporators were introduced, first invented by David Ingalls in Dunham, Quebec, and then soon updated and adopted by Vermont sugarmakers. This technological innovation, and others, allowed for the development of commercial maple syrup production. By the twentieth century, making maple syrup had moved beyond the backyard woodlot and also involved commercial production. Maple sugaring, like most contemporary farming and foraging practices, straddles between continuity and change in considering the adoption of technological innovations. One of the first was the invention of metal taps that could be inserted into trees to direct the flowing sap. After taps were inserted into maple trees to catch the flowing sap, the sap was collected into metal buckets, which were then transferred into larger containers and transported by horse and wagon to the sugarhouse. Images of such a process are still found on many jugs of maple syrup. Although taps are still central to the process of harvesting sap, at this point the majority of maple sap is transported from the sugar bush (or stands of sweet maple trees) using plastic tubing, with gravity or vacuum extractors pushing the sap down directly into the sugarhouse. Once the sap reaches the sugarhouse, machines that can perform reverse osmosis (removing much of the water from the sap) often carry out the next step. All this occurs before the sap is ever funnelled into the flat metal evaporators that a century earlier transformed the making of maple syrup, creating new possible markets for this wild food.

What is the *purpose* of such an elaborate extraction and reduction process? Sweetness, above all. However, the context for desiring such sweetness is no longer simply the reality of rural farmsteads and small villages, the means of procuring some sweetness for your family during the long cold winter. Maple syrup is now also created as an agricultural commodity, accounted for and supervised by a state agency and trade associations. Canada and the United States are the only two maple syrup–producing countries in the world.

FIGURE 3.1 *Map of the Northern Forest showing the natural distribution for* Acer saccharum *(sugar maple tress). Courtesy Elbert L. Little, Jr., USGS (Public domain), via Wikimedia Commons.*

In most years, Canada accounts for approximately 80 per cent of total maple syrup production, and 95 per cent of that syrup comes from a single province, Quebec.[15] The central and eastern part of the province is responsible for most of this maple syrup. In the United States, Vermont is consistently the number one producer of maple syrup, with the states of Maine, New Hampshire and New York making up most of the remaining production.[16] In 2012, Vermont produced 1,320,000 gallons (or 40 per cent of all maple syrup produced in the United States), with estimates of at least 1.5 million gallons produced in 2013.[17]

The striking difference between Quebec and Vermont is that Quebec now primarily sells maple syrup in bulk (85 per cent of total production in 2005) solely through the auspices of the Quebec Federation of Maple Syrup Producers. Much of this syrup is used in processing and also to redistribute maple products in bulk or prepackaged form. In Vermont, it is estimated over 3,000 people are actively tapping trees to make and sell maple syrup, with some tapping 100 trees and some tapping thousands. In fact, making maple syrup has become a new growth area in Vermont agriculture; in 2000 there were one million taps installed for extracting sap and by 2012 there were over three million taps used. Anyone who wants to sell syrup, whether from the farmstead, to the general store or one of the three major blender/packers in the state, must adhere to state regulations. Much of Vermont maple syrup is sold by individual producers to larger-scale blender-packers, but there is no central system of oversight.

In Vermont the sense of uniqueness has concerned 'purity' and 'quaintness', with maple syrup helping to proclaim the state's reputation as the site of '[t]he pastoral idyll of a clean, green, and serene place'.[18] This approach works since there has been a continuous emphasis on small-scale maple syrup production throughout the state. The increase in tapping involves many new producers with the number of larger producers staying fairly steady. Most maple syrup producers make their syrup on their own for friends, family, local markets, with some selling to the group of blender-packers dominating larger regional, national and global markets. Over 90 per cent of Vermont sugarmakers do not consider sugaring their primary economic activity. A number of regional maple sugaring associations exist but there is no central authority for the approximately 3,000 sugarmakers located throughout the state.

Folklorist Michael Lange's study of continuity and change in Vermont sugarmaking discusses the real understanding and affinity of sugarmakers for the natural environment: 'Sugarmakers know their trees and the land in which they sit.'[19] As one sugarmaker he interviewed put it, 'Oftentimes, when we're in the woods, my brother and I, and sometimes my father, we can talk about different areas, every section of our woods has a different name. We've got places like the snake run or the brown bucket run, and that all represents something that was passed down.'[20] A sense of place, therefore, informs much of the identity of Vermont maple syrup.

Vermont maple syrup is an iconic food, speaking to people's image of the state as representing a bucolic, rural idyllic place, but maple syrup is also important to the economics of Vermont agriculture. The annual Tree Tapping event, where the sitting governor of Vermont taps a maple tree symbolizing the launch of the maple season, reveals both meanings of maple. A recent statewide policy report on the present and future of Vermont's working landscape stated that 'maple syrup production is a significant economic engine for the state with a market value of over $50 million in 2011'.[21] Maple syrup is easily cast as a commodity; for example, annual reports created by the New England office of the United States Department of Agriculture discuss maple syrup in strictly numeric terms:

> The average equivalent price per gallon for maple syrup varies widely across the Region depending on the percentage sold retail, wholesale, or bulk. The 2012 all sales equivalent price per gallon in Connecticut averaged $63.40, down $9.60; Maine averaged $33.00, down $1.00; Massachusetts averaged $51.50, down $5.50; New Hampshire averaged $52.50, up $3.50; New York averaged $43.50, up $4.40; Pennsylvania averaged $39.40, down $0.60 and Vermont averaged $35.50, up $0.50. The high percentage of bulk sales in Vermont and Maine kept average prices below the other States.[22]

What is the narrative here? The generic story of a commodity, bought and sold on the marketplace, hampered by weather but improved by new technologies. Although maple syrup remains a wild food, a happenstance of a certain set of natural conditions, cultural assumptions now categorize it on the shelf, at the supermarket, next to the Domino's cane sugar and near the molasses.

The map of maple: Paying sensory attention

Maple syrup is increasingly in demand, as other sweeteners (high fructose corn syrup, cane sugar) seem fraught with problems, symbolic or otherwise. There is more demand for maple syrup in the United States than since before the Second World War; Vermont maple syrup is now regularly being shipped around the globe, including Japan, Thailand and Australia.[23] Maple syrup, thus, is not simply an artefact of the past, but remains a part of everyday life. And when we do pay attention to maple syrup, the focus (perhaps not surprisingly, given our visual-centric culture) is *visual*. Since the 1940s, the main way maple syrups have been sorted by sugarmakers and sold in the marketplace is by grade, although rules and practices vary between states and between the United States and Canada. In Vermont, since the 1970s, grade has been defined as a combination of appearance by colour and density. The four grades are fancy, medium amber, dark amber and grade B. When a sugarmaker sits in his or her sugarshack, watching the sap evaporate into syrup (it takes 40 gallons of sap to make 1 gallon of syrup) in the larger stainless steel evaporator, he or she *looks* for the moment when the density and colour are uniform. Density is determined when a small bit of syrup is poured into a hydrometer and measured; the goal is 66.9 per cent Brix (this is higher than any other state or national grade). As to colour, the syrup is poured into a glass jar, held up to the light and then compared to standard grade colours, provided in kits that contain four glass jars filled with liquid coloured to approximate each grade.

However, the traditional method of differentiating maple syrups by visual standards is being transformed. This is partially due to changing taste preferences among consumers; in earlier eras lighter grades were perceived as more desirable. There was a positive association in Vermont between fancy syrups and purity. Now people are more attracted to the more robust tastes of darker grades; for example, maple syrup has become a desirable ingredient in marinades and salad dressings. The International Maple Standards Institute has developed new standards to be adopted by all regulatory agencies in Canada and the United States. All syrup that can be sold to consumers is labelled Grade A, with any differences being described by flavour descriptors, such as *golden colour and delicate taste* or *dark colour and robust taste*.

Making sense of maple in the saturation of sweetness that defines modern cuisine is now part of the work of all sugarmakers. Increasingly there is a shared sense (from individual sugarmakers to the maple experts at the Vermont Agency of Agriculture) that the modern story of maple syrup requires an explanation that maple syrup is not just sweet; it is *delicious*. The sensual movement needs to go beyond sweet taste to the aromas and flavours that make maple *more than* sweet. The decision to change the Vermont grade to include an internationally consistent set of flavour descriptors has not been without controversy. Many Vermont sugarmakers have decried these changes as compromising traditional practices: as one sugarmaker from northern Vermont testified at state hearings on the changes, 'This going against Vermont tradition … [W]e're Vermont. Our quality of maple is superior to anything in the world. They ought to be coming to us.'[24] Others involved (in fact, the majority) see the new flavour descriptors as a necessary way to communicate with increasingly far-flung consumers: 'The person who walks into the sugarhouse is going to have the advantage. They are going to be able to have their questions answered and know the product … But the person who walks into a grocery story … or someone from out of state, they don't have that communication.'[25]

Much of the joy and pain of the sugaring season revolves around just what sort of syrup emerges after the sap has been harvested and then boiled down to a viscous liquid. Every year brings new surprises. Lighter syrups can seem floral, or have vanilla notes, or evoke the smells of maple leaves that have fallen on the forest floor. Meanwhile, the maple flavour of darker syrups, depending (among many possibilities) on the location of a sugar bush or the amount of time the sap takes to boil down into syrup, can taste woodier and earthier, with even a hint of mushroom. Soil, tree, slope, weather – it all makes a difference to the taste of maple syrup. But how do we connect such elemental forces to our actual sensory experience? In the sensory moment of tasting maple syrup, experience and knowledge often move down divergent paths.

The goal of the Taste of Place research was to embrace syrup's taste complexity, not, as often has been the case, to funnel it into one singular description or grade; *neither* the physical nor cultural qualities of Vermont maple syrup seemed reducible. Our project began with an embrace of diversity: we decided to organize our tastings geographically and geologically. Differentiating the state by prominent forms of bedrock (schist, shale and limestone), we then plotted sugarmaker and sugar stand locations onto the bedrock map. We identified people and places that best represented geology (primarily on one bedrock) and geography (a certain region). We then sourced syrup (of all grades) from over fifty sugarmakers.

Led by Dr. Montse Almena-Aliste, a sensory scientist at the University of Vermont, and Henry Marckres, the maple expert at the Vermont Agency of Agriculture, we organized a series of tastings with the research team, to see if we could identify certain aromas and flavours characteristic of a grade, a place, a rock, a season. We began to develop a list of sensory descriptors. We also consulted the work of sensory scientists at Centre ACER, the research unit supporting maple syrup production in Quebec.

In our many sensory panels, tasting hundreds of maple syrups, we found incredible diversity of flavour, aroma, taste and mouthfeel. Our sensory panels, sensory discussions and sensory observations (where we tasted syrups 'blind' or without information about what, where, how and when for each syrup) demonstrated the importance of intrinsic and extrinsic characteristics: our ability to identify unique aromas and flavours was not solely *determined* by meaning, value and symbol. We were not able to do the depth of research to conclusively connect a certain aroma or flavour to a specific aspect of the natural environment, but we did see that *paying attention* heightened our ability to taste. Our project turned either to helping others give voice to what was already known (which was the case for many sugarmakers) or to lead others to taste diversity (which was the case for chefs, retailers and consumers).

Our decision, therefore, was to create a sensory *map* of maple (Figure 3.2). We wanted to capture the sensory results, the reality of fancy syrup redolent of vanilla or dark amber with a hint of molasses but also cloves, in a manner that was both culturally explicable and compelling. We came to realize that we had to confront the classic philosophical riddle: if a tree falls in the forest and no one hears it, did it really fall? But in our case, the question was, 'If the maple syrups vary according to grades, or geography, or geology in their

the map of maple

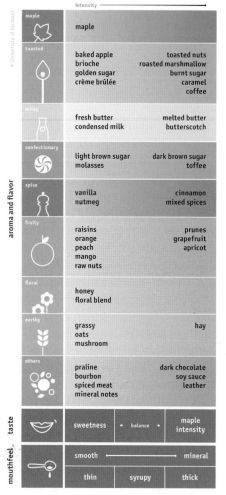

tasting maple syrup

The **map of maple** is a sensory tool, allowing you to explore all the wondrous possibilities of Vermont maple syrup. Here are some hints for tasting on your own.

Smell the syrup before tasting. Try to identify any distinct *aromas*. Take a look at the list of **aroma and flavor** descriptors as a guide.

Take a small sip of the syrup. Move the syrup in your mouth briefly, and *feel* the texture. See the **mouthfeel** section for suggestions.

Then, evaluate the taste characteristics. See the **taste** section for suggestions. For all the *sensory properties evaluated, always try to asses the quality, quantity and balance* of the descriptors identified.

Consider the *flavor* with another sip. See if the sensory "families" help you place the aroma and flavor of the syrup, allowing you to identify and describe each particular maple syrup.

If possible, taste and share your reactions with a friend. Sometimes tasting and talking with others can help your descriptions.

why taste and tell?

Maple syrup is an old-fashioned yet long-lived taste of Vermont. Exploring the differences between Vermont syrups can capture the variety of delightful and delicious possibilities the state has to offer. Learning the qualities that make each batch of maple syrup unique helps create exciting new conversations where producers, retailers and consumers engage in identifying the aromas, flavors and tastes of your favorite syrup. Though you might use this tool in a variety of ways, we hope it can serve as a roadmap on a fabulous journey through Vermont's distinctive maple syrups.

"[When] you do sip your way through a few 'syrup flights,' you quickly realize that maple syrups are wildly different once you get beyond that great bear hug of sweetness." —**food writer Rowan Jacobsen in American Terroir**

the taste of Vermont

This sensory map captures the delicious qualities of Vermont maple syrup. A team of researchers, sugarmakers and sensory panelists collaborated over several years by evaluating maple syrup from throughout the state of Vermont. It was jointly developed by the Nutrition and Food Sciences Department at University of Vermont and the Vermont Agency of Agriculture Food and Markets. Reseachers at Middlebury College were also involved. State funds for this project were matched with Federal funds under the Federal-State Marketing Improvement Program of the Agricultural Marketing Service, U.S. Department of Agriculture.

The University of Vermont   VERMONT AGENCY OF AGRICULTURE, FOODS & MARKETS

FIGURE 3.2 *The Map of Maple, a sensory evaluation tool. Courtesy of University of Vermont (TM).*

taste, but no one communicates these variations, do they exist?' We needed to identify *and* communicate this variation.

The map reflects such sensory diversity but it also creates a case for it. We decided not to determine but rather to guide. The Map of Maple was distributed to sugarmakers, chefs, retailers and others in Vermont to bring social attention to the unique deliciousness of maple syrup. Several thousand maps have been distributed and more will be produced in the future. Henry Marckres uses the map now every year when he runs the International Grading

Schools that attract producers from throughout the northern tier of the United States and much of Canada. The Map of Maple guides tasting and talking about maple syrup, making visible the cultural and environmental context for the aroma, flavours and tastes of this wild food of the Northern Forest. For many interested in the taste of place as well as traditional, local, wild and artisan food and drink the dialogical approach that our research ultimately adopted may be necessary.[26]

Conclusion

[Maple syrup] has a wild delicacy of flavor that no other sweet can match. What you smell in freshly cut maple-wood, or taste in the blossom of the tree, is in it. It is then, indeed, the distilled essence of the tree. (John Borroughs: 1886)[27]

We hunted and fished, yet sugar was our principal food during the whole month of April. (Englishman Alexander Henry's description of his Canadian sojourn from 1770–1776)[28]

And so centuries after any first accounts of sweet trees, sweet sap and sweet syrup, the practice continues throughout the Northern Forest. Politics and economics have intervened into the shared landscape of maple trees in the region of Northern Forest that now includes Vermont, New Hampshire, Maine, Quebec and New Brunswick. Long before colonization and the subsequent creation of the nation-states of Canada and the United States (and perhaps long after), sugar maple trees filled the northern forests. In many respects a distinct bioregion bisected by a national border, maple syrup remains central to the relationship between nature and culture.

Emplacing the sensory qualities of maple is part of an ongoing dialogue, without a clear cultural consensus, for as David Howes puts it, 'Sensation is not just a matter of physiological response and personal experience. It is the most fundamental domain of cultural expression, the medium through which all the values and practices of society are enacted.'[29] Thus, although sugarmakers acknowledge that sensory quality is an important shared value, there is always a tension between continuity and change: folklorist Lange points out that:

[s]ugarmakers are always negotiating a balance. The balancing act is a constant, too, though. Terroir is, in this way, no different from, say, vacuum systems. When vacuum was first introduced into sugarmaking, there were a few early adopters, and the industry watched curiously and cautiously at the results of these early adoptions. Terroir has been accepted by a few sugarmakers, but many are waiting in the wings to see what happens.[30]

So many questions about knowing emerge when the analytic gaze opens up to a wider horizon for making sense of taste. At base, we have these questions that are yet to be well answered by any scholars, be it anthropologists, geographers, historians, sensory scientists, psychologists or others: How do we know what we know about discerning and evaluating tastes? Why do we know what we know? How do food studies scholars create a nuanced analysis and discussion of how best to link values to food when trying to create *or* analyse change in a food system? And how does this nuanced analysis and discussion occur when our frames of research can involve the interdependent relationships of production, transformation, distribution and consumption on the small scale of a tiny rural state like Vermont, on the vast scale of the entire globe, or both? These are not simple questions with simple answers. What is most important is to clearly identify what values *matter*: to ourselves, to the people and community we study and to the 'resilient' functioning of a food system. In other words, in the meeting of intrinsic and extrinsic characteristics of food *emerge* the values shaping our food system. If we want to imagine future food systems that are not just virtuous but resilient and sustainable, we are well served if we focus on an ecology of values that acknowledges the power of taste. Power to inform our lived understanding of food. Power to reflect our constant interdependence with the natural world in order to subsist, survive and thrive. Power to bring nourishment, sustenance and pleasure to that most universal human experience – making, sharing and eating food.[31]

Notes

1   This comes from a banner in an exhibition of maple products in Vermont in 1915. Walter H. Crockett, *How Vermont Maple Sugar Is Made* (Bulletin of the Vermont Department of Agriculture, No. 21, March 1915), 22.

2   Heather Paxson, *The Life of Cheese* (Berkeley: University of California Press, 2012).

3   Michael Jackson's scholarship on considering being-in-the world and Tim Ingold's work on skilful practice are particularly compelling when considering food.

4   Michael Jackson, *Things as They Are: New Directions in Phenomenological Anthropology* (Bloomington: Indiana University Press, 1996), Introduction.

5   Amy B. Trubek, *The Taste of Place: A Cultural Journey into Terroir* (Berkeley: University of California Press, 2008).

6   For more information about the Working Group, consult the following website: http://www.uvm.edu/~nfsfood/?Page=about.html.

7   The Map of Maple is now distributed by the Vermont Agency of Agriculture, Food and Markets. Members of the working group do collaborative research

with Vermont food artisans and provide reports and presentations about the results of the research.

8 In this iteration, our working group was comprised of John Elder, Jeff Munroe, Lee Corbett, Montse Almena-Aliste, Amy B. Trubek and Henry Marckres.

9 In 2009, graduate students and faculty in the Department of Nutrition and Food Sciences at the University of Vermont launched a research project to document possible relationships between dairy farms, artisan cheesemaking and the sensory characteristics of Vermont farmstead cheese.

10 Jackson, *Things as They Are*, 8.

11 Ibid.

12 Crockett, *How Vermont Maple Sugar Is Made*, 11.

13 John Elder, *The Frog Run: Words and Wildness in the Vermont Woods* (Minneapolis: Milkweed Editions, 2001), 5–6.

14 Ibid., 92.

15 In Quebec, maple syrup production is vital to the province's agricultural sector, with the province creating over 70 per cent of the world's production of maple syrup. In Quebec, about 85 per cent of production is sold in bulk to packers or bulk buyers and exporters who redistribute bulk or pre-packaged maple products. These products can be sold to food stores, supermarkets and gift shops in both domestic and international markets. Producers can sell maple products of 5 litres or less directly to the consumer.

16 USDA National Agricultural Statistics Service, 'Maple Syrup Production', *USDA-NASS, New England, New York and Northeastern Regional Field Offices*, June 2013, http://www.nass.usda.gov/Statistics_by_State/New _England_includes/Publications/0605mpl.pdf.

17 USDA-NASS, 'Maple Syrup Production'.

18 Michael Lange, 'Sweet Bedfellows: Continuity, Change and Terroir in Vermont Maple Syrup', *Digest*, 2012, http://digest.champlain.edu/article1_3.html.

19 Ibid.

20 Ibid.

21 Sawyer et al., Vermont Sustainable Jobs Fund, 'Food Production: Maple Syrup', in *Farm to Plate Strategic Plan*, 1, May 2013, http://www.vtfoodatlas .com/assets/plan_sections/files/3.3_Food%20Production_Maple%20Syrup _MAY%202013.pdf.

22 USDA-NASS, 'Maple Syrup Production'.

23 Henry Marckres (Vermont Agency of Agriculture, Food and Markets), in discussion with the author, 8 April 2013.

24 Carolyn Whitney Branagan, Testimony to the House Committee on Agriculture and Forest Products, 2 April 2013. Accessed through audio files.

25 Matt Gordon, Testimony to the House Committee on Agriculture and Forest Products, 2 April 2013. Accessed through audio files.

26 Presently there is much *terroir*-inspired activity both north and south. In Quebec, the provincial ministry of agriculture recently launched the *Conseil* *des appellations réservées et des terms valorisants* (CARTV), a version of protected denomination of origin that supports and promotes quality labels for unique place-based food and drink (although maple syrup is not part of the designation system due to the singular role of the Confederation). In Vermont, we are using our scholarly research to participate in a conversation between artisan producers, chefs and the public about the sensory qualities of place-based foods. In Vermont, there are active discussions about the possibility of building place designation for maple syrup. Sensory evaluations are part of these activities.

27 Quoted in Helen Nearing and Scott Nearing, *The Maple Sugar Book* (New York: Schocken Books, 1970), 4.

28 James M. Lawrence and Rux Martin, *Sweet Maple: Life, Lore and Recipes from the Sugarbush* (Montpelier, VT: Chapters Publishing, Ltd-Vermont Life, 1993) 63.

29 David Howes, *Sensual Relations: Engaging the Senses in Culture and Social Theory* (Ann Arbor: University of Michigan Press, 2003), xi.

30 Lange, 'Sweet Bedfellows'.

31 Some sections of this chapter were previously published in the essay 'Visible Sap', *Sensate*, 2012, http://sensatejournal.com/2012/06/amy-b -trubek-visible-sap/.

Bibliography

Branagan, C. W. 'Testimony before the Vermont House Committee on Agriculture and Forest Products, "Joint resolution supporting the Agency of Agriculture, Food and Markets" proposal to adopt an administrative rule to implement international maple grading standards in Vermont' (JRS14), Hearing, April 2, 2003.

Crockett, W. H. 'How Vermont Maple Sugar is Made'. *Bulletin of the Vermont Department of Agriculture* 21 (1915): 11, 22.

Elder, J. *The Frog Run: Words and Wildness in the Vermont Woods.* Minneapolis: Milkweed Editions, 2001.

Gordon, M. 'Testimony before the Vermont House Committee on Agriculture and Forest Products, "Joint resolution supporting the Agency of Agriculture, Food and Markets" proposal to adopt an administrative rule to implement international maple grading standards in Vermont' (JRS14), Hearing, April 2, 2003.

Howes, D. *Sensual Relations: Engaging the Senses in Culture and Social Theory.* Ann Arbor: University of Michigan Press, 2003.

Jackson, M. *Things as They Are: New Directions in Phenomenological Anthropology.* Bloomington: Indiana University Press, 1996.

Lange, M. 'Sweet Bedfellows: Continuity, Change, Terroir in Maple Syrup', *Digest: A Journal of Foodways and Culture* 1 (2012), http://digest.champlain.edu/vol1/ article1_3.html.

Lawrence, J. M. and R. Martin. *Sweet Maple: Life, Lore and Recipes from the Sugarbush.* Montpelier, VT: Chapters Publishing, Ltd-Vermont Life, 1996.

Nearing, H. and S. Nearing. *The Maple Sugar Book*. New York: Schocken Books, 1996.

Paxson, H. *The Life of Cheese*. Berkeley: University of California Press, 2012.

Sawyer, Scott et al. 'Vermont Sustainable Jobs Fund, "Food Production: Maple Syrup"'. *Farm to Plate Strategic Plan*, 1 (May 2013).

Trubek, A. B. *The Taste of Place: A Cultural Journey into Terroir*. Berkeley: University of California Press, 2008.

USDA National Agricultural Statistics Service. 'Maple Syrup Production'. *USDA-NASS, New England, New York and Northeastern Regional Field Offices*, June 2013. http://www.nass.usda.gov/Statistics_by_State/New _England_includes/Publications/0605mpl.pdf.

4

Slaughtering the Pig in Kéa

Aglaia Kremezi

Setting out

From the very first winter we spent on the island of Kéa, one of the northernmost islands in the Greek Cyclades, I had spread the word that I was interested in pig-slaughtering. I was longing to witness the age-old rituals involved in this process, but no invitation came. Whenever I repeated my wish to various people, it so happened that they had just slaughtered their pig, as they said, or they were planning to do it later, and they would certainly invite me. But nobody did, not for two whole years. Finally, one day Angelos Atzakas, who owns the island's nursery, told my husband, Costas, that his father was slaughtering his pig, and we were invited to the feast. 'Don't come too early because you will probably get bored waiting for the food and drinks', he told Costas, 'just come for lunch and stay on as long as you like'. I, of course, wanted to witness the procedure – minus the actual killing, for which I had no stomach.

In the dead of winter, when seaside taverns are closed and the cold wind beats mercilessly against the deserted beaches, islanders slaughter their pigs. Pig-slaughtering is still an important annual festival for the locals on Kéa, as on all the Cycladic islands. This unique winter ritual is both old and pervasive. When previous generations withstood periods of frugality – a sense of necessary thriftiness to which we now seemed to have returned – slaughtering was an essential undertaking. Importantly, it also had evolved into an occasion, an opportunity for residents to gather, eat and drink homemade wine and *raki* (the local moonshine), while helping in the post-slaughtering process: the division of the carcass, and the making of sausages as well as other cured meats.

The *Jamón Iberico* of the Cyclades is called *loza* in Kéa, and *louza* in Mykonos, Syros, Tinos and other nearby islands. The word clearly originates from the Italian *lonza*, which is a cured pork loin. The point of origin or lineage of this foodstuff is no surprise given that that some Cycladic islands were under Venetian rule from the thirteenth to the fifteenth centuries, and others until the seventeenth century or even later.[1] By the fifteenth century, Kéa was dominated by pirates and almost deserted by its inhabitants. Around 1537, it was taken over by the Ottomans and repopulated partly by Arvanites (Albanians) as well as by people who fled from other islands.[2] My maternal grandfather's family probably came from the island of Patmos, as my mother's maiden name, Patiniotis, suggests. Others came from the mainland, but many of the sixteenth-century settlers on Kéa, Andros and other islands of the northern Cyclades were Arvanites. It is not only fascinating that traditional Venetian food habits were adopted by all – both the natives of the Cyclades and by Arvanites; it is also remarkable that these foods, and also to a degree their attendant material culture, have survived on the islands to this day.

It cannot be overestimated that the ritual of pig-slaughtering is both time-honoured and very literally present in the built environment of the island of Kéa. Every *kathikia* (or *kathedra*), as the old stone-built Kean farmhouses are called, has a sturdy hook cemented between the slates that cover the porch – the *stegadi* – connecting the two rooms of the house. Whatever it might be used for throughout the year – mainly for hanging the occasional butchered lamb or kid – come winter the *stegadi* reclaims its primary function: the place to hang the slaughtered pig. Usually, the principal places for keeping animals were either the *tsela*, a small cell-like outbuilding adjacent to the farmhouse, or *stavlia*, outer-shacks.[3] Today the *stegadia* – shaded and cool in the summer, and protected from the wind and rain in the winter – still remain the very centre of all activities. Therefore, in this particular setting, the preparation of consumables fuses with the spatial contexts: food and architecture become one. Traditional Greek farmhouses, and indeed some village homes even to this day, have no spacious kitchens, like their French or Italian counterparts, just a hearth on the side of the main room, often a few inches from the floor, not even at waist level. Food was cooked in a pot resting on a tripod in the hearth, much like in antiquity, and the cook had to lean down and sometimes sit on a small stool to stir the food. Any chopping was done over the pot, as there was no working surface. Even now that modern kitchens in Greece typically have counters all around their periphery, my mother as well as many of my friends and my local assistants cut onion, parsley and other herbs holding them with their left hand and slicing against their thumb over the cooking pot. Our forebears kneaded bread with clenched fists in a trough placed on a low stool or on a chair; to roll *phyllo*, a special round board was used, and when the work was done, it was hung on the wall. Even during the winter most cooking preparations were, and are still done in the present day, in the *stegadi*. Generations ago there was hardly any space in the small kitchen/all-purpose room of the vernacular farmstead, and today it is certainly more pleasant to peel artichokes or roll dolmades in the cool-shaded porch in the summer. Although many people now feel that their precious domestic kitchens should be kept pristine, they much prefer, even in cold winter days, to do most of the cooking and certainly to fry fish or potatoes on a small butane stove at the *stegadi*.

Pig-slaughtering (called *choirosphagia* in Greek) starts early in the morning and it may go on until very late in the night. Islanders consider the slaughtering to be a kind of *panigyri*, the village feast traditionally organized in Kéa by families on their patron saint's name day in one of the little private chapels that dot the island landscape. *Panigyri* commences with a church service in the early morning, and usually ends just before dawn the next day. However, unlike a typical *panigyri*, where only the women work preparing and serving food and drinks, during pig-slaughtering men and women share the labour. The 'man's' work – the killing, hanging and butchering of the pig – usually finishes early. The processing work done by the women continues for the next two or three days. The tedious chopping and boiling of the fat, the grinding and spicing of the bits and pieces for the sausages, the preparation of the meat that will become *loza* and the slippery 'needlework' that secures the pieces inside the pig's large intestine are all women's work. Women also cook and serve *meze* and lunch for everybody present at the feast, and do the most time-consuming of all chores: the careful washing and preparation of the intestines that will serve as the casings for both the sausages and *loza*.

Shaving the pig

The scene before me, when I arrived at the Atzakas' house around 11:00 am in the morning, was surreal. The huge slain pig was stretched out in the yard between the pots of carnation and basil, draining and drowning in its own pools of blood. Angelos' father, fitted with a pair of galoshes, was meticulously shaving the slain animal with an old-fashioned razor blade. The tedious work took almost an hour, and I still fail to understand fully the importance of this step, but apparently it is not uncommon. In fact, in Moldavia and other Balkan countries, people use a cruder if more efficient way to get rid of the hair: they cover the pig with hay and set it ablaze, before butchering the blackened carcass.

The next step was the most difficult. Transporting and hanging the massive 200-pound pig upside down took four men lifting and dragging a makeshift pulley, and two more men assisting. When I told them that in Romania pigs are butchered flat on a table, they were shocked. 'It has to hang. How else can you get rid of the blood?', they wondered. In the more frugal past, in Crete and in other parts of Greece, people used some of the blood mixed with cracked wheat or barley, to make sausages. Keans never did such a thing, they assured me, disgusted even with the idea.

It was a cold, sunny February day, and the warm water Mr. Atzakas poured over the carcass steamed excessively. I photographed the severed pig's feet, which, they assured me, were going to feed the dogs. When I mentioned the delicious slow-roasted pig's feet I had at *Brasserie Balzar* in Paris, they admitted that in the past pig trotters were boiled in order to render thick and warming soups. The real butchering was now ready to begin, and Periklis Mouzakis, the island's blacksmith, stepped in. He slashed open the belly and extracted the huge mass of intestines with the rest of the innards (I have the photo, but even I do not want to look at it again). Mr. Atzakas separated the liver and washed it, before sending it to the women in the kitchen. Cut into bite-size pieces, dredged in flour and fried in olive oil, the liver would be the first *meze* to accompany the home-made red wine. It is more than likely that in the distant past these tasty morsels would have been fried on the hearth. Periklis, helped by Andreas Manolemis, cut off the pig's head and washed his knife. The men volunteered to pose for a picture with the head as a trophy, like the images of the hunters in Africa, Mr. Atzakas said (Figure 4.1).

The pig's head

Throughout the winter, the island's butchers occasionally used to hang pig heads outside their shops. They wanted to assure the locals, and especially the Athenian customers who visit Kéa on weekends, that their meat really comes from local pigs, and this is the reason why it is considerably more expensive than the low-quality stock-pork imported from various European countries. Young people, even the locals, were startled by the sight as they probably forgot that the neatly packaged pink pieces of meat available in supermarkets were once part of a living animal with a big, imposing head. The very public display of pig heads has almost disappeared, as very few cooks nowadays make *tsiladia* (head cheese) following the traditional island recipe: the head simmers for hours in watered wine, until the meat falls from the bones. Then, after it cools a bit, the flesh is separated from the bones, chopped and mixed with plenty of garlic, lemon juice, capers and freshly ground pepper. The pieces are stirred back into the broth, and the mixture is poured into various containers. *Tsiladia* is refrigerated overnight, until well set, and it is served as a *meze*, with slices of bread. I used to make it at least once every winter, because it keeps well for a week at least, and accompanied with a green salad, it can be a wonderful and quick lunch. But I stopped preparing it, because my husband, Costas, hates it, and only takes a bite or two. It was too much work wasted, as I ended up sharing the head

FIGURE 4.1 *The slaughtered pig hangs from the hook cemented between the roof slates of the* stegadi *as the late Mr Atzakas (left) and the other men pose with the massive head. Photo by Aglaia Kremezi.*

cheese with my spoiled pet dogs. However, as a sign of the changing times, a butcher at the port offered me a pig's head for free – he was not expecting anybody to buy it, I guess. He advised me to roast it in a covered clay pot, basted with olive oil and sprinkled with chopped garlic and wild savoury, the island's herb of choice. I followed his advice and the result was memorable. My sister and her husband happened to be visiting us, and although they seemed a bit sceptical when I put the head in the oven, they loved the bits of meat with the crackling skin, and all of us, Costas included, could not stop devouring it, ears, eyes and all.

The pig's hide and lard

Periklis began to break down the carcass by methodically removing the pig's hide in equal-sized ribbons. The philosophical explanation I got when I asked why it was done in this manner was 'this is the right way to do it'. Mr. Atzakas said that he had no use for the skin, and he was going to throw it to the dogs. He reminded me, though, that in more frugal times the pig's skin was used to bind and make a kind of rustic sandal, with the soles cut from pieces of worn-out car tyres. In my childhood, when we used to visit my paternal grandmother in the port city of Piraeus, we often came across islanders who had just stepped off a boat wearing these crude sandals that had curved rubber soles. My father called these island antiquarians 'Byzantine saints' because they actually looked like the icon of John the Baptist: extremely thin, with dark and wrinkled complexions from the endless hours they spent working the fields or fishing under the sun. Up until recently, the word *gourounotsaroucha* (pig-skin shoes) was still used to describe badly made, uncomfortable footwear; now these sandals can only be found in museums.

After skinning the pig, the fat had to be removed. Mr. Atzakas beamed with pride at the considerable amount of fat his pig had accumulated. 'I was waking up in the middle of the night to feed it once more', he said. Although he was going to use only a small amount, and most of the fat would be thrown away (not fed to the dogs, I hoped), he was raising his pig in the manner passed down from his ancestors, in times when fat was a precious part of the pig.

Most cooking and baking was done with lard all over the Cyclades. Few of the islands have an adequate amount of olive trees to produce enough oil for the island kitchens, and even if the people had olive oil, pork fat was very much appreciated for its taste. In the 1960s, when 'progress' came to this part of the world, Greeks were convinced that lard was bad for them, while margarines were *the* 'healthy' fat for modern people. We all know how that story ended. Ironically, 'traditional' Keans are not entirely convinced that margarine is worse than lard, and most pork fat is still wasted today. Periklis follows the tradition and separates the fat from the inside of the belly – which people call *vassiliko* (royal) – from the outer layer of fat, under the pig's skin. 'Royal fat' is considered the best: silky and almost tasteless, it is reserved for baking. The women chopped some of it and dropped it in a blackened copper cauldron, adding some water. They set it to boil over a wood fire, at the side of the yard.

Meat in the freezer

Periklis halved the carcass with a heavy cleaver and proceeded to divide the various parts of the animal, helped by his brother, Yannis. They cut large chunks that they transported to the back of the house and piled them up into a brand new large horizontal freezer. Mr. Atzakas and his wife told us how this recent acquisition had changed their lives. They could now keep as much meat as they wanted to cook over the coming months. They did not have to slave for three days curing the various parts, like in the 'old days', they said.

The day of my first partaking of *choirosphagia* got very chilly as the sun was setting. The men's work was almost done at Atzakas' house, so we all welcomed the idea of going into the house, to warm by the fireplace. Angelos was grilling pork chops on the hearth, and his mother was frying the chopped liver and other innards, while a couple more pots were cooking on the gas stove. As we sat at the table to eat the grilled chops, I felt somewhat disappointed that I was not going to see them prepare *tsigarides* and *paspala* (Kean pork *confit*), sausages and *loza*. In fact, a year would pass before I had the chance to witness and record my neighbour Zenovia as she prepared those delicacies. I felt cold, exhausted, hungry and a bit dizzy from the wine, and stopped taking photographs. Maria, Angelos' sister, arrived on the afternoon ferry. It was Friday, and her classes had ended – she used to teach English at a high school near the port of Lavrion – and came home on weekends. The moment she stepped in, she took from her bag a neatly folded tea towel with her knives, eager to help Periklis and Yiannis cut the meat. She seemed very disappointed when she saw that the work was almost over, angry at the perpetually delayed ferry. More relatives and friends started to arrive as Costas and I were getting ready to leave. We would miss the real feast, they told us, and Angelos' mother protested that we had hardly eaten anything, and she was going to serve many different dishes. Sadly, I do not remember what she was cooking since I have no pictures to jog my memory.

Addendum: Kéa's pork delicacies

The rocky hill on the northern side of our property belongs to the Stefa family. On top of the hill is the house where the late Flora Stefa lived. Her son, Tasos, built his house down by the bay at Otzias, but keeps his animals – a couple of cows, sheep, goats, a pig and some chickens – on his mother's land. The sheep and goats graze around our property, and from the window next to my desk I often exchange glances with Taso's beautiful brown, grey or dappled goats as they nibble the meagre sprouts between the steep rocks. They clearly wish that they could climb the dry stone wall that separates them from our garden. Each day, Tasos yells in his unique way from the top of his lungs to let the goats know it is milking time; the goats return faithfully, and our dogs just as regularly bark and go crazy.

Zenovia, Taso's wife, is one of the best cooks on the island, and I often consult her whenever I have questions about the authentic Kean way of doing things in the kitchen. After seeing the Atzakas family butcher their pig, I was looking forward to learning from Zenovia how to prepare different

FIGURE 4.2 *A restored* kathikia *(stone farm house) in Poises, on the southwest part of Kéa. The length of roof's stone slates dictate the room/house's width. There is a window in one side and a door on the other. Photo by Aglaia Kremezi.*

kinds of cured pork. Taso and Zenovia's relatively new house at the beach has no *stegadi* from which to hang the pig. So they make the short trip to his mother's home where they butcher the spring lambs and kids, the pig as well as the occasional milk-fed veal in a large garage-like space that Tasos constructed for that very purpose. The long tin-roofed room has a fireplace on the far end, while next to the entrance the hooks for hanging the slaughtered animals protrude out: a thoroughly modern reinterpretation of the vernacular farmhouses that once populated the island.

When I arrived, one afternoon in February, Zenovia, her sister and a friend were preparing and stuffing the sausages at the near side of a long table set in the middle of the room. At the far end, next to the blazing fireplace, the complacent men were sitting and drinking *raki*. Their work, the slaughter and butchering, was done; now relaxed and somewhat inebriated, they were teasing the women with sexual innuendos as the sausages were filled.

Sausages

To make the sausage stuffing, Zenovia uses bits of leftover meat from the loin and the ham, after the prime pieces for *loza* have been cut and trimmed. While grinding the meat she adds fat: about a quarter to a third of the mixture should be fat, she said. She flavours the stuffing with home-made and strong red wine, salt, pepper and ground allspice, adding plenty of *thrymbi* (wild savoury). *Thrymbi* (called *throumbi* in other parts of Greece) is gathered from the hills all around the island, and tastes like a cross between wild thyme and mountain oregano. It is the herb of choice for Keans. The sausages are briefly macerated in wine and then hung to smoke for two to three days. For the low smoky fire, maintained about three feet from the sausages, Zenovia adds copious amounts of almond shells. Each garden has a few almond trees, and with these nuts Zenovia makes the most wonderful traditional flour-less cookies. She adds the woody stems of *thrymbi* to the fire, as well as the onionskins that she has been collecting for months because they produce lots of smoke, she tells me. On Mykonos and other smaller islands, the sausages are dipped in salty brine and air-dried in the wind during the cold yet sunny winter days. Mykonos is a particularly arid island, and their precious quantity of wood is not wasted for smoking meats.

Loza

The pieces of meat destined for *loza* are generously salted for a day or two, and then most of the salt is washed off in a wine bath. Meanwhile, the large intestine is thoroughly cleaned and soaked in wine. Pepper, ground allspice and *thrymbi* are sprinkled all over the meat, which is then carefully packed into the large intestine. It is a particularly difficult job, as the casing tears easily. Zenovia, needle and thread in hand, sews carefully the torn spots of intestine, fitting it tightly around the meat. Finally, pieces of string are passed through one end of the meat, and *lozes* (plural of *loza*) are hung over the fire to smoke for three days. They are ready to eat after about a month, as they need to hang in the wintry sun, a few hours each day, until firm and dark.

Paspalas *(pork confit) and* Tsigara

Well-prepared *paspalas* are the Kean equivalent of duck confit. The ribs, and other pieces of fatty meat, are boiled in well-salted water until tender. The water is then drained off, and the meat is sautéed in its own fat, then preserved in jars covered by lard. Throughout the year, pieces of *paspalas* are cooked with eggs, greens and vegetables, often together with other meats, like the local veal, to flavour winter stews. Zenovia makes the most wonderful fresh fava and lettuce stew with *paspala*, finishing the dish with *avgolemono*, the typical Greek egg–and-lemon sauce. Yannis, in his eponymous tavern in Hora (the island's main town), uses *paspala* for a much-praised Kean dish, a kind of rich scrambled eggs that combines pieces of pork confit with tomato sauce; this dish is also called '*paspalas*'.

Tsigara, the smaller pieces of meat and fat, prepared exactly like *paspalas*, take their name from the verb *tsigarizo* (to fry or sauté). Kept in a jar and submerged in lard, *tsigara* are the equivalent of modern-day flavouring cubes, but with an incomparable richness and depth of flavour. Tablespoons of *tsigara* are added to greens, vegetables and pulses, all through the winter, transforming already good dishes into sumptuous delicacies. They are also used to make *glynokouloures* (flat breads flavoured with *glyna, as* pork fat is called on Kéa). Islanders, even those who have foresworn the use of lard in the mistaken belief that it is worse for your health than butter and margarine, dreamingly describe the sublime flavour *tsigara* adds to baked or fried potato dishes.

Notes

1 Ιωάννου Ψύλλα, *Ιστορία της Νήσου Κέας* (Σύνδεσμος Κείων 1921; facsimile reprint by Βουρκαριανή, 1992) [Ioannou Psilla, *Istoria tis nisou keas* (Syndesmos Keion 1921; facsimile reprint by Vourkariani, 1992)], and J. Longnon, 'Problèmes de l'histoire de la principauté de Morée', *Journal des savants* (premier article, April–June 1946): 77–93. Also useful is R.-J. Loenertz,

'Marino Dandolo, seigneur d'Andros et son conflit avec l'évêque Jean (1225–1238)', in *Byzantina et Franco-Graeca* (Storia e Letteratura, Raccolta di Studi e Testi 118). Rome, 1970.

2 Arvanites, a minority population in Greece, originated in Albania and settled across the Greek mainland and islands during the thirteenth and fourteenth centuries. They speak their own language, Arvanitika. See P. Trudgill and G. Tzavaras, *A Sociolinguistic Study of Albanian Dialects Spoken in Attica and Biotia Areas of Greece* (London: Social Science Research Council Report, 1975). Also helpful is Ioannou Psilla, *Istoria tis nisou keas* (Syndesmos Keion 1921; facsimile reprint by Vourkariani, 1992) as well as the history page of the 'official' Kéa website http://www.golden-greece.gr/places/kyklades/kea/kea_kea.html (in Greek; accessed 19 March 2015).

3 A. Vionis, *A Crusader, Ottoman, and Early Modern Aegean Archaeology: Built Environment and Domestic Matierla Culture in the Medieval and Post-Medieval Cyclades, Greece (13th–20th Centuries AD)*. Leiden University Press (Archaeological Studies Leiden University 22) 2012: 104–106. See also T. M. Whitelaw, 'The ethnoarchaeology of recent rural settlement and land use in northwest Keos', in *Landscape Archaeology as Long-Term History: Northern Keos in the Cycladic Islands from Earliest Settlement until Modern Times*, eds. J. F. Cherry, J. L. Davis and E. Mantzourani (Los Angeles: University of California Press, 1991), 403–454.

5

The Gastro-Topography and Built Heritage of Dublin, Ireland

Máirtín Mac Con Iomaire

The word 'topography' derives from the Greek *topos* (place) and *graphia* (to write), and in Classical literature it was used to describe writing about a place or local history. This chapter discusses how place names can enlighten our understanding of the past, particularly Ireland's gastronomic and culinary history. I will explore the etymology of some food-related place names in Ireland and discuss what this data can tell us about the food habits of our ancestors. I will then focus on Dublin's gastro-topography and discuss aspects of the food-related built environment within the capital city. Place names can provide a lens to study traditions, practices or trades that were once widespread. Certain districts of both Dublin and other Irish cities were linked with specific trades, and the street names often relate to this history, although the trade or industry is but a distant memory. Dublin's Linenhall district, for example, has streets such as Coleraine Street, Lisburn Street and Lurgan Street, which reflect the northern Irish influence that dominated the Irish linen trade. The Dublin linen industry was relatively short-lived but the street names endure. Street names such as Cook Street, Fishamble Street and Winetavern Street identify the associations certain streets had with particular food trades in the past, although no cook shops and, I believe, not even one cook lives on Cook Street today! The concentration of bakers and cooks in Cook Street just outside the Hiberno-Norse north wall of medieval Dublin was logical, as their fires and ovens would have proved a potential danger to the city householders and the river would have provided an adequate source of water for extinguishing out-of-control fires.[1] Exploring food-related locations within the fabric of Dublin city, this chapter highlights how a close reading of the built environment can reveal traces of previous food-related industries and associations.

Early influences

Waves of settlers, invaders and indigenous Irish have influenced the changing urban and rural topography, and glimpses of the past are often found in the place names that have endured over time. For example, the Viking influence is to be seen in the County Kildare town of Leixlip. The Irish name of the town is *Léim an Bhradáin*, the leap of salmon. *Lax* is the Norse for salmon so the name Leixlip makes sense. Further, Norse influence is found in place names such as Ireland's Eye (an island situated north of Dublin), which stems from the Norse *ey*, meaning island. Some current place names, such as Moneyglass (*Muine Ghlas*) – literally Green Grove – have lost their original meanings in their English translations. Others have separate meanings in both languages. For example, the Irish language name for Westport in County Mayo is *Cathair na Mart*, the city of beef, which has no relation to the literal English meaning of 'Westerly port', bar to suggest what may have been a large part of the port town's export trade – beef carcasses.

The vast majority of the place names of Ireland have their origin in the Irish language, and most of these were coined before the seventeenth century; a significant number is at least a thousand years older.[2] A great deal of scholarly effort is required to establish the correct original forms of the names, a task currently being undertaken by the place names branch of the Department of Community, Equality and Gaeltacht Affairs. For example, the previously mentioned Cook Street in Dublin is *Sráid na gCócairí* (the street of the Cooks), whereas Cook Street in Cork is *Sráid an Chócaigh*, which is named after an individual by the name of Cook. The name Londonderry has become divisive, gaining the nickname 'stroke city', as it is diplomatically referred to as Derry/Londonderry.[3] The Irish name is *Doire Cholmcille* (the oak wood of Saint Colmcille), whereas the English version links the original name with the London companies that financed the settlement when the city was granted a Royal Charter in 1613 by King James I.[4]

Some place names have a purely English origin, for example, Bennetsbridge in Kilkenny, of which the Irish version (*Droichead Binéid*) is a direct translation. Less than forty place names are of Scandinavian origin, stemming from when Viking influence was at its height (ca. AD 800 – ca. AD 1150), particularly in the east and south of the country. Wexford comes from Old Norse *Ueigs – fjorðr* meaning inlet by the sandbank. The Irish *Loch Garman* has the same meaning (*garma*; *garmain* means 'a weaver's beam' and also a sand bar in toponymy).

This difference in the English and Irish versions is particularly notable in the name Dublin, which is a phonetic derivation of *Dubh Linn* or 'black pool', while the Irish *Baile Átha Cliath* literally means 'the town of the ford of the hurdles'. Some other place names originate from a tavern, inn or ale house linked with that location. Examples of this phenomenon are Horse and Jockey in Tipperary, Buck and Hounds, Fox and Geese, Swan Lane (Swan Tavern) and Lamb Alley (Holy Lamb Tavern) – all in Dublin. When exploring the gastro-topography of Ireland, there are significantly more places named after the foods eaten in the early Irish diet, such as oats, wild garlic, grouse, game, white meats, gruel, pottage, watercress, tansy and French wine, than after New World foods such as the potato, turkey and maize, which only appeared in Europe post Columbus, around the sixteenth century. Indeed, there were no tomatoes, peppers, chillies or chocolate in Europe until the discovery of the New World. Examples of these food-related place names are shown in Table 5.1.

TABLE 5.1 Selection of Irish Food-Related Place Names, with Translations and Location

Foodstuff	Irish	Place name English and county	Place name Irish
Bovine – cows, bulls, calf	*Bó, Tarbh, Lao*	Clontarf (Dublin) Drumalee (Dublin) Annamoe (Dublin, Wicklow Offaly)	*Cluain Tarbh* *Droim an Lao* *Áth na mBó*
Ovine – sheep, goats, kids	*Caora, Gabhar, Mionán*	Glenageary (Dublin) Goatstown (Dublin) Ballyminaun (Wexford)	*Gleann na gCaorach* *Baile na nGabhar* *Baile na Mionáin*
Porcine – pigs, boars	*Muc, Torc, Collach*	Swinford (Mayo) Kanturk (Cork) Glenamuc (Wicklow) Pig Lane (Dublin)	*Béal Átha na Muice* *Ceann Toirc* *Gleann na Muc* *Lána na Muc*
Poultry and feathered game (hen, grouse, goose, woodcock)	*Cearc, Cearc Fhraoigh, Gé, creabhair nó Coilleach*	Carks (Kerry) Cloonnagark (Galway) Gortagea (Tipperary) Bunacrower (Mayo)	*Na Cearca* *Cluain na gCearc* *Gort an Ghé* *Muine Creabhair*
Furred game (deer, rabbits, hare)	*Fia, Coinín, Giorria*	Dernaveagh (Antrim) Drumcuinnion (Monaghan) Harefield (Mayo)	*Dún na bhFiach* *Droim Coinín* *Gort na nGiorriacha*

(continue)

Foodstuff	Irish	Place name English and county	Place name Irish
Fish	*Iasc*	Killeisk (Tipperary)	*Coill Eisc*
Salmon	*Bradán*	Tullybradan (Leitrim)	*Tullaigh Bhradáin*
Cod	*Trosc*	Reentrusk (Cork)	*Rinn Troisc*
Herring	*Scadán*	Balscaddan (Dublin)	*Baile Scadán*
Oats	*Coirce*	Oatlands (Dublin, Limerick)	*Fearran an Choirce*
Wheat	*Cruithneacht*	Wheat Rock	*Carraig na Cruithneachta*
Rye	*Seagal*	Cappataggle (Galway)	*Ceapaigh an tSeagail*
Milk	*Bainne*	Knockavanny (Galway)	*Cnoc an Bhainne*
Buttermilk	*Bláthach*	Portnablahy (Donegal)	*Port na Bláiche*
Butter	*Im*	Kilimy (Laois)	*Coill Ime*
Wild garlic	*Creamh*	Cloncraff (Offaly)	*Cluain Creamha*
Honey	*Mil*	Clonmel (Tipperary)	*Cluain Meala*
Watercress	*Biolar*	Doovilra (Mayo)	*Dumha Bhiolra*
Corn	*Arbhair*	Corn Market	*Margadh an Arbhair*
Apples/orchard	*Úll/Úllord*	Ballynahoulort (Kerry)	*Baile an Úlloird*
Wine	*Fíon*	Wineport (Westmeath)	*Port an Fhíona*
Hostel	*Brú/Bruíon*	Bohernabreena (Dublin)	*Bóthar na Bruíona*
Potatoes	*Fataí*	Potato Islands (Galway)	*Oileáin Fhataí*
Wild tansy	*Brioscán*	Belllanabriscaun (Mayo)	*Béal Átha na mBrioscán*
Berries	*Caor*	Kilnageer (Monaghan)	*Coill na gCaor*

Methodology

This study draws on a number of sources of Irish place names as well as online sources, in particular a database (www.logainm.ie) which is a collaborative work between Dublin City University and The Place Names Office.[5] Some food-related place names are sourced from the author's previous work on Irish food history.[6] The etymology of Irish food-related place names has been explored using Irish-English and *Gaeilge-Béarla* dictionaries;[7] the *Oxford English Dictionary* (*OED*) was also used.[8] This chapter is not intended to be the definitive collection of Irish food-related place names. Rather, it explores the richness and complexity of Ireland's food-related geographical names to enhance an understanding of this aspect of our cultural heritage. More specifically, it explores how topography can illuminate the study of Irish gastronomy, focusing particularly on Dublin as a case study. Information on Dublin stems principally from two main sources: the author's doctoral research on the reciprocity of French haute cuisine and public dining in Dublin restaurants,[9] and material from the *Irish Historic Towns Atlas* project (IHTA).[10]

Food-related place names

Irish culinary and gastronomic history has been enjoying renewed attention over the last decade.[11] This chapter draws on the most up-to-date research and hopefully adds to the existing scholarship by furthering our knowledge of Irish food-related place names. The native Irish diet of cereal and milk-based products, augmented with pig meat, survived relatively unchanged from prehistoric times to the introduction of the potato, possibly in the late sixteenth century. Gaelic reverence for cattle would explain why so little beef was eaten in the Irish diet, which centred on white meats which did not require the death of the animal (such as milk, butter and dairy produce). More recent osteo-archaeological evidence now suggests that more beef was consumed by our ancestors than previously believed.[12]

Cattle and white meats (milk, butter, buttermilk and cheese)

Cattle were a sign of wealth in ancient Ireland and cattle raids such as the famous *Táin Bó Cúailnge* (The Cattle Raid of Cooley) were common. The Irish obsession with cattle is evident in Irish place names. *Bó* and *tarbh* are the words in the Irish language for cow and bull, respectively. The word *bóthar* is Irish for road and a road was defined in width by the length and breadth of a cow. Even the Irish word for boy (*buachaill*) can also mean herd boy or herdsman.[13] *Bóthar* can also appear as 'batter' as in Stoneybatter or in a direct Anglicization such as Bohernabreena, both in Dublin. H. B. Clarke notes that Stonybatter is a partial remnant of the old road from Tara, County Meath, that acted as a 'cow track' or 'drove way' for centuries.[14] Bovine Irish place names include Drumbo (Cavan), Lough Bo (Sligo) and Annamoe – ford of the cattle (Wicklow and Offaly), and also the river Boyne (from *Bóinne*, Boann or Bovinda – the goddess of the white cow). Some place names featuring the English bawn, such as Old Bawn in Wexford and Dublin, derive from *Bó-dhún* – cow fort or walled enclosure, and not from *bán*, the Irish for white.[15] In Dublin you have Red Cow Lane, Bull Wall, Bull Alley and Drumalee (*Droim an Lao*) – hill of the young calf. *Mín an Daimh* (Meenadiff) in Donegal is the smooth field of the ox (*damh*). The site of the famous Battle of Clontarf (1014) in Dublin, in which Brian Ború defeated the Vikings, derives its name from *Cluain Tarbh* (meadow of the bull). Probably the other most famous food-related meadow in Ireland is Clonmel or *Cluain Meala* (meadow of honey), which is discussed later in this chapter.

Cattle were valued principally for their milk. Fynes Moryson, the English travel writer, for example, writing in the early seventeenth century, states as follows:

> They feede most on Whitemeates, and esteeme for a great daintie sower curds, vulgarly called by them Bonaclabbe. And for this cause they watchfully keepe their Cowes, and fight for them as for religion and life; and when they are almost starved, yet they will not kill a Cow, except it bee old, and yield no Milke.[16]

Bainne is the Irish for milk and *bláthach* is the Irish for buttermilk, which could be sweet or sour. Examples of place names are outlined in Table 5.2. Where there were cows and milk, there was cream, butter and cheese. In the transhumance tradition, the milk was often preserved as butter, cheese, whey and beestings, and this practice is evident in a number of place names.

Pigs, boars, sheep, lambs and goats

Porcine place names are also found, such as *Gleann na Muc* (Glenamuck) in Wicklow, valley of the pigs; *Ceann Toirc* (Kanturk) in Cork, headland of the boar; *and Béal Átha na Muice* (Swinford) in Mayo, literally the mouth of the ford of the pigs. A boar is also known in Irish as a *collach* and this version features in a number of place names. *Log na gCollach* (Lugnagullagh) in Westmeath is literally the place of the boars. The longest place name in Ireland is *Muiceanach idir Dhá Sháile* (Muckanaghederdauhaulia), meaning pig-marsh between two seas, located in the *gaeltacht* region of west Galway where the Irish language is, or was until the recent past, the main spoken language of a substantial number of the local population.

TABLE 5.2 Information from *Irish Historic Town Atlas*, Dublin, Parts I and II

Food type or trade	Street name no longer in use	Now known as	Names still in use
Cow	Cow Lane	Beresford Street or Greek Street	Red Cow Lane
Cattle	Cow Parlour	Tenter Lane West	Bull Alley Street
Bull	Cattle Street	Location unknown	Bullring (Meath
	Bull Yard	Location unknown	Street)
	Bulrynge	See Cornmarket	
Sheep	Sheep Street (Great and Little)	Ship Street	*Sráid na gCaorach*
Goats	Goat Alley	Digges Lane	
Rams	Ram Alley	Schoolhouse Lane West	
Mutton	Mutton Lane	Ardee Row	
Lamb	Lamb Alley	Unknown	
Pigs	Pig Alley	John's Lane West	
	Pig Lane	Ewington Lane	
	Hog Hill	Andrew Street	
	Hogg's Lane	Temple Lane	
Fish	Fish Lane/Fisher's Street	St. Michan's Street	Fishamble Street
		Unknown	
	Fish Street	Castleforbes Road	
Butter	Big Butter Lane	Bishop Street	
	Little Butter Lane	Drury Street	
Sugar	Sugar House Lane	Unknown (Belleview)	
Pudding	Pudding Row	Wood Quay	
	Pudding Lane	Lincoln Lane	
Pye	Pye Alley	Unknown	
	Pye Corner	St. Andrew's Lane North	
Cooks	Cook's Lane	Unknown	Cook Street
Bakers	Bakers' Street c.1540	Unknown Possibly Schoolhouse	
	Bakhous Lane c.1370	Lane Nth.	
Cocoa	Cocoa Lane	Unknown	

(continue)

Food type or trade	Street name no longer in use	Now known as	Names still in use
Cabbage	Cabbage Garden Lane	Cathedral Lane	
Markets	Newgate or New Hall Market Ormond Market	Bridge Street Upper Ormond Place	Haymarket Smithfield Castle Market Clarendon Market
Cherry	Cherry (Tree) Lane	Unknown	Cherry Orchard
Corn	Whites Lane	Corn Exchange Place	Corn Market
Lemon	Spans Lane	Lemon Street	
Orange	Orange Street	Unknown (near Earl Street)	
Marrowbone	Marybone Lane	Marrowbone Lane	
Meat (Meath)	Meat(h) Street	Meath Street	
Mill	Mill Lane Mill Street Millers Alley	Unknown Unknown Unknown (around Temple Bar)	Milltown
Saffron(?)	Saffurin Hill	Unknown	
Wine	Christchurch Lane	Winetavern Street South	Winetavern St.
Taverns	Taverners' Street	High Street of the Taverners	

Ovine connections to Irish place names range from *Gleann na gCaorach* (Glenageary) in South County Dublin, the valley of the sheep, to *Lios na gCaorach* (Lisnageeragh), found in Offaly, Longford, Galway and Waterford. The Viking origin of Waterford, which is named *Vadre Fjord*, means the landing place for sheep. The Irish *Port Láirge* literally means the landing place of the haunch. Lamb Alley has been previously mentioned; moreover, there is a Sheep Street in Limerick and also Ship Street in Dublin, which actually derives its name from Sheep Street, mentioned in the Annals of the Four Masters (1632–1636), and still evident in the Irish original *Sráid na gCaorach*. Mutton – ovine over twenty-four months old – was more popular than lamb in Ireland and in most of Europe as it had a stronger flavour. *A Plan of Mount Merrion*, Survey'd in 1762 by Jonathan Barker shows a 'Shoulder of Mutton field' as well as a 'Pigeon Park' in this south Dublin manor land, now a well-established residential suburb.[17] Goats and kids also feature in place names, such as *Baile na nGabhar* (Goatstown) in Dublin and Ballyminaun in Wexford, which stems from *Mionáin* (kids).

Poultry and feathered game

Poultry and game birds were also part of the Irish diet. The number of place names including the stem 'cark' or 'carkfree' from *cearc* (hen) and *fraoch* (heather) is evidence of how popular and plentiful *cearc fhraoigh* (grouse) must have been in Ireland. Geese and ducks were important for their flesh and their eggs. The Irish for goose is *gé*, and Magheranagay in Mayo, Derrygay in Mayo and Gortagea in Tipperary are evidence of goose greens, woods and fields, respectively. Indeed, there is a Goose Green mentioned on John Rocque's *Actual Survey of the County of Dublin* (1760) near Drumcondra in Dublin. Today, a public house called 'The Goose Tavern', situated off Griffith Avenue, acts as a reminder and link with the district's previous name.

Furred game, deer, rabbits and hares

Furred game was plentiful in the highly wooded landscape of ancient Ireland. Many Irish place names refer to deer, from Dernaveagh in Antrim to Derrinea in Roscommon (oak wood of the deer). The Irish for doe is *eilit*, and thus Kineilty in Clare means the hill of the doe. *Poc* is the Irish for a male deer or goat, so *Lios Oboc* Lisabuck in Monaghan means fort of the stags, while Lispuckaun in Clare is the fort of the he-goats. Puck Fair in Killorglin, Kerry shares this origin.[18] Rabbits and hares were a vital part of the Irish diet. It is believed that rabbits were first introduced by the Normans. *Coinín*, the Irish for rabbit, is not a native Irish word but derived from the early-English word 'cunin'. Similarly, the word *coinigéar/coinicéar* derives from the early-English word 'cony(n)ger', meaning rabbit warren. The Irish for hare is *giorria*, and this features in place names such as *Gort na nGiorriacha* (Harefield) in Mayo and *Muine na nGiorria* (Monanagirr) in Monaghan. So plentiful were rabbits in Ireland that they were considered a pest to farmers and gardeners, and in 1954, a viral disease, *myxomatosis*, was illegally introduced which decimated the population and also changed attitudes to eating rabbits in Ireland.[19]

Fish and fishing

Being an island nation with bountiful lakes and rivers, it is no surprise to find a number of fish-related place names throughout the country from Fish Quay in Sligo; Fisherman's Quay in Limerick; and Fisherman's Green in Malahide, Dublin. *Iasc* is the Irish for fish, but a number of different species of fish such as *bradán* (salmon), *trosc* (codfish) and *scadán* (herring) also feature in the place names.

Cereals (Oats, Rye, Barley, Wheat)

Many cereal crops are mentioned in place names. *Coirce* is the Irish for oats and there are various variations, ranging from *Fearrann an Choirce* (Oatlands) in Limerick to *Gort an Choirce* (Gortahork) in Donegal. *Seagal* is the Irish for rye, and place names range from *Ceapach an tSeagail* (Cappagaggle) in Galway to *Lios an tSeagail* (Listoghil) in Sligo. Barley or *Eorna* is found in quite a few place names around the country, including *Baile Eorna* (Ballyorne) in Wicklow to *Goirtín Eorna* (Gorteenorna) in Longford. *Cruithneacht* (wheat) appears in a few place names such as *Carraig na Cruithneachta* (Wheat Rock) in Galway and a *Cruithneachtán* (Crinnaghtane) in Cork, not to mention Wheatfield in Dublin. All these cereals would be stored in a granary, which translates as a *gráinseach* or an *iothlainn* in Irish. There is a *gráinseach* (Grange) listed in over twenty-two counties on the database Logainm.ie and can also mean an outlying monastic farm.

Sweet honey

The Irish words for sweet (*milis*) and honey (*mil*) share the same root and feature in a number of place names such as Clonmel (honey meadow), found in four different counties, most famously in Tipperary. Lenanamalla in Roscommon, Coolmillish in Armagh and Milshoge in Wexford share the same etymology.

Wild garlic and other native foodstuffs

The amount of place names throughout the country related to wild garlic, *Creamh* (*Allium ursinium*), shows its popularity as a condiment in the old Irish diet. Both the leaves and roots are edible raw or cooked and were also used medicinally. Place names include *Cluain Creamh Choille* (Clooncraffield) in Roscommon, meaning the meadow of the wild garlic wood. Ireland has a long tradition of apples and orchards, particularly in counties Armagh, Wexford and Waterford. *Abhall, Úll* and *Úllord* are the Irish names for apple tree, apple and orchard, respectively. *An tAbhallort* (Oulart) and Oulartleigh in Wexford, and *Baile an Úlloird* (Ballynahoulort) in Kerry all refer directly to orchards. There is a Gartnanoul in Cavan and Clare; Knocknanool in Roscommon; Derryool in Mayo; Rossnanowl in Kilkenny; Coolanowle in Laois; Cappaghnanool in Galway; and both Corrool (Longfort) and Corrowle (Tipperary) mean round hill of the apple trees. There is also Lisheenanoul in Tipperary, meaning the little fort/enclosure of the apple trees.

Wine, claret, taverns and hostels

Ireland has a long tradition of both hospitality and wine consumption, and the Irish were reputed connoisseurs of wine (*fíon*). It is calculated that over a million gallons of wine was imported annually from 1720 to 1820, apart from the years during the Napoleonic Wars when there were embargoes on trade with France and Spain. Claretrock in Louth is a translation of *Carraig an fhíona* (rock of the wine). Claret, the red wine of Bordeaux, was considered to be the national drink and was actually known as 'Irish wine'.[20] *Port an Fhíona* (Wineport) in Westmeath literally means the landing place of the wine, and today it houses the award-winning Wineport Lodge restaurant and guest house. The early existence of the wine trade has left its topographical mark on many Irish port towns, and a trawl through the *Irish Historic Towns Atlas* series identifies Winetavern Streets, Winetavern Courts, Wine Courts and Alleys found in Sligo, Dublin and Belfast, and that Scabby Lane in Limerick was renamed Whitewine Lane.[21]

To trace every food-related place name in Ireland is outside the scope of this chapter. A number of other food-related place names are noted in Table 5.1.

Dublin

In Dublin over the last millennium, street names have come and gone due to redevelopment of city districts and renaming of streets after rich, powerful or historic individuals. A summary of such changes in food-related street names is presented in Table 5.2, which also identifies street names that have endured for centuries, such as Cook Street, Fishamble Street, Winetavern Street and Cornmarket. In early medieval Dublin, along with the fish shambles, there were also flesh shambles (meat market) on what is now High Street/Thomas Street, and its westward continuation, Cornmarket, may have begun to specialize in grain by the beginning of the fifteenth century.[22] C. Lennon points out that significant civic regulations of markets and street trading were enforced in 1683, a significant element of which was the setting up of a purpose-built facilities in Smithfield and in the Ormond Market in Oxmantown.[23] The location of the Ormond Market was originally known as The Pill, which was both the southern gate of a monastic settlement and the monks' fishing harbour. The *Oxford English Dictionary* defines pill as 'a tidal inlet on the coast, a small creek or bay', which explains the etymology of Pill Street and Pill Lane, and also explains the nearby Fisher's Lane, which is now St. Michan's Street (see Table 5.2). The Ormond Market attracted traders in butter, herbs, root vegetables and potatoes alongside the fishmongers. A map based on the 1738 trades directory shows a number of markets including Smithfield and Ormond Markets on the north side of the river and Clarendon, Castle and New Hall Markets on the south side.[24] This map also identifies food and drink trades in Dublin, which are well distributed but cluster most densely in the Smithfield and Ormond Market areas. During the Victorian era, a number of covered markets were built in traditional market sites such as the South City Markets, South Great Georges Street (1878–1881) and City Fruit and Vegetable Wholesale Market, Mary's Lane (1891–1892).[25] A study of the history of the Iveagh Markets, Dublin, shows how it differed from these covered markets or other comparable halls in Great Britain in specializing in used merchandise with the fresh food hall relegated to the back, off a side street.[26] The history of Moore Street, where butcher shops, street dealers, rabbit sellers, poulterers, fishmongers and vegetable traders have been plying their trade for generations, has recently been published.[27] A more recent phenomenon is the growth in farmers' markets in the city in the last decade in locations such as Temple Bar, Pearse Street, Christchurch, Newmarket, Coppinger Row, Marley Park, Lepardstown, Glasnevin, Ballymun, Howth, Dun Laoghaire, Clontarf, Malahide and Farmleigh.

It is interesting to note from the *Irish Historic Towns Atlas* series that certain traces of old street names remain in new guises such as the Bullring (indoor market) on Meath Street, or Suesey Street Night Club on Leeson Street, which was originally called Suesey Street and was renamed in 1728. Another example of this is the pub MacTurcaill's of Hoggen Green on the corner of Townsend Street and Tara Street. Hoggen Green was the old Norse name for the College Green area, and Ragnall MacTurcaill was a mid-twelfth-century king.[28] Other public houses and bars in that area with historic names include Thing Mote and The Long Stone.

A trawl through a modern street map of Dublin identifies a number of food-related place names including Blackberry Lane, Bull Alley Street, Bull Wall, Castle Market, Cornmarket, Cherryfield Road, Distillery Road, Haymarket, Hazelbrook, Home Farm Road, Milltown, Orchard Road, Shellybanks Road, South City Markets and Watermill Road. Some food-sounding names, however, are not as they seem, such as Marrowbone Lane (from Saint Mary at Bourne or Marylebone in London). Smithfield (*margadh na feirme*) literally means the farm market in Irish, although the *OED* defines it as a cattle or meat market. The age-old link between Smithfield, Oxmantown, Stoneybatter and the cattle trade remains in a number of relatively modern street names. The cattle market that ran for centuries at the junction of the North Circular Road, Prussia Street and Aughrim Street, was redeveloped into a public housing estate called Drumalee (*Droim an Lao*) in the early 1980s. In neighbouring Cabra, there is an Annamoe (*Áth na mBó*) Road, Park, Terrace and Drive. Oral evidence from a County Meath farmer in his early sixties confirms the age-old practice of driving cattle from Meath to the Dublin cattle market and from there the direct route down the North Circular Road past Phibsboro to the North Wall to be loaded on cattle ships and sent to England.[29] He also recalls a brisk trade in both food and drink in the City Arms Hotel on Prussia Street and in Hanlon's Corner Public House. There were numerous abattoirs also within a square mile of the cattle market which have now closed down.

Food traces in built environment

There are a number of clues in the built environment referring to Dublin's culinary past that are hidden in plain sight. Some of these are in buildings that still house some food trade (markets, hotels, restaurants). In a recent study of the City Fruit and Vegetable Market in Mary's Lane, Martin-McAuliffe draws attention to the terracotta details on the exterior of the market and tiles depicting pears, apples, potatoes, parsnips, Brussels sprouts and fish; food, she notes, were 'fundamental to the historic food economy and productive landscapes as well as seascapes of Ireland'.[30] There are also more modern sculptures such as that of the infamous fishmonger 'Molly Malone', which depicts baskets of the 'cockles and mussels' she sold on the streets of Dublin from a cart.

There are also other buildings that have long changed usage but that offer glimpses in their built fabric of previous food-related history. For example, the building on 19–20 D'Olier Street that currently houses Ashfield House budget accommodation and previously housed the Blessed Sacrament Shrine (1970–95) actually has its origins as the Red Bank Restaurant, which originates from Burton Bindon's Tavern in the 1840s.[31] Careful reading of the façade provides clues of the buildings' culinary past with references to fish (crabs and lobsters) and game (Hare and pheasant) in the carved reliefs. Similarly, a court services building, Dolphin House on East Essex Street, Temple Bar, has a golden relief of a dolphin above the doorway (Figure 5.1), and the Dolphin Hotel and Restaurant, written in stone, provides close observers physical clues to the building's history as the Dolphin Hotel which once was renowned for its steaks and a popular haunt for the city's sporting fraternity. On Nassau

FIGURE 5.1 *Dolphin House (Former Hotel) Corner of Crane Lane and East Essex Street, Dublin, Ireland. Photo by author.*

Street, the building named Morrison's Chambers was the site of the famous Morrison's Hotel, and in Wicklow Street, Glendenning House stems from George Clendenning, the former hotelkeeper (mid-nineteenth century) of the Wicklow Hotel, which was housed in that location until the 1970s. On O'Connell Street, the Revenue Commissioners offices are housed in the Hammam Building, which was once the site of the Hammam Hotel, which had its own Turkish Baths, pre-1916. It is worth noting that Dublin's first French restaurant *Café de Paris* (c.1860) was attached to a Turkish Baths in Lincoln Place. Also on O'Connell Street is a sign for 'The Confectioners Hall' dating from 1842 (Figure 5.2), which thousands of Dubliners pass daily and few ever notice. Research by D. Cashman links famous confectioner John Godey with that part of O'Connell Street (then 12 Sackville Street) in the early nineteenth century.[32]

Fading painted signage on brickwork can also point towards previous tenants of various buildings. For example, standing on Nassau Street, facing Lincoln Place, the gable end of 1 Leinster Street clearly shows a sign for Finn's Hotel (Figure 5.3), which was where James Joyce's Nora Barnacle worked. Below the hotel was the *Patisserie Belge*, run by Bob Geldof's grandfather until the 1940s. There are also a number of façades of Milk Bars (Montague

FIGURE 5.2 *The Confectioners Hall, O'Connell Street, Dublin, Ireland. Photo by author.*

Street) and Dairies (Sherriff Street) which are remnants of not-so-distant food-retailing history. Similarly, Findlater House, an office building on the corner of Cathal Brugha Street and O'Connell Street, represents a link to the famous Findlater merchant family of grocers who had their headquarters in that location.[33]

FIGURE 5.3 *Finn's Hotel (Leinster Street, Dublin, Ireland).*

Securing our culinary heritage

A close study of John Rocque's *Actual Survey of the County of Dublin* (1760) uncovers a number of links to our culinary past that have since disappeared or of which only traces remain: for example, the Raheny windmill, the coffee houses in Dun Lary [sic.], Chicken Lane in Portobello and the previously mentioned Goose Green in Drumcondra. Also on this map is Fish Street located off the North Wall, which is now called Castleforbes Road. This suggests the importance of the North Wall at the time for the fishing fleet rather than the transport and warehousing of commercial goods which followed. The *Irish Historic Towns Atlas* for Dublin identified a number of food-related street names which are no longer in use (see Table 5.2). Names such as Cocoa Lane remind us of an era from the mid-seventeenth century when chocolate houses and coffee houses were fashionable meeting places in Dublin.[34] The number of porcine place names in Ireland is a tribute to the historical importance of pigs in the Irish diet. The loss of porcine street names in Dublin belies a tradition of piggeries within the city that disappeared when legislation was introduced in 1985 and 1987 requiring the heat treatment of swill.[35]

There is a growing realization of the need to preserve place names and to gather the stories and folklore surrounding them. Will future residents of Drumalee or Annamoe Road know the origin of their street name and their links with their neighbourhood's cattle market past? The ongoing work of the Place Name Branch in researching the correct Irish-language form of the place names of Ireland is invaluable to protect this aspect of our cultural heritage, such as the case of Ship Street (*Sráid na gCaorach*) in Dublin. A more detailed study of the food-related place names of the whole island of Ireland is available.[36] There is also an ongoing Irish Field Name Project, which seeks to capture local knowledge that to date has been part of the oral tradition. Without such projects, it is feared that the majority of orally disseminated place names will disappear within the next decade if left unrecorded, with a great loss to Ireland's toponymic inheritance.[37] This chapter has identified that there are dramatically more food-related place names relating to the early Irish diet rather than the New World arrivals, such as the potato and maize, which came to dominate food discourse in Ireland, particularly since the Great Famine. Most Irish people, however, have little or no knowledge of their ancestors' diet of wild garlic, grouse, game, white meats, gruel, pottage, watercress, tansy and French wine. It is hoped that this chapter will awaken the reader's interest in Irish place names and inspire a fresh look at our culinary past and heritage. Perhaps readers will also look at the built fabric of Dublin in a new light and discover clues to our culinary heritage that are often hidden in plain sight.

Notes

1   H. B. Clarke, *Irish Historic Towns Atlas, No. 11, Dublin, Part I, to 1610* (Dublin: Royal Irish Academy, 2002).

2   D. Mac Giolla Easpaig, 'Ireland's Heritage of Geographical Names', *Wiener Schriften zur Geographie und Kartographie* 18 (2009): 79–85.

3   A. Thomas, *Irish Historic Towns Atlas, No. 15. Derry – Londonderry* (Dublin: Royal Irish Academy, 2005).

4   Ibid.

5   P. W. Joyce, *The Origin and History of Irish Names of Places* (Dublin: McGlashan and Gill, 1869–1913); P. Ó Cearbhaill, D. Mac Giolla Easpaig et al., *Gasaitéar na h-Éireann/Gazateer of Ireland* (Dublin: Oifig an tSoláthair, 1989); D. Flanagan and L. Flanagan, *Irish Place Names* (Dublin: Gill and Macmillan, 1994); A. Room, *A Dictionary of Irish Place-Names* (Belfast: Appletree Press, 1994); S. Lewis, *A Topographical Dictionary of Ireland* (*2 Vols*) (Baltimore: Genealogical Publishing Co., 1995); and P. Ó Cearbhaill, *Logainmeacha agus Sráidainmneacha Bhaile Átha Cliath Theas* (Baile Átha Cliath: Comhairle Contae Áth Cliath Theas, n.d.).

6   M. Mac Con Iomaire, 'The Pig in Irish Cuisine Past and Present', in *The Fat of the Land: Proceedings of the Oxford Symposium on Food and Cookery 2002*, ed. H. Walker (Bristol: Footwork, 2003), 207–215; M. Mac Con Iomaire, 'A History of Seafood in Irish Cuisine and Culture', in *Wild Food: Proceedings of the Oxford Symposium on Food and Cookery 2004*, ed. R. Hosking (Totnes: Prospect Books, 2006), 219–233; M. Mac Con Iomaire and A. Cully, 'A History of Eggs in Irish Cuisine and Culture', in *Eggs in Cookery: Proceedings of the Oxford Symposium on Food and Cookery 2006*, ed. R. Hosking (Totnes: Prospect Books, 2007), 137–149; M. Mac Con Iomaire and P. Óg Gallagher, 'The Potato in Irish Cuisine and Culture', *Journal of Culinary Science & Technology* 7.2–3 (2009): 152–167; M. Mac Con Iomaire, 'The Pig in Irish Cuisine and Culture', *M/C Journal: The Journal of Media and Culture* 13.5 (2010): online; and M. Mac Con Iomaire and P. Ó. Gallagher, 'Irish Corned Beef: A Culinary History', *Journal of Culinary Science & Technology* 9.1 (2011): 27–43.

7   P. S. Dineen, *Foclóir Gaedhilge agus béarla. An Irish-English Dictionary, Being a Thesaurus of the Words, Phrases and Idioms of the Modern Irish Language* (Dublin: Educational Company of Ireland, 1927); N. Ó Dónaill, *Foclóir Gaeilge-Béarla* (Baile Átha Cliath: An Gúm, 1977); and T. De Bhaldraithe, *English-Irish Dictionary* (*14th Edition*) (Baile Átha Cliath: An Gúm, 2006).

8   All names have been checked for accuracy using the placenames branch of the ordnance survey of Ireland publication (Ó Cearbhaill, Mac Giolla Easpaig *et al.* 1989) and the online database (www.logainm.ie).

9   M. Mac Con Iomaire, 'The Emergence, Development, and Influence of French Haute Cuisine on Public Dining in Dublin Restaurants 1900–2000: An Oral History (Doctoral Thesis)'. *School of Culinary Arts & Food Technology* (Dublin, Dublin Institute of Technology, 2009) http://arrow.dit.ie/tourdoc/12/.

10   Clarke, *Irish Historic Towns Atlas, No. 11, Dublin, Part I, to 1610*; and C. Lennon, *Irish Historic Towns Atlas, No. 19, Dublin, Part II, 1610–1756* (Dublin: Royal Irish Academy, 2008).

11   M. Mac Con Iomaire and E. Maher, '*Tickling the Palate': Gastronomy in Irish Literature and Culture* (Oxford: Peter Lang, 2014).

12   L. Downey and I. Stuijts, 'Overview of Historical Irish Food Products – A. T. Lucas (1960–2) Revisited', *Journal of Irish Archaeology* 22 (2013): 111–126.

13   Mac Con Iomaire and Gallagher, 'Irish Corned Beef'.

14 Clarke, *Irish Historic Towns Atlas, No. 11, Dublin, Part I, to 1610*, 2.

15 Flanagan and Flanagan, *Irish Place Names*, 20.

16 F. Moryson, *An Itinerary* (Glasgow, 1908), vol. 4, 200–201.

17 This map is located in the Pembroke Estate Papers of the National Archives of Ireland (NAI), 2011/2/2/11.

18 Puck Fair is reputed to be one of Ireland's oldest fairs, dating back at least to 1603, when King James I issued a charter granting legal status to an existing fair in Kilorglin, but the fair is believed to stem from pre-Christian times relating to the Celtic festival of Lúghnasa, the beginning of the harvest season, with the puck as a pagan symbol of fertility.

19 'Rabbit Disease Outbreak is Reported: No Diagnosis Yet by Department', *Irish Times*, July 19, 1954.

20 M.-L. Legg, '"Irish Wine": The Import of Claret from Bordeaux to Provincial Ireland in the Eighteenth Century', in *Irish Provincial Cultures in the Long Eighteenth Century: Making the Middle Sort* (*Essays for Toby Barnard*), eds. R. Gillespie and R. F. Foster (Dublin: Four Courts Press, 2012), 93–105; and M. Mac Con Iomaire and T. Kellaghan, 'Royal Pomp: Viceregal Celebrations and Hospitality in Georgian Dublin', in *Celebration: Proceedings of the Oxford Symposium on Food and Cookery 2011*, ed. M. McWilliams (Totnes: Prospect Books, 2012), 163–173.

21 Legg, 'Irish Wine'.

22 Clarke, *Irish Historic Towns Atlas, No. 11, Dublin, Part I, to 1610*.

23 Lennon, *Irish Historic Towns Atlas, No. 19, Dublin, Part II, 1610–1756*.

24 Ibid., 7, fig. 4.

25 M. Lysaght, 'Dublin's Wholesale Fruit and Vegetable Market', *History Ireland* 4.3 (1996): 42–45.

26 S. Martin-McAuliffe, 'The Ethics of Giving and Receiving: A Study of the Iveagh Markets, Dublin', in *Portraits of the City: Dublin and the Wider World*, eds. G. O'Brien and F. O'Kane (Dublin: Four Courts Press, 2012), 175–190.

27 K. Barry, *Moore Street, the Story of Dublin's Market District* (Cork: Mercier Press, 2012).

28 Clarke, *Irish Historic Towns Atlas, No. 11, Dublin, Part I, to 1610*.

29 Author's discussion with Co. Meath farmer Patrick McElroy on 12 January 2013 about his memories of the cattle market.

30 Clarke, *Irish Historic Towns Atlas, No. 11, Dublin, Part I, to 1610*; and Lennon, *Irish Historic Towns Atlas, No. 19, Dublin, Part II, 1610–1756*.

31 S. Martin-McAuliffe, 'Feeding Dublin: The City Fruit and Vegetable Market', in *Food and Markets: Proceedings of the Oxford Symposium on Food and Cookery 2014*, ed. Williams, M. (Totnes: Prospect Books, 2015), 241–253, esp. 245.

32 Mac Con Iomaire, 'The Emergence, Development, and Influence of French Haute Cuisine on Public Dining in Dublin Restaurants 1900–2000'.

33 D. Cashman, '"That Delicate Sweetmeat, the Irish Plum": The Culinary World of Maria Edgeworth (1768–1849)', in *Tickling the Palate: Gastronomy in Irish*

Literature and Culture, eds. M. Mac Con Iomaire and E. Maher (Oxford: Peter Lang, 2014), 15–34.

34 A. Findlater, *Findlaters – The Story of a Dublin Merchant Family 1774–2001* (Dublin: A&A Farmar, 2001).

35 M. Mac Con Iomaire, 'Coffee Culture in Dublin: A Brief History', *M/C Journal: The Journal of Media and Culture* 15.2 (2012): online.

36 Mac Con Iomaire, 'The Pig in Irish Cuisine Past and Present'.

37 M. Mac Con Iomaire, 'Gastro-Topography: Exploring Food-Related Placenames in Ireland', *Canadian Journal of Irish Studies* 38.1–2 (2014), 126–156.

38 Mac Giolla Easpaig, 'Ireland's Heritage of Geographical Names'.

Bibliography

Anon. 'Rabbit Disease Outbreak Is Reported: No diagnosis yet by Department'. *The Irish Times*. Dublin (1954): 1.

Barry, K. *Moore Street, the Story of Dublin's Market District*. Cork: Mercier Press, 2012.

Cashman, D. '"That Delicate Sweetmeat, the Irish Plum": The Culinary World of Maria Edgeworth (1768–1849)'. In *Tickling the Palate: Gastronomy in Irish Literature and Culture*, edited by M. Mac Con Iomaire and E. Maher, 15–34. Oxford: Peter Lang, 2014.

Clarke, H. B. *Irish Historic Towns Atlas, No. 11, Dublin, Part 1, to 1610*. Dublin: Royal Irish Academy, 2002.

De Bhaldraithe, T. *English-Irish Dictionary* (*14th Edition*). Baile Átha Cliath: An Gúm, 2006.

Dineen, P. S. *Foclóir Gaedhilge agus béarla. An Irish-English Dictionary, Being a Thesaurus of the Words, Phrases and Idioms of the Modern Irish Language*. Dublin: Educational Company of Ireland, 1927.

Downey, L. and I. Stuijts. 'Overview of Historical Irish Food Products – A. T. Lucas (1960–2) Revisited'. *Journal of Irish Archaeology* 22 (2013): 111–26.

Findlater, A. *Findlaters - The Story of a Dublin Merchant Family 1774–2001*. Dublin: A&A Farmar, 2001.

Flanagan, D. and L. Flanagan. *Irish Place Names*. Dublin: Gill and Macmillan, 1994.

Joyce, P. W. *The Origin and History of Irish Names of Places*. Dublin: McGlashan and Gill, 1869–1913.

Legg, M.-L. '"Irish Wine": The Import of Claret from Bordeaux to Provincial Ireland in the Eighteenth Century'. In *Irish Provincial Cultures in the Long Eighteenth Century: Making the Middle Sort* (*Essays for Toby Barnard*), edited by R. Gillespie and R. F. Foster, 93–105. Dublin, Four Courts Press, 2012.

Lennon, C. *Irish Historic Towns Atlas, No. 19, Dublin, Part II, 1610–1756*. Dublin: Royal Irish Academy, 2008.

Lysaght, M. 'Dublin's Wholesale Fruit and Vegetable Market'. *History Ireland* 4, no. 3 (1996): 42–45.

Mac Con Iomaire, M. 'The Pig in Irish Cuisine Past and Present'. In *The Fat of the Land: Proceedings of the Oxford Symposium on Food and Cookery 2002*, edited by H. Walker, 207–15. Bristol: Footwork, 2003.

Mac Con Iomaire, M. 'A History of Seafood in Irish Cuisine and Culture'. In *Wild Food: Proceedings of the Oxford Symposium on Food and Cookery 2004*, edited by R. Hosking, 219–33. Totnes, Devon: Prospect Books, 2006.

Mac Con Iomaire, M. The Emergence, Development, and Influence of French Haute Cuisine on Public Dining in Dublin Restaurants 1900-2000: An Oral History (Doctoral Thesis). *School of Culinary Arts & Food Technology*. Dublin: Dublin Institute of Technology, 2009, http://arrow.dit.ie/tourdoc/12/.

Mac Con Iomaire, M. 'The Pig in Irish Cuisine and Culture'. *M/C Journal: The Journal of Media and Culture* 13, no. 5 (2010): online.

Mac Con Iomaire, M. 'Coffee Culture in Dublin: A Brief History'. *M/C Journal: The Journal of Media and Culture* 15, no. 2 (2012): online.

Mac Con Iomaire, M. 'Gastro-Topography: Exploring Food-Related Placenames in Ireland'. *Canadian Journal of Irish Studies* 38 no. 1–2 (2014).

Mac Con Iomaire, M. and A. Cully. 'A History of Eggs in Irish Cuisine and Culture'. In *Eggs in Cookery: Proceedings of the Oxford Symposium on Food and Cookery 2006*, edited by R. Hosking, 137–49. Totnes, Devon: Prospect Books, 2007.

Mac Con Iomaire, M. and P. Óg. Gallagher. 'The Potato in Irish Cuisine and Culture'. *Journal of Culinary Science & Technology* 7 no. 2–3 (2009): 152–67.

Mac Con Iomaire, M. and P. Óg. Gallagher. 'Irish Corned Beef: A Culinary History'. *Journal of Culinary Science & Technology* 9 no. 1 (2011): 27–43.

Mac Con Iomaire, M. and T. Kellaghan. 'Royal Pomp: Viceregal Celebrations and Hospitality in Georgian Dublin'. In *Celebration: Proceedings of the Oxford Symposium on Food and Cookery 2011*, edited by M. McWilliams, 163–173. Totnes, Devon, Prospect Books, 2012.

Mac Con Iomaire, M. and E. Maher, eds. *'Tickling the Palate': Gastronomy in Irish Literature and Culture. Reimagining Ireland* 57. Oxford: Peter Lang, 2014.

Mac Giolla Easpaig, D. 'Ireland's Heritage of Geographical Names'. *Wiener Schriften zur Geographie und Kartographie* 18 (2009): 79–85.

Martin-McAuliffe, S. 'The Ethics of Giving and Receiving: A Study of the Iveagh Markets, Dublin'. In *Portraits of the City: Dublin and the Wider World*, edited by G. O'Brien and F. O'Kane, 175–90. Dublin, Four Courts Press, 2012.

Martin-McAuliffe, S. 'Feeding Dublin: The City Fruit and Vegetable Market.' In *Food and Markets: Proceedings of the Oxford Symposium on Food and Cookery 2014*, edited by M. Williams. Devon, Prospect Books, 2015 241–253.

Moryson, F. *An Itinerary*. Glasgow, 1908.

Ó Cearbhaill, P. *Logainmeacha agus Sráidainmneacha Bhaile Átha Cliath Theas*. Baile Átha Cliath: Comhairle Contae Áth Cliath Theas, n.d.

Ó Cearbhaill, P., D. Mac Giolla Easpaig et al. *Gasaitéar na h-Éireann/Gazateer of Ireland*. Dublin: Oifig an tSoláthair, 1989.

Ó Dónaill, N. *Foclóir Gaeilge-Béarla*. Baile Átha Cliath: An Gúm, 1977.

Room, A. *A Dictionary of Irish Place-Names*. Belfast: Appletree Press, 1994.

Samual, L. *A Topographical Dictionary of Ireland* (*2 vols*). Baltimore: Genealogical Publishing Co, 1995.

Thomas, A. *Irish Historic Towns Atlas, No. 15. Derry - Londonderry*. Dublin: Royal Irish Academy, 2005.

PART TWO

Sustainability

Commentary for Part Two: Sustainability

Green Polemics: What Are We Talking about When We Talk about Sustainability?

Samantha L. Martin-McAuliffe

Sustainability is the slipperiest of terms. Championed, co-opted, adapted, defended and abused, it is as much a designation as it is a way of life. As such, its pervasiveness across assorted disciplines and professions has rendered it nearly hollow; a ubiquitous expression turned cliché. Sustainability is now everything to everyone, thereby grouping together occupations and topics as diverse as aquaculture, sheep farming and building construction, trades which bear little or nothing in common – or do they?

In 2010 three academics published a study that explained their development of a new building material. Entitled 'Clay-based composite stabilized with natural polymer and fibre', the article states that sustainability was the driving force of the overall research.[1] The authors aimed to design and test a composite material that was not only sustainable but also 'non-toxic and locally sourced'.[2] Not long into the article it becomes clear that this new material is indeed a type of building brick. But unlike conventional bricks composed of fired clay, these specimens are derived from soil, natural fibres (in this case, sheep's wool) and 'plant-derived polymer binders'. This last component is technically called alginate, but in lay terms it can be understood as seaweed. Wool-seaweed bricks: experimental novelty, or rather the future in building construction? Several questions remain about the potential of this composite, namely its long-term resilience in harsh climates, and whether it could be considered a sustainable, ecologically friendly option in a wide variety of geographical locales. Some (but certainly not all!) sheep-farming regions in the world are conveniently situated near a seaweed-rich coastline. Yet it is important to understand this composite as something much more than a tangible rectangular brick, a mere building block. Fundamentally, the wool-seaweed brick is an exceptionally innovative vehicle for collaboration between widely different professions. It is precisely this kind of exchange and approach to living and working that is embodied by Carolyn Steel's concept of *sitopia* in her pioneering book, *Hungry City: How Food Shapes our Lives* (2008).

Steel coined the term *sitopia* as a means of articulating her argument that food must be considered the principal medium in the design of towns and cities.[3] Derived from the modern understanding of Utopia and the Greek word *sitos* (lit. grain), *sitopia* draws upon the more pragmatic aspects of utopianism, in particular its interdisciplinary ambitions.[3] Underpinning this term is the single, central premise that human engagement is the essential component of any and all sustainable development. To put it another way: even if it were possible to design and build a zero-carbon, zero-waste, self-sustaining city, it would fail without a firm commitment to and respect for community. As such, this section of *Food and Architecture* aims to provide an alternative reading of sustainability. It reaches to an underlying meaning of the word – the idea of sustenance – as a way of locating the place of encounter between eating and building. In very a basic sense, sustenance is understood as nourishment, the provision of food and drink. Yet beyond this it also embodies an awareness of both environmental and social equity, as well as disparities, within a particular group of individuals – from the home to an institution to an entire city. Each chapter in this section uses this position as a point of departure.

Food and institutions are frequently disparaged bedfellows. Together they typically elicit memories of mediocre dinners served upon polycarbonate trays – indifferent plates of fuel as opposed to considered meals. There are few other places where this assumption is entrenched as much as the school cafeteria and the university dinning hall. In fact, in some educational institutions the food is so reliably unremarkable and stodgy that it is a subject over which students bond. But change has been steadily gaining momentum. In Chapter 6, 'Open Kitchen: Tracing the History of the Hearth in the Home', Fanny Singer chronicles the remarkable origin and evolution of the Edible Schoolyard Project in Berkeley, California. A serendipitous comment made to the press by Alice Waters in 1995 ultimately culminated with the metamorphosis of a neglected school parking lot into a thriving edible garden. From its beginning the Edible Schoolyard was envisaged as an integral aspect the school curriculum, an innovative laboratory that valued experiential learning, collaboration and community engagement. Thus, instead of merely standing alongside other classrooms, it has become the nexus through which many academic subjects are taught. Through the cultivation, preparation and sharing of wholesome food, the garden, in tandem with its kitchen, teaches the fundamental principles of sustainability. Over the past twenty years, the original Berkeley garden has inspired an array of associated Edible Schoolyards and related programmes and projects, both in the United States and abroad.[4] Now, twenty years later, it no longer seems radical to rip up a dusty tarmac and replace it with a community garden; rather, it is plain common sense. Arguably, this change in perspective is due in large part to the far-reaching vision and influence of the Edible Schoolyard movement.

The following contribution in this section of *Food and Architecture* continues and extends the discussion of institutional eating. In Chapter 7, 'Sustenance and Sustainability in Higher Education', Jamie Horwitz portrays what might be termed a 'bi-focal' culture of campus dining in the twenty-first-century United States. Her chapter examines and contrasts the conventions of meal provision within both a large state university and a private liberal arts college. Both models endorse different interpretations of food preferences. Although the campuses of higher education arguably provide fertile ground for catalysing sustainable practices, few institutions have committed to reinventing their dining facilities in a wholesale manner. As Horwitz explains, Williams College in Massachusetts inaugurated a new student centre in 2007 that consciously situates the campus community within the social, economic and environmental contexts of its New England landscape. The unlikely champion of this new building is the loading dock. Too small to accommodate the large rigs that characterize industrial food suppliers, this dock has proportions that suit deliveries from the smaller vehicles typically used by local, often organic, producers. This is but one example of how Williams is constructing a new 'town-and-gown' paradigm through the cultivation of a more sustainable relationship with its neighbours.

A holistic approach to sustainability requires a commitment to the social situation but this aspect is all too often mentioned in passing, or interpreted as some sort of a by-product, a bonus achieved through better building and growing techniques. Yet the number of practitioners who are changing orientation is growing. Take, for instance, Tom Willey from Madera, a town in the Central San Joachim Valley of California. Willey operates a certified organic farm and actively participates in Community Supported Agriculture (CSA).[5] Moreover, as Barry Estabrook notes, 'Willey's definition of sustainability also extends to his workers. He specifically designs his planting schedule and crop selections to generate a twelve-month harvest, giving his employees year-round work, rather than relying on temporary laborers who are the mainstays of Big Ag in California.'[6] On his own website, Willey asserts that this approach can support not only the farm labourers themselves but also their families.[7] Put simply, children are more likely to attend school and thrive in a community when their parents have permanent, full-time employment in one locale.

The reference to Community Supported Agriculture is especially germane to this present discussion because it is an alternative movement that pays attention to the social as much as the environmental and economic contexts of sustainability. The concept of CSA originated in Japan and is referred to as *teikei*.[8] This term literally translates as partnership or cooperation, but it is most often understood by the wider public as 'food with the farmer's face on it'.[9] In other words, a central aspect of reconciling the growing chasm between producers and consumers of food is direct engagement – between growers, stakeholders (members) and the productive landscape itself. In fact, many CSAs understand community as something that resonates outward, incorporating activities other than farming.[10] It is within this model of exchange and collaboration that architects and designers have an important role to play. Not surprisingly, the first CSA in the United States started in the Berkshires of Massachusetts, the same region that Williams College calls home. The expression 'farm-to-table' is catchy and evocative, signifying transparent, sustainable communication at all stages of the food chain. It is, however, destined to remain an abstract phrase for most people unless it is situated and given a meaningful presence in our daily lives. The loading dock at Williams College is exemplary of this 'green' ambition. And, for its time, the intentionally designed open kitchen at Chez Panisse was also a dramatic experiment that quite literally dissolved a boundary between the preparation and consumption of food. It is notable that this approach later informed the principles of the first Edible Schoolyard. Other collaborations are afoot: a particularly innovative example is the Charlie Cart project, a mobile kitchen designed primarily for use in school classrooms.[11]

This section of *Food and Architecture* concludes by turning to a study of community on its most intimate scale – that of a home – and considering the ways by which domestic space stands in reciprocity with the practices, conventions and traditions of eating. In some respects, the dining table of a home is also a form of institution. Sometimes it may carry symbolic meaning, such as when it is passed from generation to generation as an heirloom. Other families may consciously refer to their table as a hearth, as Fanny Singer has pointed out in her chapter in this volume.

Although a table can take centre stage in a memorable act or ritual, like the ceremonial slicing of a wedding cake, more often than not it is the slow accumulation of daily habits that embodies this particular object with meaning. This underlying significance is part of what David Leatherbarrow has referred to as 'table talk'.[12] When an item of furniture serves its purpose without calling attention to itself, it expresses a 'quiet suitability', and by extension, a 'meal's uniqueness is conditioned on the frequency with which others like it will pass ... the particularity of an instance presupposes a history of repetitive performances'.[13] In Chapter 8, 'The All-Consuming House: Food and

Architecture in Molly Keane's *Time after Time*', Kevin Donovan casts light on the ways that food and its consumption intertwined with architecture in order to sustain the colonial culture of the 'Big House' of the Anglo-Irish Ascendancy. Using the fiction of writer Molly Keane as a lens through which to consider the idea of sustenance, Donovan illustrates how the unity of a family and an indeed entire class could be underpinned by the order of meals and their attendant spaces. Ultimately, this contribution prompts us to consider how many of the questions we face in nourishing a community, no matter how small, are nothing new.

Notes

1 C. Galán-Marín, C. Rivera-Gómez and J. Petric, 'Clay-Based Composite Stabilized with Natural Polymer and Fibre', *Construction and Building Materials*, 24 (2010): 1462–1468.

2 Ibid., 1462. It is interesting to note that bricks are also now being grown from fungus. See 'Mycotecture Brick Wall' in *Field Test: Radical Adventures in Future Farming*, edited by the Center for Genomic Gastronomy (Dublin: Science Gallery, in association with Trinity College Dublin, 2016), 40.

3 Carolyn Steel, *Hungry City: How Food Shapes Our Lives* (London: Chatto and Windus, 2008), Chapter 7, especially 307.

4 To clarify, our modern term Utopia was coined in 1516 by Thomas More in his visionary text of the same name. More's neologism is famously a pun on the Greek *ou topos* ('no-place') and *eu topos* ('good-place'). *Sitos* (s.v. σῖτος, Lidell and Scott) is first and foremost defined as grain, understood to encompass wheat and barley. It can also refer to food that is made from grain, and beyond this, to food in a general sense. Interestingly, in Greek and Roman culture, *sitos* embodied the idea of social commitment, particularly in the form of an allowance of food for the disadvantaged or for those who have worked in service to the community. An example of this can be seen in Aristotle's *Athenian Constitution* 56.7. The Latin term *frumantatio* (s.v. Lewis and Short) is defined as foraging or the act of distributing corn. During the Roman Empire the provision of corn to the citizen populace was understood as a central responsibility of the government. For a further discussion of Utopia within the context of sustainability, see Thorunn Gullaksen Endreson, 'The Essayistic Spirit of Utopia', in *Sustainable Consumption and the Good Life: Interdisciplinary Perspectives*, eds. Karen Lykke Syse and Martin Lee Mueller (London: Routledge, 2014); see especially 33–35.

4 The website of the Edible Schoolyard Project provides a searchable, interactive map of its global network of programmes, http://edibleschoolyard.org/network (accessed 30 March 2015).

5 For a working definition of CSA, see Suzanne DeMuth, *Community Supported Agriculture (CSA): An Annotated Bibliography and Resource Guide* (USDA, National Agricultural Library, September 1993). An explanation of

the background to this movement is provided in Robyn Van En, 'Eating for Your Community: A Report from the Founder of Community Supported Agriculture', *In Context* (Fall 1995): 29, http://www.context.org/iclib/ic42/vanen/ (accessed 29 March 2015).

6 Barry Estabrook, 'The Other Side of the Valley', *Gastronomica: The Journal of Food and Culture* (Winter 2011): 108–111.

7 This is noted in the 'Our Employees' section of the website http://www.tdwilleyfarms.com/employees/fremp.html (accessed 29 March 2015).

8 Stephen M. Schnell, 'Food with a Farmer's Face: Community-Supported Agriculture in the United States', *Geographical Review*, 97 (2004): 522.

9 Schnell, 'Food with a Farmer's Face', 522; and also D. Imhoff, 'Community Supported Agriculture: Farming with a Face on It', in *The Case Against the Global Economy and a Turn Towards Localization*, eds. J. Mander and E. Goldsmith (San Francisco: Sierra Club Books, 1996), 425–433.

10 Such as cooking classes, music festivals and potlucks. Schnell, 'Food with a Farmer's Face', 599.

11 The Charlie Cart was developed by Carolyn Federman, co-founder of the Berkeley Food Institute, and designer Brian Dougherty, http://www.charliecart.com (accessed 30 March 2015).

12 David Leatherbarrow, 'Table Talk', in *Eating Architecture*, eds. Paulette Singley and Jamie Horwitz (Cambridge, MA: MIT Press, 2004), 211–228.

13 Ibid., 117–118.

6

Open Kitchen: Tracing the History of the Hearth in the Home

Fanny Singer

A restaurant childhood

On an August day in Manhattan in the early 1980s, my mother, then seven and a half months pregnant, stood before a raging grill cooking Maine lobsters for her friend's wedding. The swelter of the day amplified the heat radiating from the grill, but she remained at her fireside post, rotating the crustaceans with a pair of metal tongs. Suddenly, she felt a violent lurch and tumble within her belly – something wasn't right. Two days later, safely home in Berkeley, California, her doctor insisted that she remain on bed rest for the rest of her pregnancy. She wept through the night with worry for her baby and dread at the thought of a confinement so contrary to her need to be always on the move, in the kitchen, at her restaurant. I was born before dawn the next morning.

When I was just a few months old, my mother returned to her cooking job at Chez Panisse, a restaurant she had started in 1971 in Berkeley with a couple of bohemian friends and some ideas about 'real food' she had picked up as a university student in France. Though a restaurant environment might be considered unsuitable for infants, my mother could not bear the thought of leaving me at home while she was busy in the kitchen. As she saw it, the only solution was to bring me along. During the day shift, when the downstairs dining room was empty, she would fashion a pallet of clean kitchen towels inside a stockpot, or in the largest of the nesting salad bowls. Placed in my makeshift crib on the wooden countertop, I was always within sight as she peeled and chopped vegetables; whirred sauces and vinaigrettes; and trimmed meat for the cooks working the dinner shift. I was a colicky baby, not easily soothed, but the rhythmic rapping of her chopping knife on the butcher block and the ambient sounds of the kitchen never failed to lull me.

When my mother decided at the age of twenty-seven that she wanted to start a restaurant, she and her father searched for a suitable – that is, affordable – location. In 1970, she signed a lease on a dun-coloured stucco house from the 1930s situated on a stretch of Shattuck Avenue that was then still predominantly populated by middle-class family homes. One of the few other businesses in the vicinity was the fledgling Cheese Board over the road, a bakery and cheese-vending workers collective born of many of the same ideals as Chez Panisse.

Chez Panisse, named for a favourite character from Marcel Pagnol's atmospheric *Marseilles Trilogy* from the 1930s, opened the next year following a series of handmade and improvised renovations, small and large. From the wooden sign out front carved with Art Nouveau lettering, to the interior, all offending vestiges of the original building were given a redwood-hued Arts and Crafts veneer that was truer to the dwelling's setting in the shadow of the California hills. The dining room was populated by intimate groups of tables covered with checked cloths and set with a mix of utensils and plates sourced from local flea markets – and from friends' kitchens around the corner. For the first several months, there were just two cooks (one chef and one 'sous'), with a revolving cast of friends for waiters, and my mother at the front of the house, spreading the word about what food could be. They were open from 7 in the morning until well past midnight, a herculean shift even for the most enthusiastic – and idealistic – of young proprietors.

Even forty-four years later, and with significant adjustments to the operating hours, Chez Panisse still more resembles a house than a restaurant. Growing up, I treated it as an extension of the home I lived in with my parents just a few blocks up the road. To my youthful eyes, there were few obvious differences between the two places, despite one being a commercial business. Both were built as domestic residences and both have evolved – to varying degrees – around the importance of the kitchen table, and by extension the tableside hearth. Though the old building that houses the restaurant is outfitted with what passes for a professional kitchen, the open, warmly painted space resembles our kitchen at home – with the exception perhaps of its steam-filled dish room and enormous walk-in refrigerators. To me at least, the two are identical in feel: no walls divide dining areas from cooking areas, a copper veneer covers virtually every once-offensive metallic surface and wood fires light the hearth almost every day of the year. At our home, there is no such a thing as a dining room: the kitchen merely opens out to contain a table large enough to seat however many of our friends might drop by for dinner. The hearth there – a purpose-built brick construction of open fireplace, pizza and bread oven and rotisserie – is in fact my mother's only renovation of significance in our little late-Victorian bungalow. It runs alongside the length of the dining table, and because at least one part of nearly every meal is prepared over the open flame, that side of the table is known for its 'hot seats'. 'Not for the overly warm-blooded!' my mother trills as family and friends take their places. She nearly always chooses a chair there, though she spends equal time flying around on her feet, manipulating the embers, tending to whatever's cooking that night.

Growing up at Chez Panisse, I knew the place inside out. I internalized the smells that distinguished it: the cedar of the inside of the cloak closet, the worn redwood of the booths upstairs, the ripe peaches and heirloom tomatoes that lined the shelves of an outdoor breezeway in the summertime and the freshly hoovered carpets of the downstairs dining room – to say nothing of the smells of cooking, of grape-wood fires and blackened pizza crusts, citrus salad dressings and fragrant grilled meats. And I memorized the quirks of its architecture by finger-feel, a structure that had been built as a single family home and adapted to accommodate a growing business. When it first opened, the vast hearth (now the most prominent feature of the downstairs kitchen) had not yet been built. All the grilling was performed over a steel drum in the back courtyard adjacent to where the first pastry chef, Lindsey Shere, dreamt up confections in the repurposed tool-shed that predated a proper restaurant's pastry department. The addition of an open kitchen upstairs in 1980 – to cater to a café menu distinct from the downstairs prix-fixe – was followed by a series of auxiliary buildings, storage areas, a wine room, staff locker-room and offices. Chez Panisse spread out like a new-born market town – in fits and starts, as necessity and a growing family dictated – and struggled through two significant fires, in 1982 and more recently in 2013.

As a child I used this familiarity, this inner map, to my flagrant advantage: I knew the best alcoves for games of hide-and-seek, how many of the back stairs could be cleared in a single leap (twelve was my ankle-shattering record), from which shelf in the walk-in I could pilfer a selection of pastry delights undetected. Many of the restaurant's employees also assumed informal caretaking roles: Tom Guernsey, the general manager, would crawl beneath dining tables draped with linens for secret tea parties with all the cooks' children. Mary Jo Thoresen, a pastry chef, would freeze raspberries to crown our fingertips as we gathered around her counter to watch her dust violets with caster sugar or slip ripe peaches expertly from their skin with a paring knife. Of course, my favourite place in the restaurant was the pizza station in the upstairs café, with its oakwood-burning oven. There, with Michele Perrella, our long-time Italian pizzaiolo, we restaurant urchins would receive impromptu pizza-making lessons.

Even as unrelenting dinner orders poured in, Michele would steal a moment for me to join him where he stood sentry, enveloped in a flood of wood-scented heat. As I teetered on an overturned plastic bus-tub, he led me through the steps for making a pizza. First, he would open the lid of the dough bucket for me to smell the rush of yeasty air that escaped. That smell, he explained, is what allowed the dough to rise. Then we would turn the dough out of the bucket to let it spread out over the flour-dusted counter. From its mass, we would cut handfuls, weighing each one on a scale to make sure the pizzas and pizzettas came out (more or less) uniform. Once the balls of dough had been allowed to rest – and I had finished my salad back at my table – I returned to my perch to make a pizza, starting by stippling the dough with my fingertips before gently stretching it between my hands. The rolling pin only came into play when necessary, for a few remedial flicks of the wrist. Then Michele would show me how to brush garlic-infused oil evenly over the dough and how to carefully lay down ingredients so that the flame would treat each judiciously. As the flames did their speedy work, he would hoist me up beneath the armpits to watch the transformation, our faces growing hot as embers. At the age of six, my favourite pizza topping was stinging nettles.

The hidden hearth

After the first fire blazed a hole through the dividing wall, Chez Panisse made the radical decision to open up its working restaurant kitchen to the formal dining room. Unlike the more recent restaurant fad of the 'Chef's Table', at which a small number of guests are given a privileged view of the working kitchen, face-to-face with the chef, Chez Panisse's aim was to make the preparation of the meal integral to the dining experience for everyone, rather than to perform culinary authenticity for a select few. Chez Panisse's bold redesign was effected in 1982, when allowing meals to be prepared and enjoyed in an architecturally coherent manner was still hardly commonplace in the world of fine-dining. Even many of the restaurant-focused books of the last two decades have emphasized what transpires mostly behind closed doors, and are often marketed as exposés of the brutality and chaos of the commercial kitchen. These titles include Anthony Bourdain's unavoidable *Kitchen Confidential* (2000) and Bill Buford's more thoughtful, though equally troubling, *Heat*, alongside the glut of Gordon Ramsay television series (*Boiling Point*, *Hell's Kitchen*, *The F Word*, *Kitchen Nightmares*). Together, they have perpetuated the myth that the serenity of the dining area depends for its quality on the squalor, noise and abuse of the close quarters of the kitchen – whereby the latter is proof of the excellence of the other.[1] The extraordinary success of these and other culinary figureheads in their public tell-alls – and the multiplication of this genre across the world – affirms a growing cultural fascination with that binary.

This concern with what is really going on in the kitchen is a fairly recent development. Until the early nineteenth century, only wealthy households had separate kitchens staffed with professional cooks, and it took the dramatic shifts of industrialization and urbanization to introduce the concept to the majority of the Western world. The so-called 'domestic cooking' was historically confined to the countryside where access to local ingredients was ubiquitous (there was no real alternative – you had to eat what you could grow); consequently, these houses were frequently centred around large open fires or brick ovens, much as they had been since ancient times. In ancient Rome, for example, the *focus*, or hearth, was often the point around which domestic architecture revolved. Cicero famously asserted that 'The most sacred, the most hallowed place on earth is the home of each and every citizen. There are his sacred hearth and his household gods, there the very center of his worship, religion and domestic ritual.'[2] Indeed, ancient Romans habitually honoured the *lares*, household gods intrinsically connected to the hearth. Associated both with ancestral and agricultural roots, the *lares* embodied sustenance through kinship and provision. A *lararium* then was a shrine frequently conflated with the hearth which served as a repository of foodstuffs – especially grains – following meals and festivals; conviviality and sustainability were built into the very material of the home. In *Hungry City*, Carolyn Steel's study of how modern cities eat, she affirms the historical hearth–home connection: 'Many early rural dwellings were simply kitchens in which people lived [...] and such buildings remain emblematic of the ancient marriage between hearth and home' but adds the caveat: 'Although early town houses also had open fires, as cities grew larger the fires got smaller.'[3]

Even in affluent European homes, meals were often taken informally until the late eighteenth century, and families would gather at foldaway tables in the living room.[4] With the decline of this casual approach to dining, in favour of more opulent productions (budget permitting), the idea of spatial division within the home was increasingly emphasized by contemporary architects, particularly in Britain, where huge new fortunes could be spent on capacious homes with a number of specialized rooms. For example, the prominent British architect and co-founder of the Architectural Association, Robert Kerr suggested in 1880 that 'what passes on either side of the boundary [between kitchen and dining room] shall be both invisible and inaudible on the other'.[5] In her book, *The Food Axis*, Elizabeth Collins Cromley cites even earlier examples of the kitchen/living-quarters dichotomy from the American colonies. The Brush-Everard House in Williamsburgh, Virginia, built in 1717, was equipped with a freestanding kitchen (added in 1750) so that the main house might be kept 'cool and free of cooking odors' and so that the 'conceptually clean reception rooms of the house [might be kept] from the conceptually dirty and messy food-preparation areas, particularly when they were the zone of servants' and slaves' work'.[6] As Victorian social code shifted in England, a parallel insistence on the 'upstairs-downstairs' division of the household prevailed; the relegation of cooking smells to the distant places of their origin became paramount, and, as any fan of the British television series *Downton Abbey* can tell you, labouring servants always disappeared below ground. This squeamishness regarding culinary aromas might easily be dismissed as a feature of the caricatured delicacy of the Victorian sensibility, were it not for the enduring impression it left on cultural perceptions of cooking. The rise, in the twenty-first century, of fast food, takeaway and ready-meals in the West and in the developing world, coupled with a concomitant de-emphasis of the kitchen as the centre of the home, resulted from a collision of forces. These range from the emergence of evolutionary theory and its effects on diet to the discovery of germs in the second half of the previous century (which produced widespread phobia). The equation was further ravelled by the formalization of nationalistic nutrition regimes, the individuation of social classes and the geopolitics of food provenance and distribution.

In 1926, the Austrian-born architect Margarete Schütte-Lihotzky designed what became known as the 'Frankfurt Kitchen', one of the most influential designs of the twentieth century and the first kitchen ever to be mass-produced. With the endorsement of the architect Ernst May, who had been charged with the refurbishment of the housing estates of Weimar Germany, by the late 1920s, 10,000 modules of the kitchen had been built in Frankfurt alone. Joy Parr describes the Frankfurt Kitchen's function as 'part of a civilian reestablishment project in the wake of World War I, integral to housing initiatives designed to relocate and energize their residents as productive workers and engage Germans, as democratic citizens, in the better world of their new republic'.[7] Conceived to be cheap and compact, and equipped with an abundance of space- and time-saving devices (such as a removable garbage drawer, a suspended dish rack and a compartmentalized pantry), the Frankfurt Kitchen was an early version of the cramped galley-sized kitchen ubiquitous in high-density cities today. With this design, in which space was too scarce to invite conviviality,

> ... cooking was banished to the invisible parts of the house; only this time, the mistress of the house was banished with it. Far from releasing housewives from drudgery as intended, the Frankfurt Kitchen – and the millions of galley kitchens that followed in its wake – would ensure that cooking would remain the isolated, thankless task that polite society had always believed it to be.[8]

For a brief time, in the 1940s and 1950s, homes in the United States were conceived with spacious kitchens and open-floor plans, exemplified by design of the 'typical American house' on display at the *American National Exhibition* at Sokolniki Park in Moscow in 1959.[9] This house was known as the 'Splitnik', thanks to its visitor-friendly split down the middle, its name a play on the Sputnik – or 'satellite' – launched by the Soviet Union in 1957. Though it became emblematic of a shift in thinking about the configuration of domestic space, the house's legacy suggests it was more a careful instrument of soft power than a portent of more wide-ranging architectural trends.

This was evident during the notorious 'kitchen debate', an impromptu conversation between the US vice president Richard Nixon and the Soviet premier Nikita Khrushchev at the opening of the *American National Exhibition* on 24 July. It became clear during this exchange that the US government was primarily interested in propagating the prototype as a standardized model because its architectural features, including an abundance of automated devices, conveniences and freedom of space, were intended to be transparently analogous to the freedom of the market. In this reading, the open-plan kitchen becomes – perhaps surprisingly – akin to a political arena, put forward by the US government as a tool wielded in Cold War foreign policy.[10] The electric can opener had become weaponized.

This architectural ethos followed in the wake of several forward-looking books on the subject of the future of domestic architecture, including *Tomorrow's House: A Complete Guide for the Home-Builder*, published in 1945 by the American architects George Nelson and Henry Wright. Nelson and Wright expounded the merits of the open-kitchen plan, proposing a merge between kitchen and dining room, citing examples by the architect Frank Lloyd Wright (who at that point was working on the Solomon R. Guggenheim Museum in New York). Wright and Nelson were also undoubtedly aware of earlier precedents, such as the radical Schindler House, an open floor–plan residence designed by the architect Rudolf Schindler and constructed in 1922 in which space was intended to be malleable and adaptable to function.[11] Nelson and Wright's desire was to develop a kitchen that would be pleasant to work in, suggesting that '[i]f the architect has been intelligent in his approach, the room is completely free from its familiar hospital operating-room atmosphere, thanks to the incorporation of natural wood surfaces, bright colour, and fabrics'.[12] Notionally, such a design would ensure the resurgence of the kitchen as the social nexus of the home. With the concurrent emergence of an American middle class, housewives began to assume the role of feeding their families as the tradition of maids and servants receded (in reality, becoming unaffordable in the post-war boom). In Nelson and Wright's idealized house-plan, these housewives would no longer be cut off from the living quarters of the home, as the hired help had mostly been a century earlier. Still, the modern conception of the 'family meal', for which all members gather together around the table for supper, was short-lived. As Steel explains,

> [f]amily meals as we think of them today (not only cooked by Mother, but shared by her at table) were a purely twentieth-century phenomenon; the product of the servantless nuclear family brought about by the two world wars [...] Even as it reached its apogee, the phenomenon was in decline, as the social conditions that brought it about disintegrated once more.[13]

The kitchen once again receded behind closed doors.

In 2006, average figures compiled across ten London boroughs by the Office of the Mayor of London recommended that the minimum size of a kitchen for a three-bedroom dwelling be 6.5 metres square – scant dimensions for a multi-bedroom apartment.[14] All housing built on London Development Agency land must meet the standards set by the mayor, which, according to the website for the governmental agency that regularly issues them, will 'promote better neighbourhoods, high environmental standards, better accessibility and better design'.[15] Just as the vision of American prosperity on display in Moscow in 1959 was meant to persuade Americans to live the success of their economic system, these London 'housing space standards' are testament to a hoped-for (if not mandatory) top-down implementation or decree. Such governmental policing of the private, domestic sphere arguably does little for the people whose lives such regulations are intended to improve.[16]

The two-bedroom East London apartment I lived in 2012 – and which is representative of a generation of apartment blocks built in the first decade of the twentieth century, during the decline of the New Labour government – boasted an even smaller kitchen, measuring a mere 4 metres square, with more than 30 per cent of the space consumed by oven, refrigerator, sink and dishwasher. The floor space was hardly ample enough to accommodate two bodies, and smaller appliances overtook the negligible counter space. This is not a kitchen intended to encourage the act of cooking, but, then again, neither did its designers believe it to be a central feature of the contemporary domestic landscape. Indeed, the shrinking kitchen in Western Europe could well be identified as an outcome of the shift towards convenience foods that began in the United States (and spread rapidly to Britain) just after the Second World War.

Though local culinary traditions have been to some extent preserved in parts of Continental Europe, where rural traditions persist, Britain and the United States have shown themselves to be victims of their enthusiastic embrace of 'fast food nation'.[17] A visit to virtually any Western European or American city betrays the extent to which convenience and fast foods have overtaken urban culture.[18] As Melanie Warner, author of *Pandora's Lunchbox:*

How Processed Food Took over the American Meal, has pointed out, 'We didn't know the true impact of these changes in food on our society and our health. Our diets have changed more in the last century than in the previous 10,000 years, when agriculture was introduced.'[19] Since convenience foods first appeared, their market value has increased exponentially, to the point where companies see the merit of dedicating entire stores to their dissemination and square miles of factories to their production. Though the origins of fast food lie in the *thermopolia*, or takeaway shops, of ancient Rome, with, as Steel suggests, proto-24-hour food purveyors persisting through the Middle Ages and beyond, the worrisome state of contemporary food culture now more than ever indicates our collective remove from the proverbial hearth. When Chez Panisse became one of the first restaurants in the United States to open up its kitchen to its dining space, it invited visitors to observe the cooking process; it made transparent how real, whole ingredients can be transformed into delicious, nourishing plates of food by people like themselves. And while Chez Panisse had nothing to hide, it did have something to teach.

Return to the garden

A growing detachment from the land, the kitchen and the table stems not just from the infiltration of the 'fast food nation' ideology into virtually every sphere of experience in the developed world but also from the failure of schools to educate children in how to care for the environment and, in doing so, nourish their bodies. When, in 1995, my mother first noticed a derelict car park on the grounds of a state-run middle school situated between our home and Chez Panisse, fast-food culture and the attendant obesity epidemic were not her foremost concerns. Rather, she was concerned that Martin Luther King, Jr. Middle School, which serves approximately 1,000 students representing a broad spectrum of ethnicities and incomes, should look so distressingly abandoned. Not long after, my mother was quoted in a local newspaper, in which she voiced her concerns about the appearance of the middle school she walked past daily. The school's then principal, Neil Smith, contacted her to inquire whether she might be interested in helping to rehabilitate its blighted school-grounds. As when faced with the challenges of opening a new kind of restaurant on a shoestring budget, or soothing a restless baby while prepping a sit-down dinner for dozens of patrons, she did not hesitate with her answer. It has more or less always been her conviction that any spare bit of land should be greened and cultivated with edible plants – likely a vestige of growing up in the berry patches of her own mother's wartime 'victory garden'.[20] Her vision suddenly expanded to include all school subjects being taught through a garden and a kitchen, in effect using them as laboratories to cultivate learning. The need to integrate all areas of learning – to, in effect, reinstate the hearth as the centre of the community – was immediately evident to my mother. This garden would not be a merely 'greenwash' of the school; it would become its central architectural feature. Smith could never have imagined what would transpire from his casual invitation.

Having trained as a Montessori schoolteacher in the 1960s before following her palate into the kitchen, my mother immediately saw the potential for a vegetable garden to serve as an extended classroom – one in which, in accordance with Maria Montessori's pedagogy, learning could be predominantly experiential. Her aim was to plant a garden and build an adjacent teaching kitchen that could enrich the curriculum and life of the school community. She and Smith met regularly with the faculty at Martin Luther King, Jr. Middle School to field ideas for the development of the project, and within two years, teachers and community volunteers had cleared more than an acre of tarmac and planted a cover crop. The 'Edible Schoolyard' was born. The kitchen, then situated in the forsaken school cafeteria, opened in the autumn of the Edible Schoolyard's third year, helmed by a chef and teacher named, aptly, Esther Cook. Gradually, teachers began integrating the Edible Schoolyard into their routine classroom subjects, scheduling time with their students to visit and work in the garden and using it to draw real-life connections to arithmetic and science, while also enlivening reading and writing.

By its fifth year, the Edible Schoolyard was engaged in teaching ten 90-minute classes a week in both the garden and kitchen. A director was hired to oversee the project and the staff grew to eight. A young Chez Panisse cook built a wood-burning pizza oven in the garden, in which meals could regularly be prepared when the weather was nice (which, luckily, was often in the sunny East Bay) – a playground hearth that quickly became the symbolic heart of the garden. Students cleared trees and brambles in order to place two 3,500-gallon cisterns that would collect rainwater to irrigate a hillside orchard nearby, and helped to build a chicken coop for a growing flock of chickens and ducks, which by 2012 provided more than 500 eggs annually for the kitchen classroom. Teachers began finding evermore creative ways to deploy the garden and kitchen in their lessons: measuring garden beds to teach geometry, pouring liquids into measuring cups to teach fractions, taking soil samples to analyse the mineral content of the earth and growing and threshing heirloom grains to learn about ancient civilizations.

Over the past twenty years, the Edible Schoolyard has become not only an integral part of Martin Luther King, Jr. Middle School but also a respected teaching institution and model of engaged, sustainable education. So far, I have offered two crucial examples of what might be described as 'engaged consumption' – the kitchen and dining room at Chez Panisse and the Edible

Schoolyard. Both of these are attuned to a wider understanding of sustainability, emphasizing social equity and environmental responsibility. Implicitly, they make the argument that the provision of food and the sharing of meals are the foundation for a sustainable community. This kind of education, whether or not it is a formal pedagogy (the ultimate goal of the Edible Schoolyard Project is that students be given academic credit for 'school lunch'), inevitably will inform not just our physical selves but also the tangible spaces that surround us.

The foundation created by my mother in 1996 to underwrite the project (the state schools in California, and in most other American states, are chronically underfunded) now subsidizes additional Edible Schoolyards in San Francisco, New Orleans, New York City, Los Angeles and Greensboro, North Carolina. Hundreds of other projects, modelled on the Berkeley Edible Schoolyard, are in the affiliated network. Encouraging others to grow likeminded projects has been a foremost concern of the Edible Schoolyard; all of its foundational materials, including curricula and syllabi, are made readily available online to encourage the spread of such programmes. In 2003, the Chez Panisse Foundation partnered with the Berkeley Unified School District and the Center for Ecoliteracy to implement a programme for a district-wide School Lunch Initiative. Three years later, the collaboration had transformed what 10,000 Berkeley public school children eat for breakfast and lunch in school, and how they learn about food and their relationship to the environment every day. The newly constructed Dining Commons at Martin Luther King, Jr. Middle School now serves as the central kitchen for all sixteen schools in the district, providing several thousand meals per day, made with healthy, fresh and mostly organic ingredients.

In 2005, for the Smithsonian Folklife Festival, my mother was asked to bring a version of the Edible Schoolyard to the National Mall in Washington, DC, where the site was visited by a million people. During the festival, my mother installed an open kitchen and large picnic table where politicians, activists, teachers and writers were invited to gather to discuss the real impact that 'good, clean and fair'[21] school lunches could have – a 'kitchen debate' for the twenty-first century. Since it was founded, the Edible Schoolyard in Berkeley has served more than 9,000 students and is dropped in on each year by more than 1,000 outside visitors, including California governor Jerry Brown, California's secretary of agriculture and the US surgeon general. The Edible Schoolyard Project is currently engaged in talks with the mayor of Sacramento about creating an Edible Schoolyard at a high school in the state's capital. The project will become more visible than ever to legislators who not only have the power to effect change in classrooms state-wide but who might also be encouraged to remediate farm policy run amok, diminishing water resources, pesticide abuse and other symptoms of the peril engendered by our detachment from the land. The Sacramento Edible Schoolyard will be a project-based learning programme in which the garden and cafeteria will be entirely incorporated into the high school's curriculum and students' responsibilities will include everything from designing the dining space, to sourcing raw ingredients, drawing up budgets, cooking meals and reaching out to the local community.

At a time when, in the United States alone, the World Health Organization has identified almost a third of under-twenties as overweight, and a significant portion of these as obese – leading to projected lifespans shorter than those of their parents' – alternative solutions must be sought out and supported.[22] In places where these alternatives exist, they are finally becoming mainstream: in 2004 the Oakland Children's Hospital became a partner to the Edible Schoolyard, formally endorsing the programme as a way to combat the tide of dispiriting health statistics and the gloomy future they predict. Though the obesity epidemic – and the enormous sum it has, continues to and will cost in healthcare over the coming decades – has done a great deal to propel my mother's vision of feeding every child in America a *free*, wholesome, sustainable lunch, the Edible Schoolyard was never intended as a band-aid solution for the mounting crisis. Though the dire numbers issued by the World Health Organization have given my mother's project credence, in many ways the Edible Schoolyard is still for her more about bringing children into a positive relationship with the land and with food than it is about staving off childhood obesity. It is her firmly held belief that the sensuous pleasures of the garden and the kitchen inherently encourage children to absorb the values of the Edible Schoolyard, among them, friendship, care, responsibility, cooperation, deliciousness and beauty.

The Edible Schoolyard *is* a beautiful place, lush with hundreds of varieties of vegetables, herbs, vines, berries, flowers and fruit trees. The beds zigzag organically, colourful hand-painted signs announce varietals and a kiwi vine drapes languidly over a circular gazebo meeting place where students gather to discuss the day's work. Sitting on the edge of the garden, the new kitchen classroom is awash with sunlight and the warm smells of cooking during the school day. Students hurry to tie aprons around themselves and friends before settling into their tasks: smoothing the checked tablecloths, setting down enamel plates and silverware, placing vases of just-picked flowers on the tables, chopping vegetables and cracking eggs, sautéing garlic at the (admittedly electric) hearth and filling the sinks with soapy water to do the washing up. In this kitchen, students rarely complain about doing a chore or balk at the prospect of eating the vegetables on their plates. What has become abundantly clear over the past twenty years is that if a child plants a handful of broccoli seeds and nurtures them to grow into flowering purple stems, then he or she will delight in eating them. Loris Malaguzzi, the creator of the influential 'Reggio Emilia Approach' in post-war Northern Italy, and one of the great proponents of experiential learning, referred to the environment in which children learn as the 'Third Teacher'.[23] The Edible Schoolyard is predicated on this same notion, based upon my mother's belief that children will gravitate naturally to a kitchen that is beautiful, integrated and – most importantly – open.

Notes

1 Bourdain's book details his experience of working in the kitchen of Les Halles in New York City; Buford's does the same for Babbo, also in New York City. Cited in Anthony Bourdain, *Kitchen Confidential* (New York: Bloomsbury, 2000); and Bill Buford, *Heat: An Amateur's Adventures as Kitchen Slave, Line Cook, Pasta Maker and Apprentice to a Dante-quoting Butcher in Tuscany* (New York: A. Knopf, 2006).

2 Cicero, *De Domo Sua* 41, 109.

3 Carolyn Steel, *Hungry City: How Food Shapes our Lives*. repr. ed. (London: Chatto and Windus, 2008; London Vintage, 2013), 167.

4 Ibid., 178.

5 Robert Kerr quoted in J. J. Stevenson, *House Architecture* (London: Macmillan, 1880), 2:78.

6 Collins, Elizabeth Cromley, *The Food Axis: Cooking, Eating, and the Architecture of American Houses* (Charlottesville and London: University of Virginia Press, 2010), 25.

7 Joy, Parr, 'Introduction: Modern Kitchen, Good Home, Strong Nation,' in 'Kitchen Technologies', ed. J. Parr, special issue, *Technology and Culture* 43.4 (2002): 657–667, 661.

8 Steel, *Hungry City*, 187.

9 The model home replicated a residence previously built at 398 Townline Road in Long Island, New York, originally designed by Stanley H. Klein for Herbert Sadkin's firm All-State Properties. To accommodate visitors to the exhibition, Sadkin hired Andrew Geller, vice president of the Housing and Home Components department at Loewy/Snaith to modify Klein's floor plan.

10 As was clear from the 'kitchen debate', the open kitchen design allowed for discourse (not only for competing ideologies to coexist but a place in which healthy dissent could be staged or, more cynically, stage-*managed*). The free space of the house on display, perhaps subconsciously, encouraged the (male) leaders of the two world superpowers to squabble in a *kitchen*, perhaps the most gendered of rooms in a house.

11 For more on the Schindler House, see Kathryn Smith's monograph, *Schindler House* (Los Angeles: Hennessey and Ingalls, 2010).

12 George Nelson, and Henry Wright, *Tomorrow's House* (New York: Simon and Schuster, 1945), 75.

13 Steel, *Hungry City*, 171.

14 *Housing Space Standards*, Mayor of London, August 2006, Appendix 9, 24.

15 Ibid.

16 Steel points out that:

> Families on low incomes, who could most benefit from cooking from scratch, are increasingly spending what little money they have on convenience foods and takeaways. The urban poor are the real victims of our confused attitudes towards cooking. Despite food costing a fraction of what it did a century ago, their diets have barely improved: they have simply swapped one kind of malnutrition for another. (*Hungry City* 196)

17 This phrase, now liberally deployed as a term unto itself, derives from Eric Schlosser's seminal book *Fast Food Nation: The Dark Side of the All-American Meal* (2003), in which he revealed the extent to which the fast-food industry changed the landscape of America, provoked an obesity epidemic, increased the disparity between poor and rich and re-organized global food production and distribution.

18 I use the term 'convenience foods' to mean foods that are pre-fabricated and therefore require little or no 'preparation' on behalf of the consumer. These range from packaged triangle sandwiches, to microwave dinners, to processed ingredient 'kits' that can be easily assembled and cooked at home. For an in-depth study of the development and proliferation of convenience and processed foods, see Melanie Warner's *Pandora's Lunchbox: How Processed Food Took over the American Meal* (New York: Scribner, 2013).

19 From an interview with Mark Bittman, quoted in 'Lost in the Supermarket', *The New York Times*, 9 April 2013.

20 Victory gardens, also sometimes called 'war gardens', were vegetable and fruit gardens planted by citizens at their homes and in public parks throughout the United States, United Kingdom and Canada during the First World War and the Second World War. These respective governments encouraged their citizens to plant gardens to reduce pressure on the public food supply during the war. In addition to aiding the war effort, these gardens were intended to boost civil morale and give people a sense of agency and patriotism.

21 'Good, clean and fair' is the motto of Slow Food, a global, grassroots, non-profit organization (of which my mother has served as vice president since 2002) with supporters in 150 countries. It is dedicated to promoting the connection between the pleasure of the table and a commitment to sustaining communities and the environment.

22 World Health Organization. *Obesity and Overweight*. Fact Sheet no. 311. 2015. http://www.who.int/mediacentre/factsheets/fs311/en/

23 It is worth noting that Italy, the country that bore the Slow Food movement and remains more fervently invested in the preservation of its food culture (despite the onslaughts of the fast food industry) than most comparable nations, was the fertile ground for many of the important early childhood pedagogical movements of the nineteenth and twentieth centuries – many of which insisted on the integration of the natural environment with the classroom.

7

Sustenance and Sustainability in Higher Education

Jamie Horwitz

Introduction

In the campus dining experience immortalized by Harry Potter movies, a strict spatial and temporal order connected the students and faculty with the design and furnishings of the great hall. Food and drink consumed here is less well known. Since 1529, when a meal was first served to Oxford faculty at high table, and to the students sitting on benches at perpendicular long tables below them in Christ Church's Tudor Hall, nothing much has been mentioned about food in the histories of higher education. There is barely evidence that dining even happened, particularly on English campuses.[1]

Now consider the following exchange found among the 'Frequently Asked Questions' on the dining website of a large North American university.

[Q] How can I avoid missing meals due to conflicts with my class schedule?

[A] There's always a campus dining location open between 7:00 a.m. and 2:00 a.m. You can also take-out at any of our retail operations, which offer 'grab and go' items such as sandwiches, salads, and bakery items. All of the dining commons offer carryout options, as well.[2]

The flexibility (described above) that one dining service builds into their meal plan gives a surprisingly accurate glimpse into big campus dining today: Food is ubiquitous, choices abound, class schedules overlap with other activities and eating in dining halls is optional. I am no stranger to contemporary eating

FIGURE 7.1 *Yale University's largest dining hall, the Commons, is an architectural descendent of Christ Church's Tudor Hall and has been updated to include a small retail operation with grab-and-go items. Photo courtesy of Becky Schilling,* Food Management *magazine.*

patterns, or to the design and marketing process that integrates consumer behaviour and desire with the design of products, settings and furnishings. However, this chapter represents a more sceptical view of such abundant choice: with regard to students' well-being, to the efficiencies of campus services and operations and to institutional dining's strategic (or missed) opportunity to use its enormous purchasing power and captive market towards innovations that reach across the entire food axis (Figure 7.1).[3]

Sustainable food programmes and projects in higher education are growing widely in North America. Many activists and scholars have reported that colleges and universities lead the sustainable food movement. Moreover, student-led networks that are active around the country, such as the Real Food Challenge, have commitments from hundreds of campuses that they will spend at least 20 per cent of their dining procurement on sustainably raised food from local and regional farms by 2020. An anthropologist of sustainable campus movements, Peggy F. Barlett, traces sustainable collegiate dining back to a moment when changes in dining service procurement began: to a time when students, faculty or staff were concerned about the harmful impacts of the conventional food systems, or what is called 'Big Ag'. Established campus initiatives in green building, energy, water and waste do not always recognize that dining is a strategic axis in the sustainable campus. Surveys of campus sustainable food initiatives rarely include their relationship with campus architecture or infrastructure.[4]

Campus dining: XL conventional

The dining services at Iowa State University (ISU), which is an institution located in the farming heartland of the midwestern United States, served more than 30,000 meals a day to about one-quarter of their 34,472 students enrolled in the 2014–2015 academic year. ISU students purchased customized meal contracts that were configured with a specific number of pre-purchased 'meal blocks' for use in the all-you-can-eat food stations at four residence halls, and a specific amount of 'dining dollars' and 'meal bundles' for use in the nine retail café and dining outlets dispersed across campus. ISU Dining generated 42.6 million dollars of revenue in 2014 (Figure 7.2).[5] I will refer to these kinds of large-scale dining operations here as 'XL Conventional'.

The informal interviews reported in this chapter began as conversations with my students at Iowa State University. In discussions, I learned ISU students experience satisfaction with their food choices, and their ability to plan where and when to eat with friends: 'By the second or third week in the semester, everybody knows their schedule and can figure out where they will be eating.' ISU Dining's director echoed nearly these same words and then explained some of the reasons for the abundance of choices as well as the structure and order that stands behind a fluid and flexible campus dining experience (when serving about 30,000 meals a day). Of greatest importance to ISU Dining is their use of an integrated food services information system.

FIGURE 7.2 *This ISU Dining cafeteria manager captured the revenue students spent on off-hours takeaway by preparing hot and fresh meals for pickup from 7.00 to 11.00 p.m. Photo by Jamie Horwitz.*

This digital system tracks everything they purchase, store, prepare and serve, and what time food is taken away from the stations – right down to the spoonful! Because of real-time tracking, dining staff can resupply a food station that is running short by shuttling trays between stations, even if they are located in buildings across campus.[6]

Once I was cognizant to how dining services easily managed to supply multiple venues with changing numbers of students on any particular day, I pressed the ISU Dining director to explain the benefits or challenges of having so many meal plans and options. Keller did not view the meal plans as overabundant, primarily because they enable flexible dining schedules which she views as a necessity and not a response to student desire for more choice. Instead, she explained that flexible scheduling permits students to eat at different times and in different dining locations in much the same way that academic courses are offered at multiple times in the year, and online! Much like other state universities, ISU has seen an increase in enrolment for the past decade. Following on the heels of decreases in funding allocations from the government, universities continue to thrive by making up the budget shortfalls with tuition dollars. An increase in student enrolment does not, however, translate into an increase in the number of classrooms or other types of student spaces. In a context in which academic and other collegiate activities must overlap, dining services are able to accommodate more students by using flexible schedules, having multiple venues and allowing students to spend their 'dining dollars' and 'meal bundles' in on-campus retail outlets.[7]

This discussion of these reasons for flexible dining schedules and the abundance of dining options in the context of XL Conventional may seem functionalistic or reductionist to some readers. I suggest they offer a beginning to explore further the complex factors that are linked in the nexus which is campus dining. For example, all campus dining is either self-operated or contracted to food management vendors, the largest of which are Sodexo and Aramark. Much of the new capital investment in campus dining services and operations is a result of contractual agreements with these vendors. Moreover, some campuses with dining contracts have instituted dining-related fees for all enrolled students – whether or not the students have purchased meal plans. Class action lawsuits by students have been unsuccessful, and popular interest in these additional fees and building projects has become a subject of debate within the dining industry.

Researchers who study the temporal organization of behaviour, particularly related to eating, have argued that institutional prohibitions against changes in daily routines must be well guarded if they are to be sustained. The French sociologist Francois Ascher has found that people eating in an asynchronous manner is a relatively new pattern. Interestingly, this pattern is equally present in the richest societies and among those with meagre resources: Regardless of their demographic, people are choosing what and where they eat, at what time and with whom, several times a day. [8]

It is important to mention that many types of sustainable food initiatives are identifiable at Iowa State University. Notably, there is a pre- and post-consumer food waste initiative that supplies all the composting for the student farm and a student-run project that transforms used cooking oil for the use of city buses that serve the whole campus and town. Yet, because the university is in rural, central Iowa, these initiatives tend to remain in the background: Corporate agribusiness supports research and collegiate activities here, and thousands of enrolled students were born into proud, traditional farming households across a broad region known as the American Heartland. The powerful emotional aspects of eating practices and preferences are grounded in the social and economic context of this place and its role in conventional agriculture.

This chapter now turns to consider what can be learned from the explicit use of architecture in the design of campus dining, in particular within institutions that are dedicated to cultivating a sustainable American campus. What follows here is an analysis of one institution's attempt to introduce a sustainable food system into the student dining experience.

XS sustainable

One of the best examples of sustainable practices in campus dining can be seen at Williams College, a private liberal arts school in the hills of western Massachusetts. Established in 1793, Williams has a very elegant and, by US standards, old campus. With only 2,000 undergraduates, a small group of graduate students and one of the largest endowments, Williams has established an institution-wide, top-to-bottom, commitment to environmentally sustainable practices. While green initiatives can be a source of tension in some institutions, Williams College dining services and administrators hold frequent meetings with the student Food Committee, and moreover, these groups appear to act in concert with faculty and staff across the campus.[9] This model of collegiate dining can be termed 'XS Sustainable'.

Williams' new approach to dining was launched in 2007 with the opening of the Paresky Student Center. Several years of on-campus meetings involving open sessions with faculty and students informed the planning of the new dining facility in Paresky. Both Robert Volpi, the college's (then) new director of Dining Services, and Gregory Clawson, the project architect from the Polshek Partnership, mentioned these long evenings of conversation and discussion.[10]

The construction of the new student centre would not have been possible if Williams' alumni from around the world succeeded in halting the demolition of the old student centre, Baxter Hall. Their reasons had nothing to do with planned changes in food services, or the new building's design, or the commitment to sustainable practices that hiring Robert Volpi surely signalled. Rather, the alumni wanted to keep the past alive. For them, Baxter Hall was a touchstone of memory of their time spent at Williams. This dispersed community even kept vigil on the demolition through live webcams on the college's homepage. At the end of this stage in the process, a festival of fireworks provided a finale for Baxter Hall. Ultimately, a key aspect of the original centre – an elliptically shaped dining space – was echoed in the architecture of its replacement.

For the architects of Polshek Partnership, the alumni protests were less challenging than the site itself. The project architect Gregory Clawson explained that even though the new structure is built in the middle of a tight cluster of landmark buildings, it is loaded with programme: campus kitchen and dining service facilities, seating in three venues and also a performance space for lectures and stage productions. From a distance, particularly in a photograph, there is little explicitly hospitable about the forty-foot cantilevered steel-and-glass canopy forming a double-height porch on the Paresky Student Center.

A friendly feeling in the materials emerges more slowly, with the subtle, layered permeability from its outermost exterior edges to the soft cafeteria line floating near the centre of the building. My impression is based on observing the students ramble around the building; and during warm days they tend drag chairs, laptops, food and drinks onto this wide, soft threshold. Along an entire facade, the Paresky is edged by gentle steps with a width that seems calculated to spill diners out, and onto the adjacent lawn.

I wanted to visit Williams College to ask Robert Volpi to show me what architectural design could do for sustainable dining programme. Volpi seemed slightly amused by the question and took me down to see the loading dock – perfectly sized for the small growers who deliver their full harvest and then begin to reload their truck. The dock was set up so the trucks are full on departure from the campus, taking away mounds of pre- and post-consumer food waste to be composted for replenishing soil. Dining staff load vats of used cooking oil onto their trucks to convert it for use as biofuel. Since the Paresky Student Center is a very tight fit on the site, the loading dock would never be large enough for the giant refrigerated trucks like those used by food management giants.

The kitchen is divided into a section just behind the cafeteria on the ground floor, and there is another area with heavier equipment below grade, just next to the loading dock. It is spacious, with more work surfaces and dramatically less freezer space than more conventional institutional dining facilities. The kitchen contains appliances to vacuum-pack fresh produce before flash-freezing it in a freezer that briefly drops its temperature in order to secure the nutrients and flavour. This freezer returns to a higher temperature after the intense freezing, which ensures that the staff will have ingredients for pear tarts, squash apple soup, onion pies, pesto and much more for many months.

In this manner, Volpi orchestrates a system of regional food procurement, thereby guaranteeing the continuous availability of nutritionally high-quality foods for a portion of the thousands of meals they prepare across the winter months. At the same time, this method guarantees purchase of a grower's entire season of crops just after harvest. By tapping into a network of local and regional food producers, Williams Dining assembles a continuum from procurement and delivery, to storage, preparation, service, cleanup, disposal and composting. The process unfolds out of the participation of many actors and is celebrated daily with the delicious food that helps to bring college students to the table. An institutional commitment to small and organic growers not only enables Williams Dining to ease the often impermeable boundary between 'town and gown' but also allows it to cross the boundary between a private, wealthy college and the renewal of a postindustrial regional economy and its landscape.

Inside the Paresky Student Center, there are different types of seating. Some people sit at tables, others eat sitting on couches or while reading in small booths. Each area has partial, permeable boundaries that divide it into semipublic, visible zones, rather than fully enclosed rooms with walls and doors. Eating from a tray on a cushy couch, or at a counter facing a screen or books, or on the steps of the front porch seems perfectly suited to socializing or studying, or shifting between these two activities. The spatial weaving is designed so that dining zones are interspersed with zones for studying. This co-presence allows shifting degrees of privacy and social contact, and it is found repeatedly in a new generation of elegant campus centres, such as Weiss Manfredi's at Smith College, and also the design produced for Illinois Institute of Technology's McCormick Tribune Campus Center by Rem Koolhaas' Office for Metropolitan Architecture. Yet, while the others emphasize a pedestrian movement akin to an urban arcade or passageway, Polshek's Paresky Center invites people to stay a while. It is a place to relax, not just to eat and run. This is a place where students form relationships that can make college last a lifetime (and cause them to protest when their favourite building is being torn down!).[11]

Neither architectural features nor the first photographs of students sitting around in comfortable seating are guaranteed to translate into users' experiences. Without the opportunity for extensive fieldwork during the first year that the Paresky Student Center was open, I sought the viewpoint of Darra Goldstein to help understand students' perceptions of this new building and the campus dining service it houses. Goldstein is professor of Russian at Williams College and the founding editor of *Gastronomica: The Journal of Critical Food Studies*. She is also a formidable advocate of student engagement and did not hesitate to write me back during the fall of 2009, stating: 'The students were skeptical that a brand-new building could ever have soul, but from the moment Paresky opened its doors, it became an important gathering place for the campus community, a site of both energy and ease.'

The act of dining together

Eating practices are not an entirely individual matter; they have long been considered to be the links between individuals and social or religious groups, and the landscapes on which we all depend. Yet, the perceived expression of individuality through food choices is an axiom of contemporary eating behaviour, and when considered alongside campus dining innovations, it is obvious there will be challenges to efforts undertaken to collectively eat sustainably. To be sure, the voices of students who do not want to change their food routines have been heard at Williams College as well. During discussions about a proposed 'Meatless Monday' that was being introduced in one of their four dining venues, an angry student declared, 'I pay for meals – I want what I want. Why should the choices of others dictate what I eat?' Later, the college's dining leaders responded with an even-handed letter posted on the Williams Dining Blog, discussing how they might negotiate these differences.[12]

When an institution uses the buying power of so many consumers to purchase food from local, small growers and artisan agriculture, they can change the livelihood, the economy and the ecological balance of the region. In doing so, even more people come to the table. On this warming planet, a changing climate brings new weather patterns and different patterns of growth. Changing climates and economies stress all manner of campus services as well as the students who seek higher education. There is an enduring value in sharing a meal that does not require a crisis to appreciate. Commensality with peers on campus is a special kind of opportunity for learning and unlearning during higher education. No matter what the hour, or the location, a capacity for resilience feeds on a synchrony of sustenance and sustainability.

Notes

1 The subjects of dining, meals, food services or eating do not appear in many fine histories of higher education, such as James J. F. Forest, and Philip G. Altbach, eds. *The International Handbook of Higher Education* (Heidelberg: Springer, 2007) or Mordechai Feingold, ed., *History of Universities* 20:2 (Oxford: Oxford University Press, 2005) . Histories of the collegiate campus in North America offer the richest record. The volume by Paul Venable Turner, *Campus: An American Planning Tradition* (Cambridge, MA: MIT Press, 1987), contains engravings of central dining halls in the earliest American colleges. The cafeterias situated in residential towers built for baby boomers reshaped the American campus from 1964 to 1980. In *Campus Life: Undergraduate Cultures from the End of the Eighteenth Century to the Present* (Chicago: University of Chicago Press, 1987), Helen Lefkowitz Horowitz tends to be concerned less with what or where students ate and more with how they thought about and engaged with one another. However, when she focuses on the architecture designed for men's or women's colleges, Horowitz (1984, 1985) demonstrates how dining rooms and lounges shaped social life, fostering or inhibiting communications among peers.

2 This appeared under the 'Frequently Asked Questions' page on the Pennsylvania State University's Dining website (accessed November 14, 2014). Data on the twenty-five largest university dining operations in 2014 were published in the magazine *Food Management* (a portion of the report is available online at www.Food-Management.com). Pennsylvania State

University enrolled 46,615 students at their University Park campus that year, and 14,313 students purchased meal plans that allowed them to choose where and when to eat from their five residential dining halls and eighteen retail outlets on campus.

3   The architectural historian Elizabeth Collins Cromley transformed the concept of the 'food axis' from a design term that referred to the spatial relationship between kitchen, food storage and dining spaces within a traditional house plan into a conceptual axis that 'escapes from the confines of the house plan into the section, site plan, and neighborhood map'. See Elizabeth C. Cromley, 'Transforming the Food Axis: Houses, Tools, Modes of Analysis', *Material History Review* 44 (Fall 1996): 8–22 . Cromley also explains that she 'relocates the historian's object of analysis' to the 'spaces in action that users create'. This theoretical break is the underpinning of my own work. See Jamie Horwitz and Paulette Singley, eds. *Eating Architecture* (Cambridge, MA: MIT Press, 2004) .

4   Evidences of sustainable food projects on campuses in North America are widely accessible online, particularly within the national networks such as 'Farm to Campus' and 'The Real Food Challenge'. Peggy F. Barlett's publications review sustainable campus food and dining efforts. I have learned much from the elaborated depth and breadth of her 'Campus Sustainable Food Projects: Critique and Engagement', *American Anthropologist* 113.1 (2011): 101–115 .

5   Dining industry news is found in the magazine *Food Management*. Their free online version, food-management.com, is full of discussions of developments in college and university dining services with a myriad of images. Every few years they create a list of the twenty-five largest examples of campus dining and provide interactive charts. These create rankings that show, for example, the largest number of students enrolled, proportions of students with meal tickets and dining revenue.

6   Personal communications between the author and Nancy Keller, the director of ISU Dining, occurred during the first two weeks in December 2014, by email and telephone, and meetings in her office. Nancy Keller explained the extraordinary efficiencies she helped to establish with ISU Dining's self-operated system. Perhaps most important is ISU's food information system tracking. Keller asked data managers on her staff to share information with me. After reviewing spread sheets from numerous dining halls over several weekdays in October and November 2014, I noticed what I thought was an anomaly: a larger number of burgers were eaten at one dining centre than prepared and served on that day in the in the same location. Keller explained that if one dining venue is running low, particularly on an entrée, staff from another dining centre will bring over more (burgers) where fewer students are eating on that day.

7   ISU Dining devised 'meal bundles' as a way for students to use their meal plan in retail outlets. While it is not an all-you-can-eat-style cafeteria, the meal bundle is a larger amount of food than would be purchased for the same amount of cash. The bundle includes preselected entrees, three sides and a drink.

8   The most valuable social theory on this topic is the essay by Francois Ascher, 'Hypermodern Society and the Eclectic Individual Revealed and Illustrated by

Dietary Practices', *Harvard Design Magazine* 30 (Spring/Summer 2009): 19–23 . Also crucial is John Urry, *Mobilities* (Cambridge: Polity Press, 2007) .

9 Williams College consistently ranks as one of the best colleges in the United States. For example, in 2014, both *Forbes Magazine's List of America's Best Colleges* and *U.S. News and World Report* ranked Williams as the top liberal art college. Notably, it has received nearly all A's from the 'College Sustainability Report Card', an interactive website that provides sustainability profiles of higher educational institutions across North America (see GreenReportCard.org). However, no institution is free of discord: some disagreements about the sustainable approach to campus dining have been freely discussed and aired on the 'sustainability' pages of the College's website (see www.sustainability.williams.edu). See also below, note 12.

10 Williams College hired Robert Volpi as their director of dining services prior to the process of planning its redesign; that is, he arrived before the kitchen and dining venues were housed together in the Paresky Student Center. When he was hired, Volpi had already proven himself to be a leader in forging relationships with organic growers in New England. As the Bates College Dining director, Volpi formed a buyers' group with other colleges as well as hospitals in the upper New England region to guarantee steady orders for growers who are large enough to meet the demands of institutional dining operations. Volpi became involved with the college side of dining services after nineteen years with Aramark, the largest national food distributor to institutions in the United States. When I contacted him, he in turn suggested that I speak with the Paresky Center's project architect, Gregory Clawson, of Polshek Partners. I conducted taped telephone interviews with Clawson and Sarah Anbalu of Polshek Market Relations during the fall of 2009.

11 My own interest in the relationship between architecture and food through the lens of campus dining began at the request of *The Chronicle of Higher Education*. My essay 'Following the Food: Where Students Eat' was published in *The Chronicle*'s 'Special Issue on Architecture' (March 25, 2005): B26–B28. For more focus on campus architecture and the social programme of dining and other refreshments, see: Jamie Horwitz, 'Fabricating Pluralism', *Architectural Design, Special Issue on Multi-cultural Modernism* 75.5 (Sept–Oct 2006): 24–31; and 'Replacing a Beloved Building with a Hybrid: Paresky Student Center, Williams College', *Architectural Design* (August 2009): 142–143 . Related studies of table-free eating can be found in J. Horwitz, 'Eating Space', in *Eating Architecture*, eds. Jamie Horwitz and Paulette Singley (Cambridge, MA: MIT Press, 2004), 259–278; see also J. Horwitz, 'Eating at the Edge', *Gastronomica: The Journal of Critical Food Studies* 9.3 (Summer, 2009): 42–47 .

12 I found the letter in the archives of the Williams Dining Blog named 'Purple Eats' in April of 2014. The letter itself was undated. The archive is no longer accessible, and currently (March 2016) there is no posting of announcements or comments on the blog. There are, however, photographs of food. No process of change is entirely free of obstacles or disagreements, and I find it refreshing when a community allows their disagreements to be discussed openly, and online, even for short a time.

Bibliography

Ascher, Francois. 'Hypermodern Society and the Eclectic Individual Revealed and Illustrated by Dietary Practices'. *Harvard Design Magazine* 30 (Spring/Summer 2009): 18–23.

Barlett, Peggy F. 'Campus Sustainable Food Projects: Critique and Engagement'. *American Anthropologist* 113 (1) (2011): 101–15.

Borgmann, Albert. *Crossing the Postmodern Divide*. Chicago: University of Chicago Press, 1992.

Borgmann, Albert. *Technology and the Character of Contemporary Life: A Philosophical Inquiry*. Chicago: University of Chicago Press, 1984.

Cromley, Elizabeth C. 'Transforming the Food Axis: Houses, Tools, Modes of Analysis'. *Material History Review* 44 (Fall 1996): 8–22.

Horowitz, Helen Lefkowitz. *Alma Mater: Design and Experience in the Women's Colleges from Their Nineteenth Century Beginnings to the1930's*. New York: Alfred A, Knopf, 1984.

Horowitz, Helen Lefkowitz. 'Designing for the Genders: Curricula and Architecture at Scripps College and the California Institute of Technology'. *Pacific Historical Review* 54.4 (1985): 439–61.

Horwitz, Jamie. 'Eating at the Edge'. *Gastronomica: The Journal of Critical Food Studies* 9.3 (Summer, 2009): 42–7.

Horwitz, Jamie. 'Eating Space'. In *Eating Architecture*, edited by Jamie Horwitz and Paulette Singley, 259–78. Cambridge, MA: The MIT Press, 2004.

Horwitz, Jamie. 'Fabricating Pluralism'. Special Issue on Multi-cultural Modernism, *Architectural Design* 75.5 (Sept–Oct 2006): 24–31.

Horwitz, Jamie. 'Following the Food: Where Students Eat'. Special Issue on Architecture, *The Chronicle of Higher Education* 51.29 (March 25, 2005): B26–B28.

Horwitz, Jamie. 'Replacing a Beloved Building with a Hybrid: Paresky Student Center, Williams College'. *Architectural Design* 79.2 (March-April 2009): 142–43.

Urry, John. *Mobilities*. Cambridge, UK: Polity Press, 2007.

8

The All-Consuming House: Food and Architecture in Molly Keane's *Time after Time*

Kevin Donovan

'Big House' literature

The 'Big House' has long been a term used colloquially in Ireland to refer to the homes of the Anglo-Irish Ascendancy, who, being descended from an older Protestant ruling class established through successive waves of colonization and plantation, effectively controlled the Irish territory from the seventeenth century until the establishment of the Irish Free State in 1922. This privileged social group placed itself at the centre of the Irish rural landscape, dominating its agriculture, economy and society. The War of Independence precipitated the dissolution of the social system as well as the destruction of many of the houses themselves, both henceforth peripheral to the direction of Irish history.[1] In this process of recasting Irish culture and society, families central to a type of Irish life for several hundred years found themselves displaced from a position they had assumed to be their birthright. Moreover, this landed class, previously in charge of the agricultural sustenance of the country, now was hard-pressed even to sustain itself.

The varying fortunes of this society are the subject of a genre of Irish fiction commonly called the Big House novel. The form emerged in the early nineteenth century with Maria Edgeworth's *Castle Rackrent*, and describes works typically authored by members or descendants of these families who, caught in an increasingly tense and complex relationship both with England and Irish nationalism, recorded and sometimes satirized their steady slide into improvidence. It continued to thrive alongside anti-colonial writing in the early twentieth century, reflecting the ambivalence of prevailing attitudes towards feudal relationships in the countryside. Largely marginalized in the canon of Irish writing by post-colonial redefinitions in the 1980s,[2] the form has more recently been the subject of focus in the fields of literature and Irish studies.[3]

The house

Always present in this kind of work is the building itself. It is not often as 'big' as an English stately home, but is a robust country house of what Maurice Craig describes as the 'middle size'.[4] Craig also reflects that the attribute 'big' might tell us more about the socio-economic relationship between these Protestant landowners and a Catholic tenantry, as well as a rising Catholic commercial class, than it does about the house itself. Elizabeth Bowen ponders the same question:

> ... is it height – in this country of otherwise low buildings – that got these Anglo-Irish Houses their 'big' name? Or have they been called big with a slight inflection – that of hostility, irony? One may call a man 'big' with just that inflection because he seems to think the hell of himself.[5]

In their most complete state, then, the buildings clearly mirror the ambiguous identity of the owners, marginal both in terms of England to which they looked for their religion, language and identity but also in relation to those around them who identified in opposition. The house is built of native material but in an imported form, reflecting the successive (or already superseded) English fashions for Palladian, Neoclassical and revivalist styles. It is often isolated in a park, behind a demesne wall backed by a dense wood, through which an 'avenue ... describes loops to make itself of a more extravagant length'.[6] The ensemble suggests at the same time a display of the conqueror's authority and a perceived vulnerability: 'The Ascendency built in order to convince themselves not only that they had arrived, but that they would remain. Insecurity and the England-complex remained with them to the end.'[7]

This insecurity is amplified by the characterization of these houses as imperfect. The black swamp and crumbling stone of *Castle Rackrent* set the tone for later novels whose decaying mansions reflect the increasing relative impecunity and bad fortune of their owners. The fall from grace of the declining social class is rendered more poignant by the shades of former grandeur and order still perceptible in the distressed fabric of the house: 'The indefinite ghosts of the past, of the dead who lived here and pursued this same routine of life in these walls add something, a sort of order, a reason for living, to every minute and hour.'[8]

Molly Keane's sustaining table

A latter-day example of this kind of writer is Molly Keane. Born into 'a rather serious Hunting and Fishing and Church-going family',[9] she began in the 1920s to write, under the pseudonym M. J. Farrell (ambiguous both in gender and class; she is reputed to have taken the name from the pub sign she passed during a day's hunting), a series of commercially successful novels and plays exploring the world of the Ascendancy. Following the failure of a play in the early 1960s and the sudden death of her husband, she retreated into family life to emerge again twenty years later, this time under her own (married) name with the novels for which she is best known: *Good Behaviour* (nominated for the 1981 Booker Prize), *Time after Time* (1983) and *Loving and Giving* (1988).

These three novels share the salient characteristics of the Big House novel. Their characters are members of the Anglo-Irish gentry, struggling with the demise of the politico-social system that had ensured them a place in life. In each of them a ruinous house reflects the decline of both their class and their families, described in an atmosphere of anxiety and alienation, but also with wicked humour. Female characters tend to be stronger, either when replacing the disempowered male landowner or when manipulating families with a determination to promote them. This resolve only increases with the decline of their social and political arena. The novels are, however, also distinguished by their overwhelming references to food.

Keane's daughters remember their mother's food as 'central to our sense of home',[10] lending it a richness: 'she cooked with the precision and care she spent on words, balancing sweet and sour, and creating subtle, unique flavours. Her food was really extraordinary. It was light and had a recognizable style, like her prose.'[11]

They recall feasts of lobsters costing seven shillings and sixpence per pound, produced in the family kitchen in a period when the family was heavily indebted to the bank. They remember mussel-collecting for dinner parties, friends coming to tea in the kitchen and 'broken glass pudding' (a kind of crème brulée) being assembled by a 'half praying, half swearing' cook of a mother who happily expended her energy in troublesome and elaborate dishes. The preparation and consumption of food, then, became for Keane, a writer and homemaker, a means by which to order her life and her relationships. One of her children even suggests that the twenty-year hiatus in her writing occasioned a transfer of her creative energy into cooking, allowing it to emerge as a strong theme in her later work.[12]

The relationship of the homes of the Irish gentry to food is a complex one. On the largest scale, this was the class that owned the productive landscape of Ireland and profited enormously from the agriculture of its tenant farmers. The landowners' isolation within demesnes bred a certain self-sufficiency, afforded by kitchen gardens and glasshouses, orchards, livestock and game.[13] This abundance of food supported an elaborate schedule of meals ordered around parts of the house and within a variety of habits derived from similar customs in England. Young children ate in the nursery, adults in the dining or breakfast room. Certain foodstuffs, alcohol in particular, were imported in quantity, and had a precise place both in the order of the meals and the architecture of the house, being moved from space to space with the inhabitants as custom demanded. In these houses' heyday, sequences of space, from garden to kitchen to hall to dining room, were marshalled to provide dinners, cocktail parties and teas that ensured the unity of the class.

Time after Time

Though strongly present in each of her last three novels, the twin themes of food and house are nowhere more intertwined than in *Time after Time* (henceforth *Time*). The crumbling Durraghglass is home to the Swift siblings, each of them getting on in years and each distinguished by a minor deformity or defect that blossoms with eccentricity. Thus April, the eldest, is rich, widowed, superior and deaf; May deftly restores broken china and arranges flowers despite her withered hand; June, the youngest, is 'a little slow',[14] with the 'whole memory of the illiterate',[15] though a capable farmer; and brother Jasper keeps his one good eye on them, the other having being shot out by June in their infancy. The family's petty machinations are fuelled both by 'Mummy', deceased, who prescribed that each sibling will have a claim to live on the estate and by the revenant cousin Leda, now blind, who schemes to marry Jasper for a share in the estate whose decay she cannot see.

Discussion of food and its consumption permeates the novel and is formative for each character. Jasper forms a world around his basement kitchen; 'cooking...had long provided the shields and defenses behind which he evaded interference with his thoughts or days'.[16] May tends the kitchen garden, providing for the household table;[17] April's diets set her apart at table; and June's lack of discrimination, and gullibility, is signalled by Jasper's pronouncement that she 'would swallow anything I cooked'.[18] Even outside the regularized consumption of food, references to it abound in the prose: undistinguished clothes are condemned as '*vin ordinaire*';[19] gorse in the hedgerows 'smells like sweet food'.[20]

Keane uses food and architecture as a twin support for the action of the novel. The novel's first two chapters, 'In the Kitchen' and 'In the Dining Room', announce the importance that food and the architectural spaces associated with it will have. When the dining room is inhabited for a protracted scene over dinner,[21] the architecture of the room is conjured through the order of eating and a description of the food rather than an account of the designed interior. Elsewhere spaces of the house are picked out against the smells of the kitchen: 'The extravagant upturn of radiators...the crisp incense of bay Jasper toasted on the Aga...this quelling of customary kitchen smells'.[22]

Durraghglass, then, is at once the food that is eaten there and the dining room, nursery and bedrooms where it is consumed by the household's members, together or alone. In the vertical hierarchy of the house, Jasper occupies both its foundation, his basement kitchen, and its roof space, the attic nursery where he still sleeps, whose associations with milk puddings are now overlain with his nightly critiques of recipes from the local newspaper. Each of the sisters' private spaces is equipped for some kind of private consumption necessary for survival; April's holds her dietary potions and gin, May's and June's a kettle each. Jasper takes his comforting cocktail of Complan and whiskey to his nursery bed.[23] Furthermore, the family members use a combination of food and space to undermine each other, to negotiate their entitlements. Jasper's dominion of the kitchen, May's unnoticed drawing-room flower arrangements as a backdrop to sherry and April's afternoons in the crowded shop of Ulick in the village with its 'plentiful supply of really good china tea'[24] – each of these atmospheres settles the characters into their roles. Food and corresponding place combine to enable event: Leda's bitter revelations of the suspect proclivities, sexual foibles and moral failings of the family members are made at the breakfast table in the dining room over the remains of spoiled toast and spilled coffee.[25]

Food and place combine to highlight frayed class relationships. The arched opening to the stable yard is described as once have being admired by afternoon Sunday luncheon guests.[26] In the breakfast room, Jasper berates May, unable to digest cucumber, for having a 'lower-middle-class stomach'.[27] May, at neighbouring Ballynunty House, whose household and structure are both faring rather better than her own, is obliged to eat in the morning room rather than the drawing room,[28] while, in their own drawing room, 'the sisters sipped inexpensive, though not the cheapest, sherry'.[29] Alys, the mistress of Ballynunty, refuses to eat or drink at Durraghglass and, having picked out Leda to invite to a luncheon, immediately despairs of the 'ruined gate lodge. Too ghastly'.[30]

Abject ruin

The first dining-room scene opens with a telling interplay between the formality of dining retained in the house and the building's ancient fabric:

> Late in the evening came a civilized pause before dinner. Servantless and silent, the house waited for the proper ceremony it had always expected and still, in a measure, experienced. The utter cold of the spring light shrank away from the high-paned windows. A steep distance below the house the river gave up an evening daze of fog. A lavatory clattered and slushed. Obedient to its plug and chain the contents went down the perpendicular drain to the open water. Faint pieces of paper floated among the starred weeds and iris leaves of flags. Very fat trout swam there. Once there had been an open, not a covert, drain. Every morning housemaids lifted a grill and sluiced buckets into a sloped stone spout from which the doings of the night flowed down their paved way to the river. Not any more, of course.[31]

Ellen L. O'Brien uses this extract to illustrate the importance of abjection in the work of Keane.[32] In support of her argument she appeals to two intersecting theories to unpack the issue of decay in the work of Keane. The first of these is Julia Kristeva's contention that 'abjection gives rise to subjective identity by offering an opposition against which the symbolic order, as the system of social constraints entered through language, can define itself'.[33] Abjection, the unrepresentable excesses of the body, supports the symbolic order by providing the unnamable 'other' against which this order can be defined. In doing so, the abject reveals the brittleness of the symbolic. The second theory relates to Slavoj Žižek's concept of the 'Real', elaborated from his study of Lacan. For Lacan, the 'Real' represents the body before it enters language, socialization and so on. Žižek maintains that the Real both forms and is formed by the symbolic; it is 'a grain of sand preventing [the] smooth functioning [of the symbolic]; a traumatic encounter which ruins the balance of the symbolic universe of the subject'.[34] This theoretical framework allows O'Brien to theorize on 'the relationship [in the Anglo-Irish Big House novels of Keane] between the material body and the establishment of subjectivity, class and language, and challenges [to] the way in which these bodies have been represented'.[35]

For O'Brien, the pre-dinner scene is of an architecture that struggles with the emergence of the Real through the symbolic order imposed by Anglo-Irish society. A breakdown in social norms has caused something previously unseen to become apparent and allows a confrontation of the abject. Abjection is also evident in Leda's deliberate soiling of deceased *mater familias* Violet's dresses with excrement. The (dis)function of food within the novel and its relation to place also, however, conspire to upset the symbolic order, and cause unhomely scenes. The advancing rot in the estate erupts in the processes of food preparation and consumption. The kitchen is disorderly for the want of cooks to make a cake for the drawing room table; in Jasper's domain 'nothing was ever tidied up, stored or thrown away'.[35] It produces evil smells that infect the rest of the house.[36] May struggles to keep overgrowth at bay in her walled garden[37] – something she can do by virtue of it being an enclosed architectural element, unlike the avenue of the house, with its 'riot of brambles and nettles on its once orderly verges'.[38] Rotten food is incorporated into meals. When May enquires after the 'beef I scraped all the blue mould off and left chopped up in the soup and brown bread [for the dogs' dinners],[39] she is informed by Jasper that she has just eaten it in the pigeon pie: 'Delighting in May's screams and cries of protest and disgust, he stacked a tray with plates ... [and] set off downstairs to the kitchen and the washing up, confident that no one would follow him'.[40]

As the pie is being prepared, the description moves directly from the rancid kitchen to the piggeries where 'a steep slope drained liquids from all ordure down to a pretty river'.[41]

The vital agency of food

However shaky the society of Durraghglass, there is hope. Though shackled to their depleted demesne, the characters are not marooned in their lives which, when unlocked from their moribund order by the visit of Leda, begin to flourish in unexpected ways. As if fresh, or slightly less fetid, air had entered their lives, they discover new opportunities to exercise their exposed frailties to the world for positive gain. And again, the twin forces of architecture and food are present, indeed active. In the case of May, the turnaround happens in a 'tinker's caravan' – a 'smuggler's cave of old lamps' where she drinks strong tea and plots against her hostess, unaffected by Leda's unmasking of her deceitfulness. June, also restored by tea, finds the strength to relinquish her bond with the unfaithful farmhand Christy; in the 'shelter of the stableyard' she cuts him loose.[42] April's move to the new order of a convent gives licence to the joy she has long derived from restraint in eating. Jasper finds a key to the salvation of the estate in the local monastery; his forbidden donation of a sandwich to a monk (as a way to the man's heart and, presumably, beyond) leads to an unexpected pact with the confraternity to conjoin their efforts for the sustenance of the property.

The effective and motivating attributes normally defining of characters in fiction, then, are also attributed in this novel both to the food these characters consume and to the place they are in. It is almost as if the non-organic elements in the novel had the capacity to provoke action and to be profoundly affected by it, just as the characters do. This resonates with the worldview of Jane Bennett, who has proposed that material agency emerges as the effect of shifting consonance of human and non-human forces.[43] She constructs the world as alliances of 'animate things rather than passive objects'. Things, as opposed to objects, have efficacy, 'sufficient coherence to produce a difference'.[44] Borrowing from Deluze and Guatarri, she adopts the term 'assemblage' to describe these 'ad hoc groupings of diverse elements, of vibrant materials of sorts … living, throbbing confederations that are able to function, despite the persistent presence of energies that confound them from within'.[45] Conflict of interest is, therefore, a defining element of the assembly; while it has a trajectory, striking out to provoke effects, it is not determined by intention. There is no single subject at the root of this energy but a 'swarm of vitalities',[46] composed of things and people, not working in harmony but affecting each other and consequently causing movement.

In this view, then, the affective assemblage of Durraghglass may be understood to be composed not only of the characters and their constitutional parts but also of the architecture of the place and the ever-present edible matter, which together shape the direction of events, away from the uneasy status quo and towards … well, this is not so clear, though perhaps also not so critical. Attempts at the restoration of the old order have proved unsustainable; a 'classical Austrian cake', which Jasper and Leda attempt to confect from Leda's ancient memory of the recipe, invoking rich memories of youthful seduction in a ballroom, refuses to come right and precipitates the series of scenes in kitchen and dining room that unlock the group's enslavement to memory. Rather than a restructuring of the colonial hierarchy, an uncertain but vital way out is provided when the non-human elements of the assemblage exercise their influence. The kitchen range is characterized by its unpredictability, the unreliability of the hens' eggs provokes tension among the household and the substitution of lamb with yoghurt brings off Leda's final frustration. Seakale from May's kitchen garden ('pergolas ran the lengths and richly enclosed the squares of vegetables') produces 'both love and jealousy'.[47] 'Even, plain food' is called upon to 'quieten things down'.[48]

The food, then, has a vitality, an 'ontologically real and active lively presence' actively feeding its co-components in the surrounding assemblage.[49] Unpreserved, it requires processing (picking, cooking and cooling, but also hiding, revealing etc.), which motivates the Swifts, delighting or frustrating them with its tense energy, its generative inconvenience. Alone, the architectural spaces are stuck, like the household, in unsatisfying reiterations of the old order that are increasingly unsustainable. The passage of food, through the bodies of the family, but also through the complex body of the house and the locality allow a movement that the crumbling of the demesne walls alone cannot. It legitimizes the architecture's process of becoming. As clearly as meals reinforced the routine of the Anglo-Irish house in its heyday, enforcing the dialectic of inside and out, the new narrative of food nourishes redemptive possibilities for sustainable access to space, be it a traveller's caravan, entropic outbuildings, a dilapidated kitchen or a new productive landscape made by Jasper and the monks. The effect of this action, engendered by interaction with their edible surroundings rather than by their own pure will, is a surprise to the Swifts, the kind of surprise evoked by Bruno Latour and cited by Bennett: 'There is no object ... no subject ... But there are events. I never act; I am always slightly surprised by what I do.'[50]

The vital, lively agency of food and place for Molly Keane is real as well as symbolic, as has been signalled by her daughters: 'After she died, this note dropped out of *Le Grande Meaulnes* [sic.], one of the last books she had been reading: "Well-being returns when I see sunlight glittering through a new batch of marmalade on the kitchen table."'[51]

In *Time after Time*, as in Keane's other late novels about the decline of the Irish Ascendancy, the spaces of inhabitation combine with the food grown, cooked and eaten there as well as with the remains of the old order, to make a kind of sustainable life that would be impossible without each of these components. May puts the situation succinctly: 'Jasper, we have to eat and drink to live, and we have to live here together – that's how Mummy fixed it'.'[52] What she does not yet realize is that 'Mummy', 'here', 'eat' and 'drink' will combine to provide her salvation.

Notes

1   E. Wolff, *An Anarchy in the Mind and in the Heart: Narrating Anglo-Ireland* (Lewisburg: Bucknell University Press, 2006).

2   R. Foster, *The Oxford History of Ireland* (Oxford: Oxford University Press, 1992).

3   V. Krielkamp, *The Anglo-Irish Novel and the Big House* (Syracuse, NY: Syracuse University Press, 1998); and Wolff, *An Anarchy in the Mind and in the Heart*.

4   M. Craig, *Classic Irish Houses of the Middle Size* (London: Architectural Press, 1976).

5   H. Lee, *The Mulberry Tree: The Writings of Elizabeth Bowen* (London: Virago, 1986), 26.

6   Ibid.

7   Foster, *The Oxford History of Ireland*, 194.

8   Lee, *The Mulberry Tree*, 28.

9 R. Imhof, 'Molly Keane, *Good Behaviour, Time after Time*, and *Loving and Giving*', in O. Rauchbauer, *Ancestral Voices: The Big House in Anglo-Irish Literature* (Dublin: Lilliput, 1992), 195.

10 V. Brownlee and S. Phipps, 'Memories of Molly Keane' in *Molly Keane: Centenary Essays*, eds. E. Walshe and G. Young (Dublin: Four Courts Press, 2006), 23.

11 Ibid., 21.

12 Ibid.

13 Lee, *The Mulberry Tree*.

14 M. Keane, *Time after Time* (London: Abacus, 1991), 46.

15 Ibid., 30.

16 Ibid., 16.

17 Ibid., 120.

18 Ibid., 137.

19 Ibid., 157.

20 Ibid., 202.

21 Ibid., 26–35.

22 Ibid., 100.

23 Ibid., 46.

24 Ibid., 68.

25 Ibid., 170–178.

26 Ibid., 18.

27 Ibid., 29.

28 Ibid., 69.

29 Ibid., 26.

30 Ibid., 149–54.

31 Ibid., 20.

32 E. L. O'Brien, 'Abjection and Molly Keane's "Very Nasty" Novels', in Molly Keane: Centenary Essays, eds. E. Walshe and G. Young (Dublin: Four Courts Press, 2006).

33 O'Brien, 102.

34 Ibid., 105.

35 Ibid., 102.

36 Keane, *Time after Time*, 2.

37 Ibid., 14.

38 Ibid., 120.

39 Ibid., 17.

40 Ibid., 34.

41 Ibid., 35.

42 Ibid., 16.

43 Ibid., 244.

44 J. Bennett, *Vibrant Matter: A Political Ecology of Things* (Durham, NC: Duke University Press, 2010).

45 Ibid., vii.

46 Ibid., 23.

47 Ibid.

48 Keane, *Time after Time*, 121.

49 Ibid., 200.

50 D. Goodman, 'Ontology Matters: The Relational Materiality of Nature and Agro-Food Studies', *Sociologia Ruralis* 41.2 (2001): 182–200, 183.

51 Bennett, *Vibrant Matter*, 27.

52 Brownlee and Phipps, 'Memories of Molly Keane'.

53 Keane, *Time after Time*, 31.

Bibliography

Bennett, J. *Vibrant Matter: A Political Ecology of Things*. Durham, NC: Duke University Press, 2010.

Brownlee, V. and S. Phipps, 'Memories of Molly Keane'. In *Molly Keane: Centenary Essays*, edited by E. Walshe and G. Young. Dublin: Four Courts Press, 2006.

Craig, M. *Classic Irish Houses of the Middle Size*. London: Architectural Press, 1976.

Foster, R. *The Oxford History of Ireland*. Oxford: Oxford University Press, 1992.

Goodman, D. 'Ontology Matters: The Relational Materiality of Nature and Agro-Food Studies'. *Sociologia Ruralis* 41, no. 2 (2001): 182–0.

Imhof, R. 'Molly Keane, *Good Behaviour, Time after Time*, and *Loving and Giving*'. In *Ancestral Voices: The Big House in Anglo-Irish Literature*, edited by O. Rauchbauer. Dublin: Lilliput, 1992.

Keane, M. *Time after Time*. London: Abacus, 1991.

Krielkamp, V. *The Anglo-Irish Novel and the Big House*. Syracuse, NY: Syracuse University Press, 1998.

Lee, H. *The Mulberry Tree: The Writings of Elizabeth Bowen*. London: Virago, 1986.

O'Brien, E. L. 'Abjection and Molly Keane's "Very Nasty" Novels'. In *Molly Keane: Centenary Essays*, edited by E. Walshe and G. Young. Dublin: Four Courts Press, 2006.

Wessels, A. 'Resolving History: Negotiating the Past in Molly Keane's Big House Novels'. In *Molly Keane: Centenary Essays*, edited by E. Walshe and G. Young. Dublin: Four Courts Press, 2006.

Wolff, E. *An Anarchy in the Mind and in the Heart: Narrating Anglo-Ireland*. Lewisburg: Bucknell University Press, 2006.

PART THREE

Craft

Commentary for Part Three: Craft

Repeat as Necessary

Samantha L. Martin-McAuliffe

In 2009, as the World Wide Web was celebrating its twentieth anniversary, a book decrying the virtualism of the contemporary global economy was steadily climbing the bestseller lists. Matthew Crawford's *Shop Class as Soulcraft: An Inquiry into the Value of Work* is a piercing account of the devaluation of skilled manual labour in the midst of our information age. As an academic-turned-motorcycle mechanic, Crawford quite literally uses his Hondas and Kawasakis as vehicles for investigating and experiencing what he refers to as 'pragmatic engagement', a kind of practiced absorption in a task, usually over long periods of time. This orientation, he argues, separates today's knowledge worker from the craftsperson.[1] Whereas the former encounters unremitting pressure to switch gears and perhaps even reinvent her occupation, the latter steadily develops acuity in a particular skill. In the face of flux, the craftsperson responds by deploying her specific expertise. When required, she may attune and refine her skill as necessary, but she never scrambles to retrain.

We tend to equate craft with skill, but it is so much more than technical competency. Craft, as Richard Sennett argues, takes patience, time and an uncompromising dedication to one's materials. Together, these enable one to exercise an intuitive sense of judgement. Seeking to divest the term 'craftsmanship' of its abstract and often arcane symbolism, Sennett offers a distillation of its elemental meaning: 'the desire to do a job well for its own sake'.[2] The uncomplicated tenor of this definition should not, however, distract us from the inherent temporality of craft. In other words, while a 'job well done' suggests a final result, and perhaps also a finished product, craft should always be understood as an ongoing process. It demands a recurrent cross-examination, an oscillation between the hand and the mind that ultimately develops into a competence. Tim Ingold describes this kind of development as 'embodied skill', a highly perceptive form of knowledge – be it working a tool or playing an instrument – that is acquired through practice.[3] What is important to underscore here is the role played by one's environment, not just in terms of the natural world but also through a 'matrix of social relations' that contribute to and influence the development and employment of a technical skill. Again, process and confident familiarity, rather than a fixed point of mastery, are paramount: 'Insofar as they involve the use of tools, these [technical skills] must be understood as links in chains of personal rather than mechanical causation, serving to draw components of the environment into the sphere of social relations rather than to emancipate human society from the constraints of nature. Their purpose, in short, is not to control but to reveal.'[4] Yet under what conditions does the craftsperson harness and deploy her skills in order to realize a particular form, whether it is a house, table, fork or the comestibles that we serve at a meal? Moreover, how can we reconcile the modern tendency to understand the conception of a form (or product) and its subsequent fabrication as two different processes that require separate skill sets? These questions persist as leitmotifs throughout this part of *Food and Architecture*.

Rather than limiting the discussion to the definition of craft, all of the contributions in this section, Part Three, examine and scrutinize the nature of craft through a series of common concerns and topics, such as: the relationship between craft and industry; the interplay between local environment and techniques of a discipline; the significance of observation; and the role of ambiguities, mistakes or unexpected results in our understanding of craft. The section begins with William Rubel's chapter, 'Artisan Bread', which pays particular attention to the role played by automation in bread baking. In fact, by deftly accounting for our dependence on modern machinery to produce bread, this chapter exposes and upends the common perception that a high-quality, artisan loaf is achieved through the work of bare hands. Similarly, while we might assume that the automation of bread making emerged in the wake of the Industrial Revolution, it arguably commenced at least by the seventeenth century with the assistance of a device called the 'bolting hutch'.[5] As such, how much physical labour – handwork – is now required for a bread to be termed artisan remains a thorny, unresolved question. As Rubel explains, the method of making artisan bread is easily systematized, so much so that it is virtually impossible to discern whether a loaf has been touched by human hand during the baking process. Rather than handwork, the craft of making artisan bread is instead contingent on the baker's *intentionality* – careful and learned observation, commitment to time and an uncompromising dedication to ingredients. Bakers arguably ceased making bread wholly 'by hand' once they began to obtain their flour from professional millers in the seventeenth and eighteenth centuries. But Rubel points out in his conclusion that it is towards this very juncture – the acquisition of flour – that the artisan bread movement is now turning its attention once again. Complementing the exacting standards of artisan bakers is a widening circle of agriculturalists and millers who are reintroducing heirloom grains and landrace crops, many of which were nearly lost during the rise of corporate agribusiness.[6] Out of this movement another type of craftsperson is being reinvented: the seedsman, one who collects, studies and hand selects strains of heritage seeds, year after year. This campaign not only affects the quality of the bread we eat, but it also, importantly, has the potential to reshape our productive landscapes.

Michael Pollan has done much to raise public awareness of the deleterious effects of cultivating grains on an industrial scale in the United States. One of the most extraordinary images in *The Omnivore's Dilemma* (2006) is Pollan's description of the staggeringly large agricultural tracts in the American Midwest.[7] Like yawning black tarmacs, these fields stretch to the horizon, swallowing hedgerows and fences and displacing farmsteads as well as whole towns.[8] Corn and soya are the principal culprits, but wheat is no poster child for sustainable farming. Unlike commodity-driven agribusiness, landrace farming explicitly integrates all aspects of the food system, from the grower and the miller to the baker and the consumer. Indeed, it is smaller in scale than conventional agriculture, but importantly it is also a craft that requires a farmer to develop specific expertise in regional climates, crop rotation, zero-tillage, grain history, local cultures and food literacy – a jarring juxtaposition to the work described to Pollan by one conventional Iowa farmer: 'Growing corn is just riding tractors and spraying'.[9] Landrace farming is a slow yet evolving process, and it offers the possibility of recovering a diversified form of agriculture, one that values flavour and taste over compatibility with long-haul transport and economies of scale.

In this age of offshore jobs and outsourced professions, there is a tendency to announce a crisis in architecture; to decry how the operational efficiencies of today's knowledge economy erode the traditional architect–client relationship; and to assume that the work once produced by hand in a studio is now being systematically redeployed and churned out virtually through anonymous computer terminals in distant countries. Yet these prevailing anxieties are misleading insofar as they tend to dramatize the consequence of global capitalism as well as misinterpret or overestimate the role of the computer in contemporary architectural practice. For one thing, the procurement of architecture 'by correspondence' is not at all a recent circumstance but rather a phenomenon that predates the personal computer by over a century. In 1878, George and Charles Palliser published *Palliser's Model Homes*, a pattern book of residences for the emerging middle classes in the United States.[10] For a fee, readers could order a full set of drawings for a house that included not only plans and elevations but also detailed lists of materials needed and even contractual information; mail-order architecture had arrived. From the early twentieth century, Sears, Roebuck and Co. sold home kits, complete with construction drawings and all essential building materials (even paint, though heating and plumbing were usually extra), through its eponymous catalogue. Despite these developments, the architectural profession continued to grow and flourish.

In light of the concerns about outsourcing, it is also important to clarify the place of the computer in architectural practice and its relationship to craft. The overwhelming majority of outsourced architectural work currently falls under the rubric of CAD. The businesses providing these services are not offering a comprehensive 'one stop shop' for architecture but rather technical-supporting documents at particular stages of the design process. These materials include digital construction drawings and design details, as well as 3D models based on existing plans. Ultimately, it can be argued that while the computer is an essential part of an architect's tool-kit, it is rarely the sole vehicle for design. Furthermore, in architecture, just as in bread baking, technology and craft are not mutually exclusive.

Craft plays a central but often understated role in architectural practice. Not all, but a majority of architects observe, think and problem solve through handwork. Design embodies the circular routine of sketching, drawing and model making. This is the precise pattern of work described by John Tuomey in his contribution to this volume (Chapter 10). In 'Craft and Construction', Tuomey explains how his studio commences a project (or part thereof) through free, informal sketches, which are then transferred to a computer, and finally modelled by hand from cardboard. The whole process is then revisited, sometimes even on a daily basis, and it is through this literal and figurative layering of drawing, making and scrutinizing that the design finally emerges. The computer plays a central and arguably indispensable role, but it does not generate the design for the architect. Tellingly, Tuomey notes that his typical routine in practice is not unusual: he learned his craft from his mentor, James Stirling, and likewise, as a professor, he imparts this same skill set to a new generation of architects. Sennett is also sensitive to this process or method, and in his own research he describes very similar ways of working by different architects and their studios.[11] But at the same time, craft as such remains inconspicuous to the general public. The sketches, initial drawings and models are not visible in the building itself and only live on through archives, exhibitions or publications. They are the process but not the final form.

In his description of practice, Tuomey refers to the 'mysterious jump in thinking', a moment when total immersion in a task enables the work to flow with a sense of balance and coherence. Regardless of the discipline or medium involved, this instance is almost always cited as a vital component of craftsmanship. It can be called many things – flow, absorption, feel, in the zone, wired in – and while it is characterized by a sense of effortless attention, it requires great proficiency and skill to achieve. Heather Paxson's contribution to this volume, 'Craftsmanship and Quality in Artisanal Cheesemaking' (Chapter 11), offers a lucid study of this phenomenon, bringing clarity to an experience that typically resists being defined and quantified. Through her research she has conceived the term 'synesthetic reason' to help explain how craftsmanship melds deep-seated objective understanding with acute sensory knowledge. In artisanal cheesemaking all the senses – taste, smell, touch, sight – inform every stage of the production process. While anyone can experience the multisensory properties of a particular cheese, it takes years to learn how to perceive *as well as* harness its nuances. Like any craft, cheesemaking requires habitual practice, a commitment to repeating a process over and over again, to the point where one exercises knowledge without reflection. The work simply flows.

What makes artisanal cheese such an interesting and challenging medium is its variability, both in terms of its form and ingredients. Paxson explains how a cheesemaker intentionally manipulates ('tweaks') the milk and curd, thereby varying the character of the final product, but there are also external, often unpredictable factors that influence a batch: fluctuating environmental conditions, seasonal variations and changes in the diet of the milk-making animals. The craft in making cheese lies in how to balance these variations. In her discussion of variability Paxson also offers a caveat: differences in one batch of artisanal cheese to the next are not only expected but also valued and admired because they reflect seasonality as well as stand in opposition to the monotony of industrially produced cheese; not all variation, however, is a mark of quality. In any form of craft, poor standards and skills lead to errors and unexpected outcomes. How we choose to construe such results makes all the difference in craftsmanship.

Paradoxically, contemporary food culture tends to appreciate natural imperfections in products – unevenness in texture, irregularity of form – at the same time it fears errors and mistakes in the process of making things. Newspaper columns assuredly publish 'perfect' recipes and entire cookbooks promise foolproof menus. Underlying this idealized, hyper-confident form of cuisine is the desire to control craftsmanship, to eliminate inaccuracies to the point where even variation is intentionally planned. In this volume William Rubel has explained that artisanal bread now sits at the latter end of this spectrum. Highly advanced machines are capable of producing loaves of bread that look, feel and taste as though they have been crafted by human hand. Barring exceptional one-off examples, the practice of contemporary architectural design has not yet reached this same degree of intentional imperfection.[12] What architecture does share with food and cuisine, however, is an aversion to error. Design has, in fact, arrived a point where we see what Francesca Hughes describes as a 'fetishization of precision'.[13] Digital technology, in particular CAD, operates at a level of exactitude that leads to redundancy. Hughes, among others, has noted that this overdetermination creates issues with materiality.[14]

With so much attention focused on the perfect product or final design, it is easy to lose sight of the generative experience of making, in particular the role of error as a portal to discovery. While no craftsperson excuses careless work, mistakes are implicitly understood as grist to the mill (for bakers, quite literally) and essential to the acquisition of a skill. This is more than mere cliché. Learning a craft requires the reciprocity between protocol and error: a novice complies with rules and standards, such as following a recipe or setting up a perspective drawing, at the same time as she ungrudgingly makes mistakes. This situation simultaneously hones technique and builds confidence. Eventually, through attentive practice, the novice reaches a point where she begins to modify and even discard certain rules. The circularity of repetition and routine has endowed her with a subtle awareness and sense of judgement. This, ultimately, is the very heart of craftsmanship.

Notes

1   Matthew B. Crawford, *Shop Class as Soulcraft: An Inquiry into the Value of Work* (New York: Penguin, 2009), 21.

2   Richard Sennett, *The Craftsman* (London: Allen Lane, 2008), 9.

3   Tim Ingold, *The Perception of the Environment. Essays in Livelihood, Dwelling and Skill* (London: Routledge, 2000), 292 and 414.

4   Ibid., 289–290.

5   A bolting hutch is mentioned in Shakespeare's *Henry IV, Part I.* J. Fitzpatrick explains how it was used metaphorically to refer to the large size of one of the characters, Sir John. See Fitzpatrick, *Food in Shakespeare: Early Modern Dietaries and the Plays* (Farnham, Surrey: Ashgate, 2013), 19. The play dates from at least the end of the sixteenth century.

6   Landrace grains are often understood as native cultivars but they are more specifically grains that have adapted to a particular setting through natural processes as well as the careful selection by a grower or farmer. One of the leading authorities and producers of such grains in the United States is Glen Roberts, the founder and proprietor of Anson Mills in South Carolina. See David Shields, S*outhern Provisions: The Creation and Revival of a Cuisine* (Chicago: University of Chicago Press, 2015).

7   M. Pollan, *The Omnivore's Dilemma. The Search for a Perfect Meal in a Fast-Food World* (London: Bloomsbury, 2006), 39.

8 T. Lyson argues that from 1900 there were three distinct 'revolutions' in agriculture in the United States that led the gradual disconnection of people from the land they cultivate; in other words, specific technological transformations that aimed to produce more commodity crops with less labour: tractors, which led to the displacement of farm labourers; synthetic fertilizers; and finally, biotechnology. Lyson, T. A. *Civic Agriculture: Reconnecting Farm, Food and Community* (Medford, MA: Tufts University Press, 2004), 19–21.

9 Pollan, *The Omnivore's Dilemma*, 40.

10 G. Palliser and C. Palliser, *Palliser's Model Homes* (Bridgeport, CT: Palliser, Palliser and Company, 1878).

11 Sennett, *The Craftsman*, 39–41.

12 James Wines' Postmodern designs for the Best Products Retail Stores in the United States are perhaps the most widely known examples of this kind of phenomenon. His firm SITE designed *The Indeterminate Façade* (Houston, Texas, 1974–1975), a play on the conventional big-box retail showrooms that typify the American strip mall. Its exterior façade was consciously deconstructed to appear as though it had been damaged by a hurricane.

13 Francesca Hughes, *The Architecture of Error: Matter, Measure and the Misadventures of Precision* (Cambridge, MA: MIT Press, 2014), 7 and 39ff.

14 Sennett, *The Craftsman*, 39–45.

9

Artisan Bread

William Rubel

We know from historic British tables of bread weights and prices published as part of the regulatory regime called the Assize for Bread that from the late medieval period through to the early decades of the eighteenth century there was an inverse correlation between the size of a loaf and the social position of the person buying it. If you think of each bread as a house, the poor purchased mansions and the rich small cottages and huts. The bread mansions of the poor no longer exist; the cottages and huts of the rich are the half kilo loaves and rolls of today.

Size was only one factor differentiating the loaves of the rich and the poor. There were others, too: as examples, breads were differentiated by flour type and flour refinement. Depending on the country, the leavening system used might have been seen as meaningful, but even when both the rich and the poor used the same system, like *levain* in France,[1] the level of acidity and thus also the taste and smell – sweet for the rich and sour for the poor – differentiated the breads. Underlying these and other differences were always two factors: cost and the level of intentionality brought to the recipe. At different times, and in different places, the nuances of the ideal loaf towards which high-status bakers might labour shifted, but for at least a couple of thousand years, European bread was judged against one overriding ideal: a light crumb.

If you look at a cross section of a loaf of bread and think of each of the little holes as tiny rooms, the breads of the poor were often effectively room-less. The poorest lacked the resources to produce light bread. Historically, as one moved up the social ladder, the breads on one's table required the baker to exercise ever-increasing levels of control over the choice of ingredients and the way they were handled. As one could afford breads that took more care, this also meant that the breads one bought grew smaller. It is faster and cheaper to produce a single ten-kilo loaf for a poor family than it is to break that same amount of dough up into twenty half-kilo loaves or fifty rolls weighing 200 grams each, to serve at a banquet.

The increasing democratization of life in Europe and North America that accelerated in eighteenth-century Britain was reflected in the democratization of breads. We see the product of this process in the breads offered in bakeries and grocery stores today. Virtually all loaf breads produced today have an open crumb. The inside of the bread is so riddled with air pockets that the crumb is always squishy, like a sponge. Typical breads range from the size of a roll to half a kilo, with very few loaves getting much heavier than that. In other words, our loaves all fall into the rubric of what used to be luxury breads. The large dense breads of the poor do not exist.

For most of bread history, baking took place at home. It was the work of women and started with the woman of the house (or in antiquity, if she could afford it, her slave) milling the grain. One can still see this in villages in Rajasthan, where there are women who spend hours every morning producing the flour for their family's bread. Rotary kerns – an ancient form of technology – are still in use.[2] For these women, baking bread begins with grinding the grain.

European feudalism prohibited home milling, but as late as the early seventeenth century, in England, millers just milled; and it was the home and commercial bakers refined the meal into flour. Gervase Markham, in his 1615 cookbook, *The English Housewife*, describes the ideal bakehouse for a country house in the section 'Brewing and bakerie'.[3] It includes a full set of sieves for refining meal into flour. Sixteenth- and seventeenth-century British bread recipes often start with meal and include sifting instructions. Up to the seventeenth century, the only labour-saving device bakers had access to was a brake, a pole attached to a pivot on a wall that could be worked by the baker to knead stiff dough in lieu of using his or her feet. Up to the seventeenth century, bakers sifted flour through sieves or cloths.

It can be argued that bakery automation really began with the bolting hutch, a hand-cranked, cloth-covered cylinder tumbler that radically increased flour output from the meal received from the miller. This mechanism took pride of place in the baker's coat of arms in the latter decades of the seventeenth century.

> He beareth in this Quarter five Bakers Instruments, the first and largest is the Ark Wheel which is a long Beam with Hoops, Cross pieces and Ribs, set at a distance from it, and covered with a kind of Canvas; by the help of this engine more meal will be taken from its Bran in one hour, than a person can searse or sift in a whole day.[4]

Like the brake and all subsequent automation, automated flour production distanced the baker from details of the production system by literally separating the baker's hands from materials being worked. When you sift by hand you are looking at both what is retained in the sieve, which might have been used for a grade of bread or sent through the mill for regrinding, and at what falls through the sieve. When hand sifting, the baker decides when to stop shaking the sifter, which means deciding when this step in refining the flour is over, a decision based on skill. Yet, when refining flour through a rotating drum the flour moves, as in a screw, at a fixed rate. The operator has much less control as it is the construction of the drum sieve that determines the outcome for any given batch of meal. The drum sieve deskills the bolting process.

By the mid-eighteenth century, bakers had largely stopped refining flour. Flour refining in Britain had moved from the bakery to the flour mill. The miller, who had mostly provided meal, now provided refined flour. While early nineteenth-century commercial bakers might still occasionally bolt flour, for all practical purposes, by 1800 flour was purchased by both home and commercial bakers from the miller, as is the current practice.

With control over flour production transferred out of the bakery, the production of flour was professionalized and thus made more consistent. But it also meant turning control over flour, the principal ingredient in bread, to a third party and it took some of the hand work out of bread baking. In fact, it eliminated the entire first part of the recipe: preparing the flour.

The earliest bread recipes in English we know of that have the precision of a modern recipe are those recorded by someone we only know by the initials 'TT'. His manuscript was purchased by Sir Hugh Plat (ca. 1552–1608) and bound into Plat's manuscript.[5] Plat's biographer, Malcolm Thick, attributes TT's work to the 1550s. For one of the breads TT instructs to 'Searse the flower wth the finest searse and go not to farre therwyth'.

What TT is saying is to stop sifting as soon as the finest of the fine flour has fallen through the sieve. Do not strive for efficiency; do not keep working the sieve until every last particle of white flour has fallen through, because by then you will have contaminated the white flour with something a little coarser. Once flour production was, firstly, shifted to a tumbler, and, secondly, ceded entirely to a third party, the baker himself or herself stopped evaluating exactly when to stop sieving to get the product he or she wanted. The potential for nuance was lost. With this loss of control, it was easy for flour to become the commodity product it is today.

At the start of the nineteenth century, bread dough was mixed by hand and baked in wood-fired brick ovens. Most milling was still reasonably small scale, and yeast was variable as it was acquired from brewers and distillers as a waste product, or grown in the bakery itself.

By the end of the nineteenth century, milling was fully industrialized through the proliferation of steam-driven and later electrified steel roller mills; ovens had been reinvented as rectangular metal boxes fired with gas; and yeast was standardized and produced for bakers in factories. As electricity use became universal, bakeries introduced mixers that would both mix the ingredients into a dough and then knead the dough. These devices took the baker's sweat, literally, out of the bread. They also radically reduced the time that a baker's hands are covered with flour and dough.

Universal electrification in the twentieth century fundamentally transformed bakeries. Today, when we think of making bread by hand, even most home bakers reach for the electric mixer. Master bakers do not work the dough with their own backs. At the most, they observe the work of a machine and (possibly) adjust water and flour based on an observation of the dough. In the context of baking, 'by hand' does not necessarily mean 'with hands'. This applies to the mixing and kneading, and it can apply to all other processes as well.

When baking was very much with hands, the trade carried with it the risk of a skin condition known as 'baker's itch'. Lest we look back with too much romance at the time when bakers mixed and kneaded the bread using their own bodies, here is a description of baker's itch from the mid-nineteenth century:

> Frequently, the affected parts to the tips of the fingers become hard, stiff, and dry; the hand remains in a state of semiflexion, and cannot be opened without great pain; the lines, naturally observed on the palm, are greatly increased in depth, and the spaces between them are covered with thick laminated scales. In protracted cases of the disease, these lines change into fissures, which bleed, whenever attempts are made to use the hand. The parts are always highly inflamed, and in general acutely sensible.[6]

The home bread machine is a version of a fully automated commercial bakery. The bread machine simplifies the in-line bakery that takes ingredients in one end of a production line and spits out baked loaves on the other. In the bread machine, mixing and baking take place in the same location. There is no venue for craft.

In all bakeries today the mixer stands between the baker and the mixing and kneading of the dough, processes that are central to the character of a loaf. For any given dough, the length and strength of the kneading process determines the baked loaf's structure. As all bakeries use mixers, it is clear that there is general agreement in the baking trade that there is actually no need for a human to do this, ever. Commercial bread recipes often specify what kind of mixer is used (all mixers are not created equal) and the mixing times at different speeds. These instructions can be thought of in the context of instructions directing the motions and time spent by a labourer.

Thus, the two first steps to making bread – preparing the flour and mixing and kneading – have both been automated. Where is the handwork in making bread? Where handwork comes in, if at all, is later in the process. In many bakeries, even reasonably small ones, there are also other machines that stand between the kneaded dough and the oven. Never assume a loaf you purchase, no matter what it looks like, has actually been touched by a human.

There are machines to scale the dough (scalers); form the scaled pieces into loaves (rounders), and conveyors to load loaves into the oven. One discussion that surrounds artisan bread is the question: how much handwork does a loaf of bread require to be 'artisan'? While the term 'craft' rarely appears in the context of discussions about artisan bread, the nature of craft is in some senses at the heart of the discussion.

In terms of taste, texture and appearance of the finished product, it can be impossible to tell how much automation was used to produce a bread. Thus, it can be impossible to tell how much craft, in the sense of handwork, goes into a loaf or whether the handwork that did go into the bread contributed anything notable.

While the dense roomless loaves of the poor no longer exist, the significance of the amount of machinery involved in making a bread is a contested space. It is possible to see within the varying definitions of artisan bread a playing out in a modern context the ancient underlying distinction between the breads of the rich and those of the poor: one is created with more intentionality and labour than the other. Thus, we assign to the more affluent the bread that requires purposeful shaping (not just dough dumped in a tin) and a slower rise to produce a more open, chewy crumb; whereas the soft, quickly leavened breads that are formed in tins are associated with those who by choice or necessity pay less for their bread.

There are reasons why a culture may decide to pay a little more for a bread with handwork, even if it is a token amount of handwork. Bread is an invention of culture. But in some ways it is like performance art. Bread itself might be eternal but the loaf itself is designed to be destroyed. It is the idea of the bread that is permanent, not the loaf. In its plasticity, loaf bread expresses cultural ideals. Each loaf is its own little sculpture, a form to be admired in its own right with a surface to excite through an interplay of colour and texture. The surface is especially important with crusty breads that are not baked in a tin as the entire outside crust is on display. The crust-centric display in French bakeries of loaves baked with pattern-enhancing slashes leaves no doubt that the surface is an important aspect of the French bread aesthetic. In contrast, a display of tin-baked loaves reveals most of the surface to be unimportant as the patterns on the sides are just an artefact of the tin they were baked in. The free-form shape of most French breads requires no technology but folding and so removes the loaf from an obvious connection with time and place. It is a form that is utterly simple to make. If formed by hand, it connects us through the gestures of bakers who must have performed the same movements for thousands of years. The *boule*-shaped loaves in the painting preserved from a Pompeii bakery and the same shaped loaves produced by bakers today are directly connected by their form, which implies a similar underling structure to the recipe.

It can be – and today it often is – an explicit cultural decision to pay a little more for certain breads to support people who want to work as bakers in small-scale enterprises producing objects that can by association tie the loaf (and by extension, us) to the past and to archaic practices. Given that increasing automation, the prospect of robot cars and the growing internet of things is the context of most of our life, the archaically touched loaf, folded but not moulded in metal, is an idea that seems to be culturally appealing. Less profoundly, these smaller, minimally automated bakeries can more easily innovate compared with bakeries that are more fully mechanized. They can thus more easily contribute to and respond to changes in fashion which, after all, is appropriate for producers of a product that ventures into the realm of an elite (if cheap) designer-like foodstuff.

Up until very recently, there was little discussion around shades of baking professionalism or the importance of handwork in the baking process. For thousands of years, right up to the last few decades, it was understood that bakers were professional and that the women who baked for their families were not. The two groups also often baked very different breads. This distinction was explicitly addressed in early modern texts. For example, the extensive bread section of the many-editioned *Maison Rustique* (sixteenth through eighteenth century) was addressed to the housewife. In the last quarter of the eighteenth century, the French author Antoine-Augustin Parmentier (1737–1813) wrote one book for professional bakers, *Le parfait boulanger, ou Traité complet sur la fabrication et le commerce du pain* (1778), and another for housewives, *Avis aux bonnes ménagères des villes et des campagnes, sur la meilleure manière de faire leur pain* (1777). If a housewife baked fortnightly (a common pattern in the era of wood-fired ovens), then she produced 26 batches a year and 260 batches in ten years. In contrast, the baker who worked six days per week produced a minimum of 312 batches per year and 3,120 batches in ten years, and very likely twice or three times that quantity. Furthermore, the baker had trained. He had apprenticed. His craft skills vis-à-vis the home bread maker were implied by his title—baker.

Today, however, bread baking is in flux. It is in flux for multiple reasons. One reason has to due with changes in technology. There are now machines – we could call them robots – that under the supervision of a skilled baker can make excellent bread, by any standards. In rich countries, the woman who bakes bread for her family has been eclipsed, and probably effectively replaced, by male home bakers, many of whom have in large numbers acquired quasi-professional skills – at the least, the ability to replicate in their home kitchens difficult breads, like the baguette.[7] Perhaps not unexpectedly, the male home bakers (this is especially true in the United States) who bake breads that emulate those of professional bakers, particularly those who are identified as artisan bakers, differentiate themselves from the millennial tradition of female home bread bakers by calling themselves 'serious home bakers'. These 'serious home bakers' often sign SHB after their names in internet bread groups. The moniker speaks for itself.

Bread is no longer a staple in rich countries. Even in France, it is effectively an optional side dish. Bread can be dispensed with entirely at a meal without damage to the integrity of the meal. If you serve bread at dinner and a guest does not eat it, you take no notice, while if that same guest were to leave all of the rice or potato on the plate, it would suggest something was wrong. This, at least, is true in Anglophone countries. As bread has receded from being a staple it has nonetheless kept a central place in the culture of food. In fact, in many discussions at international gatherings like Slow Food's biannual Terra Madre conference, and also at bread forums in the United States, such as the Maine Grain Alliance's annual Kneading Conference, bread itself functions as a proxy for working out larger issues relating to craft, food and technology. A critique of centralized corporate agriculture, manufacturing and distribution is often explicit in the assessment of soft white breads. And that is where artisan bread comes in.

Bread in America had been effectively industrialized in the first half of the twentieth century. Yet it was only during the 1990s, with the coinage of the term 'artisan bread', that people began to notice that all but a small percentage of bread was being baked in industrial-scale mega-factories; in these institutions, the values of craft as they had been understood within the bread trade for centuries, were no longer the primary concern. The following three pronouncements about artisan bread from the 1990s clearly illustrate this situation:

The popularity of artisan bread products – those crusty, oddly shaped breads found in upscale restaurants, delis, and fast food chains such as Au Bon Pain – is surging.[8]

Although the Empire was not the first bakery in the state to make what has come to be called artisan bread, it was in the vanguard. Today, all of

Texas' big cities have one or more boutique bakeries that specialize in the kind of old-fashioned, handcrafted bread that was the norm before commercial bakeries sent it packing decades ago. The basic definition of artisan bread, which is also called rustic or European style, is simple: hand-shaped bread made from untreated flour, using natural starters in place of commercial yeast. The resulting bread is generally round or oblong – but never conventionally loaflike – and crisp crusted.[9]

When they were not baking bread, they talked about baking bread. The kind of bread they discussed was called artisan bread, which Coppedge said accounted for about 5 percent of all bread consumed in the United States. Most of the bread sold in the United States is white, presliced, and stacked on grocery store shelves in colorful plastic bags. Artisan bread had become enormously popular recently.[10]

Given the ubiquity of the term artisan bread, it may come as a surprise to realize how recent an expression it is. But it is clear from these written attestations in the late twentieth century that artisan bread was, indeed, a new term. Readers might have been familiar with the breads themselves but not with calling them artisan. While artisan bread and the related but not necessarily paired 'artisan baker' entered the language in the 1990s, searching Google Books suggests it did not become a common term in books until 2000. Authors of bread books embraced the term and the style of bread it referred to, as did an increasing number of bakers. The early innovative bakers who introduced the bread style to America may have ushered in a purity of vision but they did not give it a name. However, by the time the style was named, it was already a multi-pronged tradition encompassing both 'upscale restaurants', and here we can name Berkeley's Chez Panisse as an exemplar, as well as bakery chains like Au Bon Pain. Needless to say, the craft ethos of Chez Panisse and that of Au Bon Pain are mutually exclusive.

Today, although artisan baker and artisan bread are expressions, what they might mean beyond reference to a style of bread is still in flux. There is no agreement over the relationship between the breads and the way they are produced. That the terms are central to an active conversation is evident by the fact that if you do an internet word search on the terms, you will find that a substantial number of bakeries that identify themselves as artisan offer their own definitions tailored to their practice. Even still, a full fifteen years after the terms entered the cookbook literature, authors of bread cookbooks continue to define what the artisan in artisan bread means.

One tension inherent to artisan bread is that while the common-sense meaning is bread made by an artisan, first and foremost, the term refers to a style of bread, specifically, a subset of the breads of France. In contrast to American breads, even the counter-cultural hippy breads of the 1960s in America, the breads that came to be known as artisan breads were unsweetened, unenriched – no fats added to dough – and with the notable exception of the baguette, they were usually unyeasted. The breads of most interest were those made with sourdough or *levain*. The widespread use of sourdough starters is a radical departure from historic Anglo-American bread culture as is bread made from unenriched dough.[11] By way of an example, the bread that the San Francisco Diggers distributed for free in Golden Gate Park in the early 1960s when Haight Ashbury was the centre of the West Coast hippie movement was yeasted, included some sugar and was enriched with 6 per cent dried milk by weight of flour. They were baked in tins, even if those tins were reused coffee cans, and thus transgressively outside standard capitalist bakery practice. The breads were clearly in the tradition of the Anglo-American tinned sandwich loaf.

The crisp, crackly, thick crusted, hand-formed, sour, leavened, unenriched loaves that came to us from France were in every way the opposite of the iconic American or British sandwich bread, the quickly leavened, whiter than white, pre-packaged, pre-sliced, tin-formed loaf produced by the iconic American Wonder Bread Company with its lovely soft, even crumb;[12] or the equally soft British bread produced by the Chorleywood process.[13] The exemplars brought from France were never bright white, even if made with white flour, as the preferred wheat flour used by French bakers had a yellow tinge; and the baking formula specifically addressed ways to preserve crumb colour. These breads were chewy rather than cottony soft, and it is worth observing that they often had big holes, and thus were not good for the iconic American peanut butter and jelly sandwich or the butter-sodden British toast.

Of overriding importance is the fact that none of the breads were baked in tins. The shape itself confirmed that the loaf was indeed formed by hand, and thus its very form attested to the fact it was a bread produced by artisan bakers – hence, artisan bread. The spirit of the French artisan baker – one who apprenticed as a teenager and worked in a small bakery – was implied by the form. This and the whole imaginative power of French old world craft and culinary culture was baked into the loaves. Anglophone culinary cultures could not possibly master the totality of classic French cuisine, but we could master baking a loaf of bread!

It is difficult for foods to jump borders and be widely adopted. In this case, there was not even a large immigrant group to back up the adoption of French-style breads in the United States. But there was mass tourism, which meant millions of Americans wanted to bring home to our dinner tables a bit of Paris, where millions of us were now regularly eating. More profoundly, central to the successful adoption of this style of bread by large portions of populations outside of France was the understanding that the breads were an integral part of a culinary culture that celebrated taste, flavour, sensuality and cooking process. This intellectual package found fertile ground outside its home culture in the counter-culture of the 1960s, part of which evolved into a counter force to the industrial food systems that seemed to have a strangle hold over what and how we ate. The dark, deep-cracked crusts of these hand-formed French breads, each one different, were in total contrast to the uniformity of the machine-made plastic-wrapped breads of everyday commerce and spoke to a widespread feeling that our food systems were impersonal and out of our control and that we needed to make them personal, as we imagined they used to be. This argument remains as topical as ever. These French-inspired breads are part of the dream of taking back personal control over what we put into our mouths. These breads speak to a new or at least revived cultural focus: eating food created for us by real people who take care.

Ironically, however, unlike many other foodstuffs, bread lends itself to the kind of systematization that makes it possible for fully mechanized production lines to produce breads that compare favourably to breads produced in craft bakeries where craft means at least some of the production is handwork. Bread making is a time and temperature process. This is what makes it possible for bakeries to reliably produce identical batches of bread on a schedule day after day.

Artisan bread, as a style, is defined by its recipe. There are broad similarities that unite all breads baked under the mantle of artisan bread. Most are made with 100 per cent wheat flour. Flour plus water produces glue. Bake a mass of flour and water and you get a brick. Add leaven and time and dough bakes into a loaf of bread. Wheat flour contains a protein, gluten, that forms strong chains when exposed to water and then either worked (kneading) or given time (a long, slow fermentation). Of all the grains, wheat produces the flour with the most potential for trapping gas within the dough. To the best of our ability to know, it seems that as far back in time as it is possible to surmise, wheat has always been the flour of choice for high-status breads. Gluten is the physical scaffold on which breads are built. It is an internal scaffolding or, more accurately, the membrane that supports a foam. The primary function of a bread recipe is to influence the character of the foam in the finished loaf.

Bread, as a subtle food, is altered by any change in the ingredients, formula or procedures with which it is made. That is how every bakery can produce a named bread (like baguette or *pain de campagne*) that is recognizable as that bread yet different from a competitor's bread. There is an overarching formula for making artisan bread: make relatively wet dough, use sourdough or a minimum of yeast and give it as much time to rise in a comparatively cool place as you can. While a bread made with 50 per cent water by weight of flour will make an excellent bagel, and one with 60 per cent water by weight of flour an excellent sandwich bread, artisan breads, like *pain de campagne*, usually call for 70 per cent water, or more. That is how you get the big holes. A bread made with 70 per cent water but 2 per cent yeast will make a horrible artisan bread – it will rise too quickly so the mouthfeel will be wrong – while if the yeast were reduced to 0.5 per cent and the dough given longer to rise everything would be fine. Artisan bread requires gentle dough handling including, compared with many other breads, minimal kneading.

The *reducto ad absurdum* recipe for artisan bread is the very popular (and very excellent) bread produced by the 'no-knead system' popularized in the United States by Mark Bittman of *The New York Times*. In the spirit of full disclosure, I have been making bread to what amounts to the Bittman formula for approximately thirty years. Gluten, the protein in wheat flour that produces webs of protein chains, develops on its own if given time. Kneading speeds up gluten development but is not a prerequisite. With a small amount of yeast (so the dough will rise slowly), a long rise and a wet dough so it can form large holes, kneading becomes unnecessary. Let a bowl of dough rise overnight in a cool kitchen (or the refrigerator) and in the morning it is a mass of glutenous webbing. All that is required to create a professional-looking finished product is folding the dough over itself a few times at a couple of intervals before forming and baking. The taste of the bread will always be exemplary, and as even the most devoted commercial baker is under time constraints – time is the ultimate creator of flavour in bread, sourdough starters being, in some senses, a short-cut to time – it is simple to create a bread with a more complex taste than nearly anything a commercial bakery can put out. And yet, the home baker, like me, who simply dumps the ingredients together and waits, has no real baking skills. This approach to bread is offered in the hugely popular *Artisan Bread in Five Minutes per Day* by Jeff Herztberg and Zoë François (2007). The no-knead artisan bread lacks the artisan. Like bread made in a bread machine, it requires no craft – at least, no craft that implies handwork.

I recently watched a YouTube video of a house in China being printed with a 3D printer. The video is noteworthy, not because the house is not being built by the architect—few buildings are—but because it is an early example of construction workers being replaced by software and an extruder. It is uncontroversial that architects design and that builders build. Artisan bread offers a challenge. If a perfectly credible loaf can be created through automated processes, that is, loaves produced with intellectual intentionality but through industrial expediency (labour replaced by equipment), then is there a reason to see it as different from the loaf produced by less mechanical means? Large baking firms like the American multinational La Brea Bakery argue that all that matters is intentionality. If we use the best ingredients and make the breads with care and never cut corners on process, particularly as regards issues of time and temperature, then we are artisan bakers. In their words,

> La Brea Bakery Artisan Flatbreads are made with the same dedication to the artisan traditions and uncompromising standards that we have prided ourselves on for 25 years.[14]

This can be dismissed as cynical corporate-speak. But I do not think it is. The concept of artisan bread as it was first used in American English did not focus on the loaf as a hand-crafted object. It is well within American English to understand an artisan tradition as being attention to detail but without requiring handwork throughout the entire process.

The definition of 'well-crafted' that comes up in large type at the top of the browser page from a Google search is 'skillfully constructed'. The iPhone is indisputably skilfully constructed, but it is not handcrafted. Within American culture, at least, this can be understood as a splitting of hairs. There is no discourse in which an object well crafted by machine and that which is well crafted by hand are conceptually differentiated from each other.

While it is exceedingly rare as of this writing, in both the United States and the United Kingdom, one sometimes finds the ambiguity of artisan bread and artisan baker resolved through the term 'craft artisan baker'. The following job posting by an Edinburgh bakery pinpoints the single area in which many self-styled artisan bakeries insist on handwork.

> We are looking for an energetic, enthusiastic and flexible craft artisan baker to join our team. You should have great hand moulding skills and a love of high quality, properly made bread.[15]

In other words, all mixing and kneading is done by machine. All you will do by hand is form the loaf. The following excerpt comes from an anonymous letter posted to a British website for commercial bakers. The author clearly struggles with what it means to make bread with intentionality, but for all the work to be by machine:

> I've not yet found a bakery that doesn't use at least a mixing machine, so when does a bakery lose its 'craft' status, because it uses machinery [sic]? Sourcing the best raw materials and turning them into top-quality finished products is a craft, at whatever level.[16]

Rather than focusing on descriptive words – like artisan and craft – perhaps the baking community and the culture at large would find it more constructive to think of terms like artisan bread as conceptual, rather like architectural styles. A building can be made with many different types of materials and still be Italianate. A great building may, or may not, include handmade materials. If it does, then it will have an added layer of meaning but whether it does or does not has no bearing on whether it is a pleasure to look or whether its spaces work for the purposes intended. Applied to bread, if you substitute process for materials, then you come up with a democratic approach to artisan bread in which production systems are depreciated in favour of results and craft is extended to cover the controlled manipulation of dough to achieve a desired result regardless of how that manipulation is achieved.

If, as a culture, we wish to favour hand-crafted bread, whichever way it may be defined in a modern context – for example, through the use of a mixer and scaler, but not a rounder – that is, of course, our prerogative. There could be a term for well-crafted industrial products, like those Apple products that feel so perfect, or that could differentiate the loaf produced entirely by machine from those touched by hands, but there seems little indication that these are distinctions our Anglophone culture is particularly concerned with. Bread production is already so highly automated that the small windows of handwork that remain in craft bakeries are implicitly understood to stand on the edge of the production system.

The discussion over what is an artisan bread within the Anglophone artisan baking community is undercut by the fact that time and temperature are such important features to bread making and that one can, in fact, make a credible loaf of artisan bread in five minutes a day. What remains at the core of the artisan bread critique is mass production, profit over intent and satisfaction with commodity products. Through a remarkable power to organize around a belief in bread as a soul-centering food that should not be made in a factory, even if it can be, the artisan bread movement is currently resurrecting the first part of the recipe that was lost so long ago: a focus on the wheat itself and on milling. In many countries, including the United States, Canada, and the UK, the artisan bread movement is responsible for bringing wheat cultivars to market that were long lost to agricultural production. It is reviving wheat growing in areas where no wheat has grown for 100 years, or more. This also means bringing back grain storage systems that work for small farmers and small-scale milling.

Over time, as automated baking systems become ever-more sophisticated and as a new generations of bakers with a focus on loaf quality and innovation come to the fore, a more sophisticated language will evolve to talk about bread and craft and the role of handwork, if any, in the production of breads that feed our imagination as well as our bodies. Humans remain much easier to reprogramme than a machine, and crucially, we are creative. If our culture wishes to support bakers who want to outwit automation, it will be easy to do so. For example, there is a myriad of ways to decorate the surface of bread; in fact, many options have never been explored and thus no robotic system would be able to keep abreast with this creativity and inventiveness. Bread, as subtle food, is ever flexible. As a plastic medium, dough is ever-mouldable. And once you start bringing back choice in grain cultivars and real choice in flour formulation the options for bread culture are truly limitless. Even if some of those breads are eventually made by robots, it is nonetheless a good bet that visionary bakers will continue to bring us artisan loaves, however artisan is defined.

Acknowledgements

I would like to thank the American Master Baker Craig Ponsford, the first American to place in the *Coupe de Monde de Boulangerie*, in Paris, winning gold for the best bread in 1996, for his wide-ranging insights into artisan bread as we know it in the United States. In particular, I owe Craig the insight that bread recipes depend on careful control of time and temperature and are thus amenable to full-scale automation. In his own bakery, in San Rafael, California, there is a mixer but all other work is done by hand by Craig, who is the only baker.

Notes

1   'Sourdough' in standard English, 'leaven' in an older English, but in texts written by followers of the 'artisan bread' movement, the French *levain* is often the word chosen for sourdough starters.

2   A small mill with a moveable top circular grindstone turned with one hand by the miller who sits beside the rotary kern on the floor. *The Academy of Armory*, Printed for the Author, (Chester: Randle Holme, 1688), Book III chapter VII, 316.

3   The implements in the bake house are described on the last page of the book, page 128 of the 1615 edition of *The English Housewife* by Gervase Markham Printed by I.B. London.

4   Holme, Randle.

5   British Library Manuscript SL 2189.

6   R. Dunglison, *The Practice of Medicine: A Treatise on Special Pathology and Therapeutics* (Philadelphia: Lea and Blanchard, 1848), 64.

7   The baguette was (is) often leavened with yeast. Thus, among the group of breads deemed artisan this one is often yeasted. The only non-French bread regularly regarded as artisan is the Italian ciabatta. This bread is usually yeasted, but includes its own set of challenges: It is made from a dough that can be so hydrated as to resemble a batter. Some bakers work with a dough that employs equal weights of flour and water, though hydration levels of 75 per cent and 80 per cent are more common.

8   Bakery, Confectionery, and Tobacco Workers International Union, *Bc&T Report* 19 (Kensington, MD: The Union, 1995), 145-146.

9   P. Sharpe, 'Bread Winners', Texas Monthly, July 1996, http://www.texasmonthly.com/content/bread-winners (accessed 7 January 2015).

10 M. Ruhlman, *The Making of a Chef: Mastering Heat at the Culinary Institute of America* (New York: Henry Holt and Company, 1999), 161.

11 Sourdough breads were reserved for the poor with virtually no exceptions in the Anglo-American bread tradition as recorded in texts from the mid-sixteenth century to the mid-twentieth century. Sugar and oil began entering the mainstream bread supply in the UK and the United States in the later decades of the nineteenth century.

12 Now owned by Grupo Bimbo, the Mexican multi-national bakery product manufacturing company.

13 The Chorleywood process is a system for producing a softer (40 per cent softer) bread faster (3½ hours) start to finish employing high-speed mixing, a stiff fat or oil, enzymes and a larger-than-usual dose of yeast. It does not require an industrial setting. Approximately 80 per cent of British bread is made by this process, which was invented in the early 1960s. As a side-benefit of the process, it makes it possible to make light loaves with soft British-grown flour as opposed to harder imported flour from North America. It is thus a baking system that reduces food miles.

14 This description of 'artisan flat breads' was originally published on the La Brea Bakery website in 2015. www.labreabakery.com.

15 This was a job posted at the website vacantwork.co.uk in March 2015.

16 Sara Reid, letters: What Is a 'Craft Baker'? 12 Februrary 2010, published at the website of *British Baker Magazine*, http://www.bakeryinfo.co.uk/news/archivestory.php/aid/6437/Letters:_What_is_a__craft_baker__.html (accessed 5 March 2016).

10

Craft and Construction

John Tuomey

We want to make our buildings feel permanent, to make a lasting thing, robust and ready for a long and useful life in the world. I think that is why we like to work with raw materials, with the archaic stuff that will weather naturally and wear out slowly: brick, concrete and timber seem to offer some sort of aesthetic resistance – resilient as they are to time and season.

But for the builder, this makes his or her life a little more difficult. The structure is the first thing to be made, in mostly wet and often windy outdoor conditions of a building site. And then these primary elements have to be protected through all the messy stages of the process of construction, eventually to emerge intact as a precious finish. The first thing made becomes the first thing visible – in a world where final finishes do not conspire to cover up early work.

This is difficult to achieve in real life. Sometimes we have seen a well-made piece of work suffer from the untimely drop of a scaffold pole or a belt from the end of a passing ladder. But the builder is a necessary part of the team, and has to feel part of the family that is working together to make a good building. Architects must be ready to praise the work and learn to love the person who is doing one's best.

Rainer Maria Rilke, in his efforts to seek out space for poetry, told his patron to:

> *Praise this world to the angel*
> > *so show him*
> *something simple which, formed over generations,*
> *lives as our own, near our hand and within our gaze.*
> *Tell him of Things. He will stand astonished; as you stood*
> *by the rope-makers in Rome or the potters along the Nile.*
> > > (Rilke, *Duino Elegies*, 'The Ninth Elegy')[1]

We could translate Rilke's lyrical advice (to send praise to the angel) to more practical, but no less poetic, ends. Architects should speak directly to clients, contractors and tradespersons, talking simply about qualities near our hand; qualities that inhere in what Rilke liked to call 'Things' – or in what we call buildings.

Architecture is a craft-based art. The architect's concept has to be carried across to live in the building itself, and this transference is realized through the active commitment of the contractor and the measured skill of manual work. Bricklayers, carpenters, shuttering contractors, site engineers and general supervisors are the unsung actors who make actual architecture out of architects' intentions. These are the people worth talking to, worth taking into our confidence and whose advice is worth listening to. Ideas are born in the mind, but architects' ideas live on in the practical, poetical things we call buildings. Or, as Denys Lasdun said,' You can go and see it, and the building, if it has anything to say, will have to speak for itself.'[2]

Professional training inclines our profession towards the view that craftsmanship is a thing of the past, and by this way of thinking, architectural design should avoid the demands of difficult construction and instead it should provide for the norms of the industry. Taken literally, it is as if the building process should be, or could be, reduced to the assembly of standardized components.

On the contrary, we have found that the whole construction team can rise to the satisfaction of seeing a difficult job done well. And we have had the good fortune to work with master-craftsmen and very careful colleagues who attend to the discipline of their craft at every stage in the difficult journey from design to completion. Strangely enough, it seems that the more difficult the challenge, the better the chances of getting the work done well. This is one further reason for us to try to approach simplicity through complication; because if it is too easy to do, no one seems to think its worth trying to do it particularly well.

We practice our own craft through a studio-based way of working. First, thoughts are sketched out in soft pencil, then quickly drawn up on computer and roughly modelled in cardboard. The process is repeated on a daily basis and designs are gradually developed with overlay drawings on A3 sheets of *Skizzen* paper. There is nothing novel in this routine: it is the technique we learned at Jim Stirling's office. It is the means by which fluency emerges, continuous in many respects with the methods of student project work; and, sometimes, on a good day, a mysterious jump in thinking happens when the work itself is in flow.

Constant practice in the studio helps to develop a surer sense of scale, and some practical experience on site helps to keep the mind's eye and the hand's action connected to each other. Working closely with trusted colleagues in the studio and cooperating with expert consultants is one of the tangible benefits of professional practice. Unlike in college or academic life, where the hard question always seems to be 'Why?' in practice more often the interesting question is 'How?' This is the craftsman's question, and the search for an adequate answer can open up directions for collaborative investigation into the capacities of materials and methods of construction.

The technology of communication has changed completely in our generation. The principles of the tools of the trade have changed somewhat less. The raw materials of construction have changed very little. However, the really big change in building technology happened long ago, by the end of the nineteenth century, with the separation of structural frame from enclosing fabric.

Walls these days are not monolithic. Weight no longer requires massive thickness for its support, and buildings provide added protection from the weather in purpose-specific layers of construction. This is the breakthrough that, after countless centuries of masonry-based building, brought about the revolution in twentieth-century aesthetics of construction. Nowadays this news is no longer new.

Timber, always a scarce resource, requiring management at source and maintenance in use, is still sawn in planks and joined in sections to allow for movement along and across the grain. And the technology of glass and steel is amazing in its complexity and refinement, but the difference is in degree, not in kind. Bricks have changed not at all: 175,000 bricks for the London School of Economics Saw Swee Hock Student Centre were individually made from clods of clay, hand thrown in wooden moulds, sprinkled with coloured sands and baked in the oven-like loaves of bread.

Construction sites are social settings, settings where the social art of architecture takes on its substance. And the quality of craftsmanship is always appreciable, and ready, like Rilke's angel, to be recognized with human respect at every stage from setting out to finishing off.

Notes

1   Rainer Maria Wilke, 'The Ninth Elegy' in *The Selected Poetry of Rainer Maria Rilke*, ed. and trans. Stephen Mitchell (New York: Random House, 1984), 200.

2   Lasdun was speaking in reference to the Royal College of Physicians in London during a talk which he delivered at the Royal Institute of British Architects, February 9, 1965. See Denys Lasdun, 'His Approach to Architecture', *Architectural Design 35* (June 1965): 271–278.

Material Matters

Samantha L. Martin-McAuliffe

John Tuomey and Sheila O'Donnell have been practicing architecture together for over twenty-five years. In 1988 they founded O'Donnell + Tuomey, a Dublin-based firm which focuses on educational, cultural and social buildings, both in Ireland and abroad. Their projects are noted for their craftsmanship, especially in terms of materiality. Static components such as brick, timber and concrete weave together and interlock to shape spaces that embody an astonishing sense of movement. Whether set in rural surroundings or within constrained urban sites, their buildings invariably draw their historical and spatial contexts into conversation. Both O'Donnell and Tuomey teach at University College Dublin and in 2015 they received the Royal Gold Medal from the Royal Institute of British Architects (RIBA).

The following photographic essay is designed to stand in reciprocity with, as well as productively extend some of, the key points in John Tuomey's written contribution to Part Three, 'Craft' in this volume. With the exception of Figures 10.1 and 10.14, all the buildings and projects illustrated are by O'Donnell + Tuomey.

FIGURE 10.1 *A view of the studio of O'Donnell + Tuomey in Dublin. Photo by Alice Clancy. For over twenty-five years, John Tuomey and Sheila O'Donnell have based their practice in a stone schoolhouse at the heart of Dublin's Victorian south side.*

FIGURE 10.2 Vessel, *13th International Venice Architectural Exhibition (2012).* *Photo by Alice Clancy. O'Donnell + Tuomey have participated in the Venice Architecture Biennale on three occasions, most recently as part of the* Common Ground *exhibition, which was curated by David Chipperfield in 2012. Vessel, a perforated tower of timber, was a site-specific response to the setting of the Corderie in the Venice Arsenale. A commodious warehouse of brick and timber, the Corderie was originally the heart of the Venetian Republic's shipbuilding enterprise. The layered and stacked planks of Vessel reference the construction methods of the industrial facility while also drawing allusion to the wider symbolisms of seafaring.*

FIGURE 10.3 *View of the auditorium of The Lyric Theatre, Belfast, Northern Ireland (2011). Photo by Dennis Gilbert. The Lyric is also a vessel of sorts, an acoustical container for the voice. The auditorium is intimate in size – it seats 400 – and it is designed to maximize the reciprocity between the stage and the audience. The timber floor and lining create a warmth that enhances the familiarity and closeness of the space. The Lyric was shortlisted for the RIBA Stirling Prize in 2012.*

FIGURE 10.4 *Exterior view of The Lyric Theatre (2011). Photo by Dennis Gilbert. Although situated along the bank of the River Lagan, the theatre directly responds to the brick streetscape of Belfast. Pictured here (right) is the outdoor auditorium.*

FIGURE 10.5 *An Gaeláras Irish Language Arts and Cultural Centre, Derry, Northern Ireland (2009). Photo by Dennis Gilbert. Built on a constrained urban site with limited street frontage, An Gaeláras folds inwards towards a skylit central courtyard. The building was shortlisted for the RIBA Stirling Prize in 2011.*

FIGURE 10.6 *An Gaeláras Irish Language Arts and Cultural Centre, Derry, Northern Ireland (2009). Photo by Dennis Gilbert. Elsewhere John Tuomey has argued that components of a building are 'not neutral ingredients of a recipe, neither do they come readymade of any and every architectural design. Cooked up in the brain and played out on the page, such fragmentary phrases must be thoroughly tested for spatial composition and rhythmic volume'.[1] Any recipe, whether for a building or a dish, must espouse fundamental principles and standards, yet neither can be wholly controlled by absolute prescriptions or rigid formulae. They rely on a combination of intuition, inventiveness and even wonder.*

FIGURE 10.7 *GMIT Furniture College Letterfrack, County Galway, Ireland (2001). View of the Machine Hall and Chimney beneath Desmond Hill. Photo by Dennis Gilbert. Letterfrack Furniture College has its early roots in a Quaker community and it rises from the ashes of Ireland's dark history of industrial schools. The project retains the foundational architecture of the site but transforms and remoulds it within the surrounding landscape, thereby rehabilitating the site as a whole.*

FIGURE 10.8 *The Lewis Glucksman Gallery, University College Cork, County Cork, Ireland (2004). Photo by Dennis Gilbert. Taking inspiration from Seamus Heaney's poem 'Lightenings viii', Tuomey has described the Glucksman Gallery as both a 'hovering timber vessel' and a 'ship in the air'.[2] Situated within a meadowland besides the River Lee, the building has a small footprint yet stands tall amidst a pre-existing grove of trees. The gallery was shortlisted for the RIBA Stirling Prize in 2005.*

FIGURE 10.9 *View of the limestone-clad podium and undercroft of the Glucksman Gallery. Photo by Dennis Gilbert. In addition to exhibition galleries, the building contains a riverside café and bookshop.*

FIGURE 10.10 *A bay window juts out from the timber-clad Glucksman Gallery. Photo by Alice Clancy. The entire building was designed to fit within the woodland. It bends around the trees and opens into the canopy.*

FIGURE 10.11 *The view from an upper bay window in the Glucksman Gallery. Photo by Alice Clancy. The height of the building allows for expansive views and long sightlines down the River Lee. Standing at the edge of the campus of the University College Cork, the Glucksman Gallery could be understood as a hinge between the city and the university.*

FIGURE 10.12 *Saw Swee Hock Student Centre, London School of Economics, London, United Kingdom (2013). Photo by Dennis Gilbert. London, as Tuomey has noted, is a city of bricks.*[3] *Many streets of the city still echo their ancient urban patterns, but over time the medieval buildings have given way to thousands of brick structures. The campus of the London School of Economics is typical in this way. Its student centre rises and stretches out of a tangle of passages. The building was shortlisted for the RIBA Stirling Prize in 2015. In 2014 it won the RIBA London Building of the Year Award.*

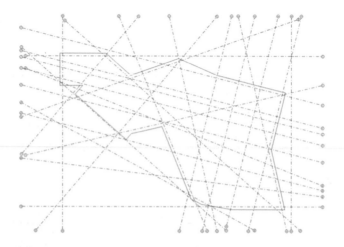

FIGURE 10.13 *Underlying gridlines for the Saw Swee Hock Student Centre. O'Donnell + Tuomey. Although largely built of a most typical and mundane building material, the student centre runs counter to any preconceptions about standard parts and practices. This plan clearly communicates the complexity inherent to the LSE site. Not only did the project have to accommodate a constricted and unusually shaped plot, but it also had to comply with height restrictions in relation to the neighbouring buildings. Beyond this, the final building needed to house a diverse range of activities.*

FIGURE 10.14 *Bricks and wooden brick moulds. O'Donnell + Tuomey. Much like loaves of bread, bricks are baked in moulds in an oven. There are 175,000 hand-made bricks in the London School of Economics Student Centre, and many of these are customized shapes, called* specials, *which deviate from the standard rectangular form.*

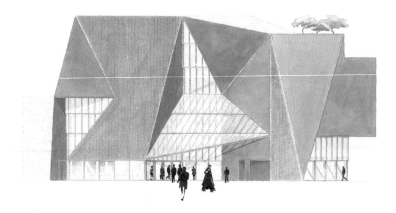

FIGURE 10.15 *Saw Swee Hock Student Centre, London School of Economics, competition elevation design. O'Donnell + Tuomey. In addition to fabricating specials,* the brickmakers adjusted the colour and tone of the bricks by finishing them with different kinds of sand. These types were based on Sheila O'Donnell's watercolour studies for the project.

FIGURE 10.16 *Detail of the Saw Swee Hock Student Centre, London School of Economics. Photo by Dennis Gilbert. Depending on the time of day and the quality of light, the facetted brick exterior of the building resembles a mottled textile.*

FIGURE 10.17 *Internal spiral stair of the Saw Swee Hock Student Centre, London School of Economics. Photo by Dennis Gilbert. To some degree, the entire interior of the building manifests as a slowly unfolding spiral. The stairs act as streets, vehicles for communication as well as movement.*

FIGURE 10.18 *Exterior view of the Saw Swee Hock Student Centre, London School of Economics. Photo by Dennis Gilbert. The exterior was constructed using Flemish bond, but patterns were created by perforating the brick envelop. During the day, these openings bring light into the building, while at night they create the appearance of a latticework lantern.*

Notes

1 Sheila O'Donnell, and John Tuomey, *Space for Architecture* (London: Artifice, 2014), 164.

2 John Tuomey, *Architecture, Craft and Culture: Reflections on the Work of O'Donnell + Tuomey* (Kinsale, Ireland: Gandon Editions, Edge Series: Ideas on Art and Architecture, 2008), 58; Sheila O'Donnell and John Tuomey, *O'Donnell + Tuomey: Selected Works* (New York: Princeton Architectural Press, 2007), 160.

3 *Space for Architecture*, 200.

11

Craftsmanship and Quality in Artisanal Cheesemaking

Heather Paxson

A few years ago, a wine shop opened in Cambridge, Massachusetts, featuring a cheese counter specializing in domestic artisanal wares. Walking into the shop one afternoon, I found the cheesemonger surrounded by co-workers seeking to learn whether, in his absence, they had properly labelled the cheeses in a new display case. One of the shop's owners held up a wedge of cheese, in one hand, and a wheel, in the other, saying, 'I don't understand how *this* can be Weston Wheel, when *this* is Weston Wheel, and they don't look the same to me!'

Artisanally made cheese resists standardization. Indeed, in the course of anthropological research into American artisanal cheesemaking (undertaken between 2004 and 2011), I heard repeatedly that the most difficult skill to master in making cheese is achieving consistency: the ability to work with ambient microorganisms, seasonal changes in milk chemistry and fluctuating climatic conditions to turn out a self-similar, if necessarily variable, product batch after batch, month after month. In grasping what makes cheese artisanal, I find helpful furniture designer David Pye's insight that, in craftsmanship, the 'quality of the result is not predetermined, but depends on the judgement, dexterity and care which the maker exercises as he works'.[1] Pye names this a 'workmanship of risk', in which product quality remains 'continually at risk' throughout the manufacturing process. Such risk may be introduced from human error or from flaws in the materials used. Whereas industrial manufacturing seeks to obviate both sets of errors by deskilling production and by standardizing materials (thereby ensuring what Pye names a 'worksmanship of certainty'), the craftsperson works to accommodate natural variations, though only so far as these may be harnessed to help realize an intended form. So, just as a woodworker might incorporate a twisted knot of wood into the design of a hand-turned bowl, a cheesemaker works to incorporate natural variations – in concentrations of milk butterfat, in ambient microbial populations, in the seasonal composition of pasture flora or browse ingested by sheep, cows or goats – into what is nonetheless a safe, tasty and recognizable food.[2]

To be sure, being made 'by hand' is no guarantee of product quality; indeed, Pye acknowledges that the workmanship of risk 'can produce things of the worst imaginable quality'.[3] Quality in craftsmanship begs the question of what qualities are valued as markers of especially 'good' quality in a given craft. Pye suggests that quality in workmanship can be judged by two criteria: 'soundness' of structure and 'comeliness' of aesthetic expression.[4] A well-worked object, on Pye's view, is both free of hidden structural flaws and true to the craftsperson's aesthetic intent. But while Pye would judge both criteria 'by reference to the designer's intention', the sociologist Howard Becker reminds us that the crafts have come to be distinguished from the fine arts by virtue of their *utility to someone*.[5] For commercial crafts, that someone is frequently a consumer; not all aesthetic choices sell well. Therefore, as Becker suggests, market values – that is, saleability – must be added to soundness of structure and comeliness of form in assessing skilled craftsmanship.

In working to realize multiple material and aesthetic qualities simultaneously, cheesemakers have much in common with architects. The quality values I have just outlined resonate remarkably well with what John Tuomey identifies as the three 'components of character' in architecture: substance, form and 'appropriation by use'.[6] In this chapter, I outline how artisan cheesemakers work to bring into being, simultaneously, the *material qualities of soundness or substance* (e.g. the material integrity and 'keeping quality' of a foodstuff; although ultimately perishable, a soundly made cheese will not 'go off' sooner than anticipated) and the *aesthetic qualities of form* (i.e. organoleptic properties of flavour, texture and odour that should be not only palatable but also self-similarly recognizable from one batch to the next). The fundamental significance of both substance and form in constituting cheese is reflected in its very name: *cheese* and *Käse* come from the Latin *casein*, referring to the milk protein solids precipitated from coagulation that form the basis of cheese; *fromage* and *formaggio* refer to cheese forms – the moulds that give shape to cheeses as well as the forms that result when curd is moulded. Although I will not elaborate it here, market qualities of utility (i.e. what will sell as food to be eaten) are also at issue.[7] These three types of qualities or components of character are all present in a 'good' cheese. It is no easy task to manage at once all three sets of qualities – each entailing a somewhat different set of risks and, therefore, skills. And that, in no small part, is because *cheese is alive*.

Teeming with the metabolic activity of bacteria and fungi feeding on the enzymes and carbohydrates in milk, cheese is continuously ripening (or, from another angle, decomposing). Awake to cheese's aliveness, artisans who encourage the surface formation of edible moulds to create so-called natural rinds – and whose handicraft leaves its mark in lopsided shapes and mottled surfaces – often personify their cheeses as if they were organisms: cheeses *develop, age* and *mature*. For example, fresh wheels of Vermont Shepherd cheese, after ripening for about a week in an aging 'cave' (fashioned, in this case, from repurposed concrete culverts sunk into a hillside), sprout a powdery bloom of the yeast-like fungus *Geotrichum candidum*. At this stage the cheesemaker, Vermont sheep farmer, David Major, speaks of the cheeses as 'toddlers'; in a few weeks, they will 'hit puberty' and 'graduate' to drier boards around the corner, where they will 'mature'. Cheeses when anthropomorphized can be spoiled or go rotten.

Such anthropomorphizing language – by no means restricted to this farm[8] – reflects the artisan's sense that cheese *does stuff* of its own accord. Under artisanal conditions (more so than industrial), cheese development cannot be fully predicted or controlled – it has a life of its own; this is precisely what many artisans love about their craft, and what safety regulators may fear. To impart a 'life of its own' to an individual or batch of cheese might seem to absolve a cheesemaker for less than scrupulous care. However, from interviews conducted with more than forty cheesemakers (owner-operators of small businesses as well as hired artisans) primarily in New England, Wisconsin and northern California, I found that such language generally expresses artisans' sense of responsibility to make cheese *well* by exerting selective pressure on its microbial ecologies to direct fermentation and cheese development towards preconceived outcomes.

In view of this, in speaking here of how *appropriation by use* is a quality feature of craftsmanship, I choose to investigate not the utility of the end result (i.e. marketability and consumption) but rather the usefulness or value to the artisan of the production process itself. What do cheesemakers get from making cheese by hand within an industrialized food system? In conclusion, I return to reflect on the aliveness of cheese through the lens of what the anthropologist Tim Ingold, following Heidegger, has termed a 'dwelling perspective'. Craftsmanship in cheesemaking, on this view, entails living-in-place, whether at a microscopic or a human scale. One of the 'uses' of artisanal cheesemaking, I suggest, is the life that it affords, the human dwelling that it constitutes and is constituted by it.

Substance

Echoing Pye on the workmanship of risk, the dairy scientist Paul Kindstedt writes of artisanal cheesemaking, 'The goal should be to achieve the appropriate level of control to ensure safety and consistently high quality while at the same time giving nature enough free rein to encourage the diversity and uniqueness of character that make artisanal cheeses special.'[9] To strike this balance, proficient cheesemakers develop an intimate understanding of their materials – not of milk chemistry in the abstract, but of *their* milk and curd. Diana Murphy, who makes goat cheese on her Wisconsin farm, said to me, 'Part of the artisan feel of it is knowing your milk, knowing what cultures complement your milk, what rennet complements your milk, [and] how to manipulate that.' By having 'a feel' for how their materials behave under fluctuating conditions, cheesemakers are able to adjust their recipe and tweak elements of practice – the temperature to which curd is heated, the duration of time curd is allowed to set before being cut, the size of the pieces into which curd is cut to release either more or less whey – so as to realize the end in view. 'As in any craft', writes Ingold, 'the skilled maker who has a feel for what she is doing is one whose movement is continually and subtly responsive to the modulations of her relation with the material.'[10]

Elsewhere, I have described 'having a feel' for one's milk and curd – the ability to respond reflexively in light of one's cross-sensory apprehension and experienced evaluation of empirical data – as an exercise in 'synaesthetic reason'.[11] Related to the concept of 'flow', or total absorption in a task,[12] synaesthetic reason is exercised at the edges of consciousness. Caught up in the rhythm of practice, the proficient craftsperson makes reflexive self-adjustments that are nevertheless informed by experiential knowledge – habituated, rather than instinctual. Farrar and Trorey similarly describe how, caught up in the 'flow' of dry stone walling, a skilled waller can immediately 'see' the right stone to pick up and where to place it without conscious deliberation; they quote a waller as saying, 'How do you know it's the right stone? It fits... you know, you put one down there and it just fits. You can feel it – that's it, that's what it's going to be.'[13] I heard similar accounts from cheesemakers, although with cheesemaking one's 'flow' has to keep pace with seasonal and environmental fluctuations.

Despite never having taken a formal cheesemaking class, Sue (let me call her, as she requested anonymity), a goat farmer in New England, had been making chèvre for ten years when I interviewed her. She learned to make cheese – this cheese – by working alongside a friend, who also sold her the goats. Even after ten years, Sue described cheesemaking to me as an experimental enterprise. She records meticulous data on what she does, taking note of what works well and what does not. Although she has followed the same recipe for a decade she continuously modifies her practice, mostly in response to fluctuating conditions. 'Goats are seasonal', she explained. Hers kid in February and produce milk until December, when she dries them off in preparation for another round of kidding. 'When you do that, the milk when they first give birth is different than at the end of the season…That's kind of the fun of it, that the cheese in the spring doesn't taste the same as in the winter', she told me. But such variability also introduces practical challenges. Late summer milk is more concentrated, she elaborated: it has 'more fat and solids' in it. Trying to get a handle on how, in concrete terms, artisanal practice responds to fluctuations in the materials used, I asked, 'So, do you use less rennet at the end of the season?' She thought about it for a second and replied, 'Yes. I would use less rennet at the end of the season. When you use more rennet it reacts more': this is how she tried to articulate her feel for it. 'It's because you have more of the solids, the proteins, you actually want it to react a little bit less, because you have more quantity there, and the more it reacts, then there's more structure happening and it gets a little grainy or whatever. So, when you're using less [rennet], there's kind of less action. That may not be right but that's how I see it', she said with a smile.

In acknowledging 'that may not be right', Sue was suggesting not only that scientific knowledge of milk chemistry and fermentation could explain the phenomena that she observes and responds to yet struggled to articulate but also that science would *properly* explain it. Implicitly, she was privileging scientific knowledge as more 'correct' or complete than her own practical knowledge. But is that the case? Would scientific knowledge of (say) acidity levels and their effect on coagulation necessarily *improve* or importantly *legitimate* Sue's experiential knowledge? I think not. After all, inability to articulate the *why* behind the *what* and *how* of practical knowledge is a hallmark of what Polanyi called its 'tacit' dimension.[14] Absence of critical self-awareness can aid in the fluent exercise of craftsmanship.

Scientific and practical knowledge need not be mutually exclusive or antithetical to one another. Not only do laboratory and field scientists rely on practical knowledge of instrumentation and the ability to tinker with equipment in order to get 'good' experimental results,[15] scientific understandings of how biochemical properties of materials (acidity, microbial ecologies) are affected by environmental conditions (temperature, humidity) can add to the craftsperson's problem-solving toolkit without undermining their reflexive 'feel' or synaesthetic reason. Scientific knowledge, in other words, might aid in the mastery of a 'workmanship of risk' – in the ability to work with and respond to material and environmental variability – just as much as to a 'workmanship of certainty' driven by goals of efficiency and standardization. Such a view inspired the convening of a conference devoted to the 'Science of Artisan Cheese', which I attended in the United Kingdom in 2012 (I discuss about it further in the following section).

Sue's modest articulation of having an experiential 'feel' for a process that she concedes has a scientifically knowable basis might be viewed as a *vernacular* understanding of what enables her to engage in successful cheesemaking. Sue's success is borne out commercially; she has made cheese for a decade, selling as much as she can produce through her farm store and at area farmers' markets. No one is challenging her legitimacy as a cheesemaker – *certainly not in scientific terms*. Her cheese is recognized, and appreciated, by others *as* vernacular; the fact that it is made without the intervention or approval of professionally trained food scientists can be part of what distinguishes artisanal from industrial food. If anything, Sue herself suggested that some might question her legitimacy as an artisan because she is not as *artsy* as others: she makes a simple cheese, 'kind of a boring cheese', as she put it – namely, fresh goat cheese. Sue seemed to be suggesting that her fresh cheese, compared to one aged to develop a natural rind, is more *substance* than *form*. But, as I detail below, I have come to view these as inextricable.

Form

In his essay, 'The Art of Cheesemaking', the artisan and consultant Peter Dixon writes as follows: 'In the same way that the set of six mugs our neighborhood potter made for us are slightly different in form and appearance, my wheels of cheese are different in size and coloring of the rinds. I believe that it is precisely this quality that distinguishes artisanal cheese from its industrial, mass-produced counterpart.'[16] However, when I took a two-day workshop with Peter Dixon to better understand for myself how cheesemakers begin to acquire the practical knowledge requisite for proficiency in a workmanship of risk, I learned that not all variability of form is *quality* variability. Lecturing us each morning on chemistry and craft, Peter extolled the virtues of working with raw milk, pointing admiringly to the natural variation it generates in the quality characteristics of artisanal cheese. From one batch to the next, spring season to fall, the colour, texture, flavour and odour of a cheese varies – particularly when it begins with unpasteurized (raw) milk. 'That's what consumers value', he said to us at the workshop. But one of my classmates, coming from a career in catering, interjected that she hears the opposite: that what consumers are looking for is *consistency* from one purchase to the next (recall the puzzlement over Weston Wheel with which I began this chapter). Peter explained that, thanks to industrialization, consistency is expected of most American cheese but 'not twenty-dollar cheese' – not the sort he was teaching us to make.

At this point, however, our host for the workshop, Mark – a cheesemaker in his own right – called out from the next room that variation owing to material flaws or environmental conditions is one thing, but not 'variation from poor skills, which is what most American variation is'. Humidity, temperature, what the milk-making animals are eating – all of that affects cheese development, Mark acknowledged – but so too does the *skill* of the artisan. Mark's tone hinted at some frustration with those who might pass off genuine mistakes or flaws as 'natural' marks of seasonality or of *terroir*, the notion that material elements of the place of production can influence flavour development in an agricultural product.[17] Form and substance help to realize one another.

In August 2012, I travelled to England to attend a two-day conference on 'The Science of Artisan Cheese', organized by Neal's Yard Dairy (a London-based retailer specializing in domestic farmhouse cheeses) and hosted at Manor Farm in Somerset, where farmhouse Cheddar has been made by three generations of the Montgomery family. As an afternoon excursion, Jamie Montgomery gave group tours of 'the store', the warehouse-like building in which the cylindrical wheels, called truckles, of Cheddar are aged. With a nod to the vernacular of artisanal cheesemaking, he began, 'Every traditional Cheddar maker has a different theory about what's going on on their rinds. My theory is that I want the molds to eat the lard by three-to-four weeks.' To encourage the moulds to accomplish this task, he keeps the humidity in the store relatively low and gives the muslin-wrapped cheeses only a light coating of lard. He told us of a novice employee who once slathered a fresh batch with something like thrice their usual amount of lard; that batch, Montgomery noted, 'tasted like a Keen's', likening what was for his farm and store an unusual flavour profile to the Cheddar made similarly but not identically (since 1899) by the Keen family at their Moorhayes Farm, also in Somerset.

Keen's Cheddar and Montgomery's Cheddar – these farmhouse cheeses have patronymics, signalling distinct lineages of familial resemblance reaching back and forward in time. In his narration as tour guide, Jamie Montgomery drew on an organismic model of cheese vitality – treating individual cheeses as organisms or beings – in describing the practical knowledge enacted in nurturing the development not of cheddar, but Montgomery's Cheddar. That work begins in the vat, with the acidification of milk, well before individual cheeses are formed from curd. Montgomery's Cheddar is inoculated with 'traditional pint starters', concentrations of bacteria that, in feeding on enzymes in milk, produce lactic acid as a by-product, thereby starting the fermentation process. Pint starters (while purchased commercially) are 'bulked up' in heated milk before being added to the vat. On the West Country Farmhouse Cheesemakers' website, the page devoted to Montgomery's elaborates as follows: 'The cultures used to create acidity…are difficult to handle and produce a wide variation in flavours, but they have lots of character.'[18] Standing before us in the cheese store (i.e. aging facility), Jamie explained that they rotate seven different starter culture cocktails, one for each day of the week, in order to prevent the unwanted development of bacteriophage, a virus that infects and replicates within bacterial hosts. While harmless to human health, phage thwarts fermentation and interrupts the development of a cheese's desired substance and form.

Thinking of these seven different strain mixtures, someone on the tour asked, 'Do different starters make better cheese?' 'Different starters make *different* cheese. And I celebrate that', Jamie replied. Just as Montgomery's and Keen's Cheddar represent distinct variants of the classificatory form known as cheddar, Montgomery's Cheddar, I came to realize, embodies a variety of qualities that nonetheless share a characteristic *form* associated with Montgomery's Cheddar. Jamie Montgomery and his team 'grade' the cheeses at three, six and ten months of age. Cheese grading entails pulling a core sample from the interior of a truckle, or wheel, and subjecting the sample to sensory analysis: the grader looks at, feels, smells and tastes the sample before plugging the small borehole with the bit of rind that was removed (moulds and bacteria grow over the cut, resealing the rind). As implied by the name, grading entails empirical evaluation and classification. Cheeses exhibiting different flavour profiles will be slotted into different markets, including (for Montgomery's) international ones (the American market was said to be partial to sweeter flavour profiles). In addition, as with wine, some cheeses are assessed as having the capacity to be 'aged out' longer than others. Sensory analysis is an important skill employed in cheesemaking's workmanship of risk. Jamie Montgomery knows his cheese – or rather, cheeses – meaning that he knows what range of flavours and odours to expect as characteristic of 'Montgomery's Cheddar'. Divergences from this range signal that something has 'gone off' and suggest the possibility of phage infection, a problem with the silage fed to the cows, or a technical error in production. Each of Jamie Montgomery's seven starter cultures, he told us, generates a distinct flavour profile. 'The seven [starters] are like I've got seven children', he said. 'As long as they are behaving according to character, I know I'm okay.' Conversely, he knows he has a problem if a batch starts mimicking the behaviour of one of the other children.

A cheesemaker in California described this skilled and embodied practice to me as having a 'house palate'. It can lead to developing a taste – meaning not only capacity for discernment but also preference – for one's own product 'because you're so familiar with it', a familiarity that is reinforced by the developmental metaphors personifying cheeses as organisms, even as children. Such language also reflects an artisanal understanding that cheeses have a 'life of their own', a life that must be carefully monitored and nurtured, but which is not – and, to Montgomery's mind, should not be – subjected to total human control. Montgomery celebrates the diversity of his cheese's character – such diversity of form is what David Pye named as the ongoing value of craftsmanship in an industrial age – but he also wants each of the seven strains to behave recognizably as 'itself', true to type. A Montgomery's

Cheddar, after all, should not more closely resemble a Keen's (which is by no means to disparage a Keen's!).

A principle challenge for the commercial artisan is to become sufficiently skilled in the workmanship of risk that she turns out batch after batch of cheese that may vary, but is nonetheless self-similar. Having a 'house palate' is essential to producing a recognizably consistent product. Typicity of form (colour, consistency and flavour) is well established by custom for British and European classics, and seasoned creameries such as Montgomery's have developed their own vernacular takes on those classics, which they strive continuously to replicate. But when it comes to the new American artisanal cheeses, there is no à point. There is no collective knowledge of ideal type for a cheese named and made – and introduced relatively recently – by a single artisan.

I spoke about this with Mateo Kehler during a visit to Jasper Hill Farm and Cellars, which he runs with his brother, Andy, in the remote region of Greensboro, Vermont. While touring their vast aging facilities, designed to be a regional centre of affinage (cheese-aging), we talked about the extensive growth in American artisanal cheesemaking over the last decade. Mateo shook his head at the thought of newcomers selling product when they 'don't even know their own cheese', as he said, meaning that they cannot define (or are uninterested in defining) typicity – a definitive aesthetic and flavour profile (typicality) for a cheese (type) they have created, named and launched on the market. Not all practicing cheesemakers, in other words, have developed a 'house palate', let alone learned how to use it as a tool in artisanal manufacture.

Mateo located his dissatisfaction with current trends in American artisanal cheesemaking in what he characterized as an overly 'artistic' approach. Drawing an analogy to a woodworker creating a table, Mateo argued that 'Cheesemaking is not an art, it's a craft'. If one leg of a table comes out shorter than the other three, he pointed out, that table is not celebrated as 'unique' – it is a problem. In the cheese world, Mateo sees 'the ability to celebrate or explain away the short leg' as indicative, in his words, of 'the immaturity of the industry'. In fact, he continued, artisanal cheese is not yet really an industry in this country; it's more of a social 'movement'. The Kehler brothers, serious about their business and its potential to revitalize the rural economy of Greensboro and beyond, describe themselves as working to achieve recognizable typicality in form towards establishing their cheeses as distinct types: as forms that have a recognized place in an established taxonomy – (supposedly) independent of context. Their goal is to establish cheeses in the world that will have a social life beyond the Kehler brothers and even Jasper Hill Farm. It is rather the inverse of Jamie Montomery's project. Whereas Montgomery works to distinguish a range of qualities that are recognizably typical as 'Montgomery's' rather than a more generic 'cheddar' type, the

Kehlers dream of a day when they can retire but yet watch their Bayley Hazen Blue or Winnimere live on as 'Vermont' cheese, no longer exclusively typical of Jasper Hill. However, as the professor of architecture Peter Carl notes, 'a type is far less determined by any intrinsic properties than by the mode of isolation that is the context for its use'.[19] The Kehlers' is an ambitious goal within a cultural context in which artisanal quality/qualities remain associated with the 'hand' and name of an individual artisan or farm/house, rather than a collective, regional patrimony.

Building, dwelling, aging

In 2013, Anne Topham retired from commercial cheesemaking (but not goat-keeping) at age seventy-three. She had been milking goats and making cheese for twenty-five years when I visited her Wisconsin homestead in 2007 and she told me the following story. A few years previous, when her ailing parents required her attention, Anne boarded her goats with a neighbour. Each morning she would drive over to say 'hi' and collect some milk, but the cheese she made that summer was atypical; to Anne's 'house palate', it suffered. It was not simply that her goats' milk was being mixed with the milk of her neighbours' goats (their flocks were already interbred and familiar to one another); what mattered was that Anne's goats were away from home. When she brought the animals home, the cheese improved – it became more itself. Anne explained:

> I always have thought it was because of having that close-tied relationship to the animals. I remember one Sunday afternoon, it was just really, really quiet, it was a beautiful day, and I was hand-ladling the cheese and I was feeling all of the goats in the room. It's like they're there every time I do the cheese. And I need that. I need that relationship. I make lots better cheese when I have that. I don't think you could measure the difference in the milk [as with seasonal changes between early and late-lactation milk; or as the composition of pasture flora change]. It's another kind of difference, it's about their [i.e., the goats'] life here.

The quality of Anne's life and the quality of her cheese are, in her estimation, mutually constitutive.

In 'Building, Dwelling, Living: How Animals and People Make Themselves at Home in the World', which is Tim Ingold's meditation on Heidegger's 'Building Dwelling Thinking', Ingold advances a 'new way of thinking about organisms and about their relations with their environments; in short, a new ecology' that he calls a 'dwelling perspective'.[20] To conclude this chapter, I would like to explore connections between Ingold's dwelling perspective, Pye's workmanship of risk and what I have called elsewhere an 'ecology of production'.[21]

Building on Heidegger, Ingold bases the dwelling perspective on the understanding 'that the forms people build, whether in the imagination or on the ground, arise within the current of their involved activity, in the specific relational contexts of their practical engagement with their surroundings'.[22] It is not so much that we as humans live in a built environment, but that the built environment lives in and through our ongoing activities – with 'us' encompassing not only human dwellers but also animal and plant denizens. Ingold takes inspiration from Jakob von Uexküll, who upheld the figure of an oak tree to example his theory that species can have different *Umwelten* – perceptions of their surroundings – even as these share ostensibly the same environment. While the fox seeks shelter beneath it, the tree provides 'support for the owl, … hunting-grounds for the ant', a resource of raw material for the logger and so on. Ingold invites us to imagine a house as Uexküll imagined the oak tree. The house, too, offers habitation for many organisms, some provided for (e.g. the litter box), while others, uninvited, 'find shelter and sustenance in its nooks and crannies, or even build there'. Regardless of welcome, all the inhabitants (mammals, rodents, insects), 'in their various ways, contribute to its evolving form, as do the house's human inhabitants in keeping it under repair, decorating it, or making structural alterations in response to their changing domestic circumstances'.[23] Houses, like trees, 'have life-histories, which consist in the unfolding of their relations with both human and non-human components of their environments'.[24]

So, too, do cheeses have life histories. If you order a wheel of Vermont Shepherd directly from Major Farm, your cheese will arrive packed in fresh straw with a card announcing notable conditions characterizing the farm on the date your cheese was 'born' in the vat. Perhaps it was a fine spring day when three lambs were also born, or on that day a late-summer thunderstorm darkened the sky. The 'birth' announcement speaks to how the particular life history of an individual cheese, a cheese spoken of by its maker in personified, developmental terms, unfolds through formative relations with humans, pastures, ruminant livestock and microorganisms, both ambient and introduced. Not unlike Uexküll's tree and Ingold's house, Major's cheese materializes organic, social and symbolic forces that he and his collaborators nudge into productive assemblage to generate not only an agricultural product but also a form of life, for himself, his family and his few employees, 'that seeks to work with the agencies of the natural world in a way that revitalizes rather than depletes those forces'.[25]

Artisanal cheeses both embody and propagate 'ecologies of production'. The word *ecology*, derived by Ernst Haeckel in 1869 from the ancient Greek *oikos*, meaning 'house' or 'home', may be viewed as the study of the 'home life' of living organisms. If we view cheese as a dwelling place for microorganisms, as a landscape 'constituted as an enduring record of – and testimony to – the lives and works of past generations who have dwelt within it, and in so doing, have left there something of themselves',[26] that microbial dwelling unfolds within a set of broader and more diverse ecologies. There is first the cheese house and aging facility (whether cave, store, or basement room) in which humans dwell alongside collaborating microorganisms and, often as not, uninvited residents: cheese mites and the stray fly. It is here that the cheesemakers, no less than the microorganisms, work and live and build. Far from being rural isolates, working farms are connected to urban markets and are embedded in county, state and national polities. In suggesting that farmstead cheese – cheese made artisanally on a dairy farm – emerges from an ecology of production, I mean to call attention both to the multispecies activities and agencies that contribute to the substance and form of a cheese and also to how that generative ecology is made possible, organized and constrained by broader forces of market capitalism and government regulation.[27]

Ingold writes, 'it is in the very process of dwelling that we build'.[28] On farms such as David Major's, Jamie Montgomery's or Anne Topham's, the substance and the form of cheese emerge through the dwelling of microorganisms but also within and through the cheesemaker's process of dwelling, of making a life and a living from making cheese. How do cheesemakers decide what types of cheese to make and what forms to aim for? They follow a recipe given by a friend, they adapt favourite European recipes to fit the equipment at hand and local regulatory limitations and they investigate market niches to fill. If they sell much of their cheese at local farmers' markets, they will work to diversify their offerings (customers buy more when they have options from which to choose) and they may produce a fresh cheese (e.g. chèvre or ricotta) to provide a quick source of cash flow while they await aged cheeses to become ready to take to market. If they do not care for the task of spending hours on their feet chatting with potential or repeat customers, or would prefer to spend their Saturday mornings in the company of livestock or at their kids' soccer matches, then a cheesemaker might instead work to sell cheese through a distributer or directly to a retail chain. If this is the case, then consistency rather than variety will be a primary guide. Form and substance are not simply technical criteria, but take shape in and through the dwelling of the cheesemaker that constitutes his or her own home life.

Ingold's 'dwelling perspective' adds a new dimension to Pye's characterization of craftsmanship in terms of a 'workmanship of risk'. For Pye, what is at stake in the workmanship of risk is the quality of the result – the substance and form of an artisanal product as evaluated within particular markets and (in the case of a food product) regulatory guidelines for safety. But if we think of craftsmanship as unfolding within ecologies of production, as an element of generative dwelling, then we can recognize how, for producers, at risk, too, is the quality and character of their lives as artisans.

By bringing a dwelling perspective to bear on the workmanship of risk, we can recognize that one of the qualities at stake in craftsmanship is quality of life for the craftsperson. The question of scale, of how big is big enough to grow a business to make artisan enterprise financially viable, carries this risk: the risk of getting too big. Getting 'too big' can mean having to hire employees to do what jobs can be taught and delegated, but 'once you start hiring people', as a Vermont cheesemaker said to me, 'you move away from the actual work itself' – the hands-on, sensory work that draws many into artisan enterprise in the first place – 'and become more of an administer'. Getting 'too big' in a farm-based business can also mean disrupting one's dwelling place: 'if it puts distance or borders between you and your children and your partner, your wife or husband', another cheesemaker commented, 'then what's the point?' In working towards achieving consistently desired forms, artisans – those who craft for a living – remain mindful that the productive outcome of their craft labour is made manifest not only in the craft objects they produce but also in the quality and character of their daily lives and relationships, their dwelling.

Notes

1   D. Pye, *The Nature and Art of Workmanship* (London: Studio Vista, 1968), 7.

2   P. Kindstedt, *American Farmstead Cheese: The Complete Guide to Making and Selling Artisan Cheeses* (White River Junction, VT: Chelsea Green, 2005).

3   Pye, *The Nature and Art of Workmanship*, 9.

4   Ibid., 13.

5   H. Becker, 'Arts and Crafts', *American Journal of Sociology* 83.4 (1978): 862–889.

6   J. Tuomey, *Architecture, Craft and Culture: Reflections on the Work of O'Donnell + Toumey* (Oysterhaven, Ireland: Gandon Editions, 2004), 11.

7   H. Paxon, 'The "Art" and "Science" of Handcrafting Cheese in the United States', *Endeavour* 35.2–3 (2011): 116–124.

8   S. Ott, *The Circle of Mountains: A Basque Shepherding Community* (Reno, NV: University of Nevada Press, 1981); H. West and N. Domingos, 'Gourmandizing Poverty Food: The Serpa Cheese Slow Food Presidium', *Journal of Agrarian Change* 12.1 (2012): 120–143.

9   Kindstedt, *American Farmstead Cheese*, 37–38.

10 T. Ingold, *The Perception of the Environment: Essays in Livelihood, Dwelling and Skill* (New York: Routledge, 2000), 357.

11 Paxon, 'The "Art" and "Science" of Handcrafting Cheese'. *Endeavour* 35.2–3 (2011): 116–124.

12 M. Csikszentmihalyi, *Flow: The Psychology of Optimal Experience* (New York: Harper and Row, 1990).

13 N. Farrar and G. Trorey, 'Maxims, Tacit Knowledge and Learning: Developing Expertise in Dry Stone Walling', *Journal of Vocational Education and Training* 60:1 (2008): 35–48, 44.

14 M. Polanyi, *Personal Knowledge: Towards a Post-Critical Philosophy* (Chicago: University of Chicago Press, 1958); H. Collins, 'Tacit Knowledge, Trust and the Q of Sapphire', *Social Studies of Science* 31.1 (2001): 71–85.

15 S. Schaffer, 'Glass Works: Newton's Prisms and the Uses of Experiment', in *The Uses of Experiment*, eds. D. Gooding, T. Pinch, and S. Schaffer (Cambridge: Cambridge University Press, 1989); F. Nutch, 'Gadgets, Gizmos, and Instruments: Science for the Tinkering', *Science, Technology & Human Values* 21.2 (1996): 214–228.

16 P. Dixon, 'The Art of Cheesemaking', in *American Farmstead Cheese: The Complete Guide to Making and Selling Artisan Cheeses,* ed. P. Kindstedt (White River Junction, VT: Chelsea Green, 2005), 198.

17 A. Trubek, *The Taste of Place: A Cultural Journey into Terroir* (Berkeley, CA: University of California Press, 2008); M. Demossier, 'Beyond *Terroir*: Territorial Construction, Hegemonic Discourses, and French Wine Culture', *Journal of the Royal Anthropological Institute* 17 (2011): 685–705.

18 http://www.farmhousecheesemakers.com/cheesemakers/montgomery_s _cheddar/, accessed 28 March 2013.

19 P. Carl, 'Type, Field, Culture, Praxis', *Architectural Design* 81.1 (2011): 38–45, 43.

20 Ingold, *The Perception of the Environment*, 173.

21 *Life of Cheese*, chapter 2.

22 Ingold, *The Perception of the Environment*, 186.

23 Ibid., 187.

24 Ibid.

25 Paxson, *The Life of Cheese*, 31–32.

26 Ingold, *The Perception of the Environment*, 188.

27 Paxson, *The Life of Cheese*, 32.

28 Ibid., 188.

Bibliography

Becker, H. 'Arts and Crafts'. *American Journal of Sociology* 83, no. 4 (1978): 862–89.

Carl, P. 'Type, Field, Culture, Praxis'. *Architectural Design* 81, no. 1 (2011): 38–45.

Collins, H. 'Tacit Knowledge, Trust and the Q of Sapphire'. *Social Studies of Science* 31, no. 1 (2001): 71–85.

Csikszentmihalyi, M., *Flow: The Psychology of Optimal Experience*. New York: Harper and Row, 1990.

Demossier, M. 'Beyond *Terroir*: Territorial Construction, Hegemonic Discourses, and French Wine Culture'. *Journal of the Royal Anthropological Institute*, 17 (2011): 685–705.

Dixon, P. 'The Art of Cheesemaking.' In *American Farmstead Cheese: The Complete Guide to Making and Selling Artisan Cheeses*, edited by P. Kindstedt. White River Junction, VT: Chelsea Green, 2005.

Farrar, N. and G. Trorey 'Maxims, Tacit Knowledge and Learning: Developing Expertise in Dry Stone Walling'. *Journal of Vocational Education and Training* 69.1 (2008): 35–48.

Ingold, T. *The Perception of the Environment: Essays in Livelihood, Dwelling and Skill*. New York: Routledge, 2000.

Kindstedt, P. *American Farmstead Cheese: The Complete Guide to Making and Selling Artisan Cheeses*. White River Junction, VT: Chelsea Green, 1995.

Nutch, F. 'Gadgets, Gizmos, and Instruments: Science for the Tinkering'. *Science, Technology & Human Values* 21, no. 2 (1996) 214–28.

Ott, S. *The Circle of Mountains: A Basque Shepherding Community*. Reno, NV: University of Nevada Press, 1981.

Paxson, H. *The Life of Cheese: Crafting Food and Value in America*. Berkeley, CA: University of California Press, 2013.

Polanyi, M. *Personal Knowledge: Towards a Post-Critical Philosophy*, Chicago: University of Chicago Press, 1958.

Pye, D. *The Nature and Art of Workmanship*. London: Studio Vista, 1968.

Schaffer, S. 'Glass Works: Newton's Prisms and the Uses of Experiment'. In *The Uses of Experiment*, edited by D. Gooding, T. Pinch, and S. Schaffer. Cambridge: Cambridge University Press, 1989.

Trubek, A. *The Taste of Place: A Cultural Journey into Terroir*. Berkeley, CA: University of California Press, 2008.

Tuomey, J. *Architecture, Craft and Culture: Reflections on the Work of O'Donnell + Toumey*. Oysterhaven, Ireland: Gandon Editions, 2004.

West, H. and N. Domingos. 'Gourmandizing Poverty Food: The Serpa Cheese Slow Food Presidium'. *Journal of Agrarian Change* 12.1 (2012): 120–43.

PART FOUR

Authenticity

Commentary for Part Four: Authenticity

Variations on a Theme

Samantha L. Martin-McAuliffe

In a profile article from *The New Yorker* in late 2012, Jane Kramer gives an account of a communal dinner at the home of Yotam Ottolenghi in London. The main course, a take on a central Asian dish called *plov*, is described as a 'one-pot Sephardic-hybrid'.[1] *Plov* is often cited as a cornerstone of Bukharian Jewish cuisine, and like many dishes that evolved along the Silk Road, it embraces and is inflected by the foodstuffs of multiple cultures and communities.[2] Essentially a slow-cooked rice meal, *plov* typically contains meat (lamb, chicken or beef) in addition to carrots, onions, cumin and currants. Yet there is no canon of ingredients, no definitive – much less original – recipe. During the nineteenth and twentieth centuries, waves of Bukharian Jews emigrated from Central Asia, taking with them their culinary traditions and adapting them to new contexts and climes. The vast majority ended up in the United States and Israel.

Ottolenghi could be described as a kind of Silk Road incarnate: born in Israel to parents of Italian and German descent, he spent a year in the Bay Area during his youth and then a longer spell in Amsterdam as a graduate student before enrolling at the London campus of Le Cordon Bleu. London remains his principal home, although anyone who has eaten at Ottolenghi's eponymous deli-cafés will understand without reservation that he is rooted in the eastern Mediterranean. His food is culturally elastic, drawing together not just ingredients but also recipes and techniques in an imaginative yet meaningful way. In explaining to Kramer how *plov* made its way to Jerusalem, Ottolenghi stressed the resourcefulness of the Bukharian Jews in the city:

> You have to remember that, for Jews, Jerusalem was never an affluent town ... It was different for Palestinians. The Arab middle class was affluent.

But for most Jews it was a poor immigrant town. They cooked with what they had. There is no one recipe. In fact, we never replicate recipes. We replicate the *idea* of a dish [emphasis in original]. We replicated the idea of *plov*.[3]

Thus, instead of attempting to resurrect a 'pure' recipe, Ottolenghi's approach to food entails respectful and informed adaptation. It is a form of cookery mediated by a genuine sense of engagement with people and place. Although it can be challenging, both in terms of its ingredients and methods, the food is also assuredly experiential rather than forced or sanctimonious. Put a different way, the dishes developed by Ottolenghi and his staff in London have become the mainspring their own distinctive, authentic cuisine.

'Authenticity' is one of the most controversial terms in food studies and architecture in the present day. Bandied about within academia, practice and the media in equal measure, the concept typically aligns with the topics of tradition, heritage and originality. When an object or thing – be it a cooking ingredient or building material, an edible dish or architectural structure – claims historical continuity, it is often interpreted as a legitimate and veritable example of a given type. Yet, supporting each isolated and preserved type there are, as Kimberly Dovey has argued elsewhere, a whole spectrum of processes and relationships which are often overlooked – intangible qualities that are ultimately paramount to formal appearance.[4] As such, all the contributions in this final part of *Food and Architecture* broaden the dialogue on authenticity by assessing its underlying conditions. In doing so, they help illuminate the reasons why this concept retains such a persistent foothold in both professional and academic debates.

This section opens with Tom Hudgen's contribution (Chapter 12), 'The Possibility of an Authentic American Cuisine: Catherine's Corn Pasta.' In questioning whether it possible to achieve a form of authenticity that is independent of both ethnic and geographical provenance, this chapter calls attention to the easy fluidity of American cuisine. Hudgens, a chef and cookery-writer, walks us through the execution of a single dish – an amalgamation of fresh Californian produce, Italian components, Mexican technique and French nuance – which he helped create while working at Chez Panisse in Berkeley. In a matter-of-fact fashion, and without a hint of irony, he describes the resulting dish as both 'fusion' and 'Californian', two terms that habitually draw scorn and provoke the ire of cooks and critics alike. Felipe Fernández-Armesto, in his volume *Near a Thousand Tables*, is forthright in his criticism of such culinary genres: 'Fusion food is Lego cookery.'[5] Notwithstanding the miscalculated degradation of Lego, Fernández-Armesto's argument is understandable insofar as it rebukes the practice of haphazardly assembling food from cheap and ready-made components. Yet while he cites the wide variety and availability of ingredients as harbingers of despoiled cuisine, Hudgens arrives at an altogether different perspective. For him, a diversity of ingredients that reflects seasonality and respects locality can produce innovative, not to mention delicious, food. Both writers arguably represent different sides of the same proverbial coin. Moreover, for Hudgens, the corn pasta experiment is authentically American – a dish deeply connected to its place and time. Quoting David Chang, the chef-proprietor of *Momofuku*, Hudgens describes this approach to cooking as 'reaching past tradition'. It stands on the shoulders of venerable culinary practices but does not champion a single custom or provenance. It cannot be overstated that this kind of authenticity is not based within a set of ingredients or the appearance of a dish. It is rather about the experience of creating the dish and the relationship it holds with a particular place.

When authenticity is discussed within the context of food, other factors often arise with regard to its setting, such as utensils and tableware. In restaurants, cafés and pubs, the aim for authenticity may extend beyond the table to the décor, interior design and even sometimes the architecture of the venue itself. This kind of 'staged authenticity' is well documented, both within food studies and architecture.[6] Ethnic restaurants frequently create a romanticized version of a particular culture for local culinary tourists. Indeed some iterations of this practice are now commonplace to the point of being hackneyed: for instance, diners have come to expect Thai restaurants to display photographs of the Thai royal family, or decorative objects associated with Thai culture, such as painted wood carvings and ornamental fans;[7] likewise, vermillion-coloured walls and lacquer-style furniture remain the presumed décor of Chinese restaurants, regardless of geographical location.[8] Increasingly common in the global tourism market is the carefully constructed restaurant that idealizes an indigenous culture and repackages it as a multisensory authentic experience solely for visiting foreigners.[9] At the other end of this spectrum are the phenomena of 'post-tourism' (a canny appreciation of the inauthentic) and 'rootless cosmopolitanism', a term which has been redeployed to describe the premium yet standardized aesthetic of global coffee chains.[10] Weaving through these different strands of authenticity is Henriette Steiner's chapter (Chapter 13) 'Café Chairs, Bar Stools and Other Chairs We Sit on When We Eat: Food Consumption and Everyday Urban Life'. Taking an innocuous dining chair as a point of departure, this contribution calls attention to the (often-overlooked) supporting or background materials that characterize and typify where and how we eat. It ultimately evaluates the assumptions that predicate the understanding and interpretation of authenticity, framing it as a condition of Modernism.

While the term 'authenticity' itself suggests sensitivity to certain principles, standards and customs, what happens when these are manipulated at the expense of others or deployed for political or economic gain? In the final chapter of this section of *Food and Architecture*, Ruth Lo investigates how a single, typical foodstuff – the grape – was used to affirm authenticity during the fascist regime in Italy. Her contribution (Chapter 14), 'Celebrating the *Festa dell'Uva*: Invented Traditions, Popular Culture and Urban Spectacle in Fascist Rome', chronicles a most unusual and elaborate food festival, an event which brought together food and architecture on an extraordinary scale. Although it explicitly referenced Italy's august heritage, both in terms of agriculture and the built environment, the annual Festival of the Grape was ultimately an exercise in staged authenticity by the twentieth-century regime. Reappropriating history and tradition for political advantage is nothing new, but it is rare that an entire city is given over – *dressed* – as a stage for the display of comestibles. Some of the most striking and memorable descriptions in Lo's chapter concern the festival's exploitation of Rome's street system and major historic monuments. Extravagant floats festooned with grapes and inscribed with fascist symbols paraded through the city, linking major avenues with key sites such as the Vatican, Villa Borghese, Trajan's Markets. By self-consciously harvesting and reinventing earlier culture, the festival amplified the complexities inherent to 'authenticity'. In short, it exposed the term as a moving target.

Notes

1   Jane Kramer, 'The Philosopher Chef', *The New Yorker*, 88.38 (December 2012), 86ff.

2   For an excellent overview of Bukharian Jewish cuisine, see Claudia Roden, *The Book of Jewish Food: An Odyssey from Samarkand and Vilna to the Present Day* (London: Penguin, 1999), 389–409.

3   Kramer, 'The Philosopher Chef', 96.

4   Kimberly Dovey, 'The Quest for Authenticity and the Replication of Environmental Meaning', in *Dwelling, Place and Environment: Towards a Phenomenology of Person and World*, eds. David Seamon and Robert Mugerauer (New York: Columbia University Press, 1985), 33–49.

5   Felipe Fernández-Armesto, *Near a Thousand Tables: A History of Food* (New York: Free Press 2002), 222.

6   The term 'staged authenticity' is largely attributed to Dean MacCannell, in particular his article 'Staged Authenticity: Arrangements of Social Space in Tourist Settings', *American Journal of Sociology* 79 (1973): 589–603. It is worthwhile noting that MacCannell has more recently updated and expanded his appraisal of authenticity, specifically within the context of contemporary architecture and urbanism. For this, see MacCannell, 'Staged Authenticity Today' in *Indefensible Space: The Architecture of the National Insecurity State*, ed. Michael Sorkin (New York: Routledge, 2008), 259–276.

7 Jennie Germann Molz, 'Tasting an Imagined Thailand: Authenticity and Culinary Tourism in Thai Restaurants', in *Culinary Tourism*, ed. Lucy M. Long (Lexington, Kentucky: University Press of Kentucky), 53–75, especially pp. 58–61.

8 Rafi Grosglik and Uri Ram, 'Authentic, Speedy and Hybrid: Representations of Chinese Food and Cultural Globalization in Israel', *Food, Culture and Society* 16 (2013): 223–243, especially pp. 227–229.

9 A quintessential example of this is the well-known and highly respected Bumbu Bali restaurant, which is located in the tourist enclave of Nusa Dua, Bali, Indonesia. The restaurant bills itself as the first and only authentic Balinese restaurant on the island. Its spatial setting, which is modelled after a traditional Balinese village, is an essential part of the dining experience: teak tables are spread across a tropical, open-air courtyard that is romantically lit and decorated with Indonesian textiles; a temple adorns one side. Balinese dancers, accompanied by musicians, provide live entertainment for diners. Ironically, the restaurant was founded by a Swiss chef, Heinz von Holen (www.balifoods.com).

10 Benjamin Aldes Wurgaft, 'Starbucks and Rootless Cosmopolitanism', *Gastronomica: The Journal of Food and Culture* 3 (2003): 71–75.

12

The Possibility of an Authentic American Cuisine: Catherine's Corn Pasta

Tom Hudgens

The process

Peel about ten heads of garlic, cut each clove in half and pry out the bitter little green sprout. You must not smash the cloves of garlic, or they will oxidize and taste old. Cover and place in the walk-in. Now make pasta: measure six pounds of all-purpose flour into a large mixer bowl. Crack about thirty brown eggs into a pitcher, whisk in a generous half-cup each of water and olive oil and carefully pour the egg into the flour with the mixer running at its lowest speed, just until the mixture coheres. You must not add too much egg, or the noodles will be flabby. You must not overmix the dough, or it will be harder to roll out later, and the noodles will be tough. Turn the dough out onto the wooden counter and knead briefly to uniformity. Divide into grapefruit-sized balls, wrap tightly with plastic and flatten the balls into thick disks. Let the dough rest at room temperature while you go to the upstairs kitchen to wash and spin all the lettuce and greens for the day's salads. After lunch, haul out the pasta machine and begin the long process of rolling the balls of dough into successively thinner sheets, cooking a sample batch of noodles for the chef's approval, then sending the sheets through the cutting rollers, dusting the noodles with rice flour to prevent sticking, trimming to serving length with a bench knife, arranging them in a layer that is not too thick on parchment-lined sheet pans, covering with cotton kitchen towels and placing on a rack in the walk-in refrigerator. In the hour remaining, ask the chef for a prep task, for example, shucking and cutting a case of sweet corn. Working rapidly, shuck all forty-eight ears of corn, wiping each with a damp cloth to remove the silk and neatly cutting the kernels from each cob with your knife. You must not cut too deeply, or the kernels will be tough; nor too shallowly, or too much is wasted. Scrape out all remaining juice and germ from each cob with the back of your knife. Transfer the corn to containers, label, place in walk-in, compost all waste, recycle the box, clean up your area and go home.

That, essentially, was the job I was lucky to have at Alice Waters' celebrated restaurant Chez Panisse, in Berkeley, California, over twenty years ago, when my passion for cooking was as fresh as my liberal-arts degree. Even from my lowly status among the kitchen's cooking team, I was able to observe, wide-eyed with wonder, the daily creative process of determining the menu for the upstairs café. (Chez Panisse comprises two restaurants: a more formal, prix-fixe, set dinner menu is served downstairs, and a more casual, à-la-carte lunch and dinner menu is served upstairs.) The café chef wrote the menu each morning based on a long list of all available ingredients that I or a fellow-underling compiled. Mid-morning, the chef and prep cooks (including, democratically, me) sat around a table to go over the menu, sometimes in great detail. What dishes to serve depended on the given circumstances of the day and took into account not only the available ingredients but also the season. Even the weather was considered – what dishes are most appealing on a cold, blustery evening or on a brilliant, hot, late-summer afternoon? How best to realize those dishes? Those questions were at the root of almost every kitchen conversation, and for all of us passionate about the craft of cooking, those conversations continue today.

From me, the pasta-maker, the chefs sometimes requested fettuccine, sometimes delicate linguine. On some days, I would roll the sheets extra-thin for ravioli, and the entire team gathered to assemble them; on other days, I would get out a pizza cutter and make wide hand-cut pappardelle noodles. We might put a bit of finely chopped rosemary in the dough for noodles destined to be tossed with sautéed chanterelles, black pepper in pappardelle served with lamb stew (you had to grind the pepper and sieve it into three different grinds and use only the middle grind for the pasta; otherwise the noodles turn out grey), or lemon zest and parsley in linguine for clams or crab. Often, Catherine Brandel, a beloved café chef, would challenge me and request *palia i fieno* – green and plain fettuccine, tossed and cooked together. Green pasta dough, containing pureed spinach, is moister than regular pasta dough. For successful *palia i fieno*, the two types of noodles must cook at the same rate, and so must be rolled to different, but very precise, thicknesses: a technical challenge. Once, having saved the inky liquid left in the pan from roasting beets, we used it to make bright pink fettuccine. Sometimes we would use buckwheat flour in place of some of the regular flour; these fine noodles would often be tossed with sautéed nettles and strewn with walnuts and *ricotta salata*. And occasionally in the summer, we would include some wholewheat flour in the dough. One morning, Catherine requested wholewheat noodles, so I dusted off a small electric grain mill I had found in a storage area, and used it to grind wheat berries into the freshest possible flour. I used this for about 20 per cent of the dough's flour. The resulting noodles were still supple, silky and delicate, but they were intriguingly flecked with bran, and had a deeper flavour, with a whisper of wholewheat's characteristic bittersweetness, excellent for balancing the sweetness of summer vegetables. These noodles were to be tossed with a sauté of sweet summer corn cut off the cob, red onion, tiny dice of summer squash, minced hot green chillies and cilantro. Catherine liked referring to fresh cilantro as 'coriander' on the menu, echoing the French usage. The pasta was finished with a good spoonful of butter, and topped with crème fraiche. Here is how it appeared on the menu:

Wholewheat fettuccine with sweet corn, summer squash, coriander, and crème fraiche

Among the myriad pasta dishes served there during that time, this one, a Mexican sauté of vegetables (essentially, the dish known as *calabacitas*) atop Italian noodles, has haunted me for years. Chez Panisse's cooking has always been inspired chiefly by French and Italian culinary traditions, yet the kitchen has also long explored many other ethnicities – Latin American, Spanish, Russian, Indian and American Southern – always with the aim of authenticity. A plate of curried lamb would invariably include basmati rice and a yogurt raita. If there was to be couscous, it always came with harissa sauce. Once, the downstairs chefs cooked a Mexican menu I still remember: orange and jicama salad, duck mole with tortillas and caramel flan for dessert. They hired a skilled Mexican woman to come in and pat out corn tortillas all night and cook them on a *comal* in the fireplace. They even festooned the front captain's table with colourful Mexican oilcloths. Dishes were seen to have a provenance, almost a history, that was best kept clear and distinct. Rarely was that provenance blurred or blended, but it was those blurred, blended moments that fascinated me most, such as Catherine's wholewheat pasta with corn and chillies. The more 'authentic' menu offerings seemed to hearken to a specific other place (such as the southern French countryside), and even to an earlier time, when all food was grown and made by hand. If a dish was worthwhile, so the thinking went, its ingredients and techniques must be firmly rooted in long-standing tradition. By that strict logic, cooks in the United States, still a relatively young country, lacking established, long-standing culinary traditions of our own, must look to other places that have such traditions, and emulate them closely, even reverently.

The currents of influence

For much of the past century, Americans looked to France and served French food when they wanted to be 'fancy'. Gradually, the focus shifted to Italy; increasingly 'authentic' Italian restaurants opened throughout the 1980s and 1990s, and still figure prominently in the US fine-dining world.[1] Chez Panisse itself reflects that shift: it began as a much more distinctly French restaurant than it would ultimately become. Alice Waters opened the restaurant in 1972, flush with inspiration from her experiences in France. Her chefs helped continually define the mission of the place. Jeremiah Tower pioneered the restaurant's emphasis on California regional cooking, and Paul Bertolli embodied the United States' gravitation towards, and increasingly sophisticated knowledge of, the cuisines of Italy. So how does Catherine's dish of noodles with chillies and corn fit in? Traditional Mexican cuisine does not include noodles like that, and sweet corn is not traditionally served in Italy. Chez Panisse cooks of that era never dared to utter the word 'fusion', and many even scoffed at the designation 'California', so badly bandied about it had become. The more culinarily conservative members of the kitchen crew might have called dishes such as Catherine's corn pasta 'a mishmash of flavours willy-nilly on a plate'. But set it down in front of them (or a favourite café variation with corn, garlic, thyme and chanterelles), and how could they resist? In that creative midst, given the ingredients on hand and the circumstances of the day, sometimes innovative dishes such as Catherine's corn pasta – most definitely fusion, most assuredly California – naturally, and deliciously, arise. A dish such as wheat-flecked delicate noodles tossed with fresh sautéed corn speaks, I think, not of any far-off land or long-lost time, but of where I live, here and now. This dish is, in a simple sense, true American food.

Catherine attributed the dish to Diana Kennedy, the renowned Britain-born authority on Mexican cuisine, and would sometimes call it 'Diana Kennedy's whole wheat fettuccine' on the menu. In Kennedy's most personal cookbook, *Nothing Fancy*, she includes a recipe for *Tallarines a la Mexicana* – simply white onion, roasted poblano chillies and corn kernels, sautéed in butter and tossed with wholewheat taglierini. She writes:

I like to 'mix-and-match' my cuisines and often use, for instance, Mexican vegetables with Italian pasta. Last year, when friends arrived unexpectedly, they were surprised to be eating wholewheat tagliarini (*tallarines*) with

FIGURE 12.1 *Catherine's Corn Pasta. Illustration by author.*

brilliant blue mushrooms and yellow corn. A fascinating combination is linguine with chopped *cuitlacoche* (corn fungus) and chilli strips. I quite often julienne zucchini, chayote, or fennel root, or blend the dark-green *chilaca* (substitute *poblano* in the United States) with thick cream and serve that along with a *picante* tomato sauce over the pasta. Anything goes so long as we don't call it authentic.[2]

The core of Kennedy's life work, her books on Mexican cuisine including *The Cuisines of Mexico* and *Recipes from the Regional Cooks of Mexico*, are painstakingly researched, towering monuments to culinary authenticity.[3] With scholarly, ethnographic rigour, she has documented thousands of Mexican recipes from all parts of the country; named and described the cooks that taught her the recipes; and offered thorough, intelligent advice on tracking down then-exotic ingredients such as cilantro, tomatillos and whole chillies. That those ingredients are ubiquitous in American supermarkets today, coast to coast, speaks, perhaps, to Kennedy's influence, or at the very least, to her foresight. Judging by those books, one might never suspect that any 'mixing-and-matching of cuisines' takes place in her kitchen. And yet, there it is: Italian pasta with Mexican corn. *Anything goes so long as we don't call it authentic.*

David Tanis, along with Catherine Brandel, was one of my era's Chez Panisse Café chefs, and fellow cooks from that time associate the pasta-and-corn dish with him. No such dish appears in the wonderfully improvisatory *Chez Panisse Pasta, Pizza and Calzone*.[4] David spent a few years in Santa Fe, New Mexico, incorporating the deeply rooted, serious cooking there into his Mediterranean repertoire. He authored *Corn: A Country Garden Cookbook*, in which the very last recipe is 'Fettuccine with Corn, Squash and Squash Blossoms'.[5] He sautés onions, garlic and thyme in olive oil, and the pasta is finished with butter, lemon juice, basil, parsley and chives – a very southern French-northern Italian treatment of purely American corn. David likely served this version in the Chez Panisse Café, and thereby brought it into the repertoire. In his cookbook *A Platter of Figs*, he offers this account of his thought process in creating a menu:

> You are probably not surprised to learn that I am not a fan of fusion. They can keep their wasabi aioli, thank you very much. But though my training and inclination usually push me in a European – or at least a Mediterranean – direction, there's a dim sum-eating, noodle soup-slurping part of me too. [...] In both cities where I live – San Francisco and Paris – robust Asian communities have seductive markets offering such enticing ingredients it's impossible for a curious cook to remain stubbornly, foolishly Western. [...] Recently I was at the market, prowling for dinner as usual. I thought I wanted to make a spring duck stew, had nearly decided on a ducky variation of a spring lamb navarin, and had just bought some duck legs, when I noticed little bunches of sweet young turnips with their bright green tops smiling up at me. Duck with turnips is a traditional combination in classic French cooking. Nothing wrong with that. But suddenly the notion of duck and turnips turned Asian on me. I am a great fan of Chinese-style roast duck, and also of those heavily griddled turnip cakes served in dim sum

parlors. So I changed gears, went with the new idea, and bought some fresh ginger. The result was a French-style braise with Chinese flavors. It might sound like fusion or new-wave cooking to you, but the result is extremely subtle, and it doesn't overpower a good bottle of red wine.[6]

Essentially, he is saying that, for cooks who pay close attention to both our own hunger and cravings, as well as to today's world of previously disparate culinary influences right at our fingertips, 'fusion' food sometimes naturally and deliciously arises.

The dish of corn and pasta still echoes today. Judy Rogers, the exacting chef of San Francisco's Zuni Café, influenced by Chez Panisse in many ways, includes a recipe for 'Pasta with Corn, Pancetta, Butter, & Sage' in her compendium *The Zuni Café Cookbook*.[7] Michael Tusk, who cooked at Chez Panisse in my era, now chef-owner of the two-Michelin-starred San Francisco restaurant Quince as well as the more casual California-Italian eatery Cotogna next door, frequently often offers a corn-and-pasta combination on Cotogna's summer menus.

Other chefs address issues surrounding culinary authenticity in different ways. Russell Moore, originally hired by David Tanis to cook at Chez Panisse in the mid-1980s, is now chef-owner of the Oakland restaurant Camino, where he cooks almost everything with live fire, mostly in an enormous stone fireplace containing multiple grills. There is also a wood-burning oven, but significantly, he does not serve pizza, nor pasta of any kind, on his short, daily changing, seasonal menu – a firm statement of 'provenance' in our era where American fine dining is dominated by Italian restaurants. Often, a Camino entrée includes two or more cuts of meat, each fire-cooked in a contrasting way – a few pink slices of grilled lamb leg, for instance, alongside a tender chunk of lamb shoulder slow-cooked in the wood oven. There are French, Italian, Spanish, Middle Eastern and Indian influences all over his menus, but the dishes rarely possess any discernible ethnic 'stamp'. He uses Japanese rice for his signature paella. For the overarching descriptor of his restaurant, Moore has unapologetically taken up the designation 'California cuisine' – by working to define it on a daily basis, he has refurbished it and given it new respect. Given the ingredients he has on hand each day, as he sits down to compose the evening's menu, certain combinations become obvious. He makes a practice of discarding those obvious ideas in favour of something not yet tried. The results can be stunning: at Camino I once had a dish of wood-oven-roasted chanterelles with sheepsmilk ricotta, nettles and mint. Each bite revealed new levels of flavour. The nettles were cooked, cooled and dressed with a vinaigrette, enhancing their deep greenness; the mushrooms were brushed with an infused oil; the cheese was pristine; the mint subtle but present. It all balanced, every component enhancing the others. It did not bring to mind another place or time; rather, it somehow brought the present moment into sharper focus. It was absolutely authentic – to itself, to that place and that time where I was.

Beginning barely a decade ago, a very different chef, David Chang, began what has become a culinary empire, the Momofuku restaurants of New York (now with outposts in Toronto and Sydney), that among many other things could be described as a subversion of the paradigm of authenticity. Born to Korean parents in Virginia, he grew up in the American South, trained in ramen shops in Japan and developed a great love for the Chinese restaurants of New York. All these influences are brought together and discernible in his food, in a way that makes absolute gustatory sense: many of his dishes taste like classic, comfort-food recipes that were made by, well, your Korean-American-Southern-Japanese-Chinese grandmother, had she existed. In Chang's cookbook *Momofuku*, written with Peter Meehan, there is a long introduction to the recipe for 'Shrimp & Grits', which shows his thought process about authenticity:

I imagined what it would be like if my ancestors had ended up in Charleston, South Carolina, a few generations before I was born. They would have eaten corn, they would have eaten grits, they would have cooked with bacon. Or, if Southerners were magically transported to Korea, they'd eat jook instead of grits at breakfast. And you know a people who can handle the salty power of a country ham certainly could have gotten down with kimchi. I imagined a Japanese cook making grits – you know he'd boil it in dashi and season it with soy. I guess these were all conversations I was having with myself. I didn't want to be cooking shitty fusion food. I consoled myself by thinking about how Vietnamese cuisine and Cajun cooking adapted French techniques into something that might have looked French but tasted totally different. But it was this dish that I decided – or accepted – that if we reached past 'tradition' to create the truest and best version of a dish for our own palates, then what we were doing wasn't bullshit. Momofuku was going pretty strong at this point, but this is the dish that allowed us – or me, certainly – to really look outward and onward.[8]

The recipe is simple: grits cooked with dashi, bacon, soy sauce and butter; shrimp seasoned only with salt and very simply pan-cooked; a slow-cooked egg; little piles of chopped crisp bacon and sliced scallions. The complexity of the dish resides in the grits; the shrimp, bacon, egg and scallions are left absolutely simple and unadorned: it is balanced, delicious and comforting, much 'cleaner'-tasting than the traditional Southern version with tomato gravy and cheese, yet just as unctuous. Its Asian aspects make sense, and meld seamlessly with the corn and bacon.

Until *Momofuku*, in my own cooking, I long avoided tackling East Asian cuisines. The demands of authenticity were far too great, I thought. In a kind of reverse-self-gastro-racism, I thought only Asians could convincingly cook Asian cuisines. (What did I mean by 'convincing'?) Chez Panisse, in my experience, never played around with East Asian flavours or dishes, so neither did I. But perusing *Momofuku* when it came out, suddenly a new light was cast on those assumptions. Chang's recipes (and inspirations derived thereof) have greatly enriched my cooking: the simple rice-vinegar pickles, kimchi, traditional dashi, bacon dashi, slow-cooked eggs, noodles, miso, Korean seasoning pastes and so on – I cannot imagine cooking without them now. Through the doorway of Chang's approach, with authenticity requirements freshly waived, I felt a great sense of creative liberation. Having now cooked many a meal in Momofuku's paradigm, I find myself emboldened to investigate, yes, more authentic Chinese, Japanese and Korean culinary practices.

Twenty years ago, 'authentic', when used in a culinary context in the United States, seemed to contain an implicit, veiled criticism of food's status quo here; most of the food generally available was seen to be tainted, if not with pesticides, then at least with industrialism and commercialism. The pursuit of authenticity, as we understood it, subverted that status quo. 'Authentic' food brought to mind another place – Italy, France – and/or a pre-industrial time. We respected, reverentially, the knowledge embodied in other cuisines and their traditional combinations of foods – duck with turnips, for example. Cooking an authentic meal was laborious. You had to scour the ethnic markets for the correct ingredients, and bring out all the bells and whistles – the Mexican oilcloths, the Russian samovar and the Moroccan tagine. This was how I observed the cooks at Chez Panisse in my time exploring other cuisines. After years of this approach in my own cooking, I began to find it creatively stifling. If there are Middle Eastern flourishes in your menu, dessert must always feature pistachios and rosewater. Blinis with caviar must be served with anything Russian. A Mexican dinner? Go hunt for those flan moulds. You did not 'mix-and-match' cuisines, regardless of what Diana Kennedy suggested. What was there to learn from that? What would your grandmother think? Nobody in Italy – or Mexico – ever put *calabacitas* over pasta (an erroneous, and perhaps even condescending, assumption), so why do it? The best reason, of course, is that it is delicious. And it makes sense: here we are in California, a place with Italian and Mexican influences all over the place, and if someone really never made *fettuccine alla calabacitas* before, they should have, so let's now be that someone. David Chang's words come to mind: *if we reach past tradition to create the truest and best version of a dish for our own palates, then what we're doing isn't bullshit.*

Once at a special luncheon at Camino, I met James Oseland, then the editor-in-chief of *Saveur* magazine, a journal founded in the mid-1990s, whose tagline has always been 'Savor a world of authentic cuisine'. Bearing that in mind, I asked if he thought the definition of authenticity, in a culinary setting, had changed. He said, 'Well, authenticity is whatever you want it to be.' If that is the case, there is little reason to use the word, and in fact, I hear it far less often than I once did, but perhaps it was overused. I think our definition of the word has shifted. Yesterday's authenticity was about following the recipes of other, more established, culinary traditions in order to better develop our own; today's authenticity is more about the physical provenance of food – local, organic, farm-to-table, the idea of *terroir* – than ethnic provenance. With tongue very consciously in cheek, the Momofuku website, in the FAQ section, to the question 'What type of cuisine is it?' answers, 'We try our best to serve delicious American food.' For the Momofuku restaurants in Toronto and Sydney, the answer is simply, 'We try our best to serve delicious food.' The subtext is that ethnic provenance need no longer define a meal, menu, restaurant or repertoire; it is a label that we once thought useful and necessary, but have found no longer is.

It is a rich, but perhaps ironic, moment for creative American cooks: we no longer need to doggedly imitate the culinary traditions of far-off shores, our own traditions having been richly developed at this point in our culinary history. Our food increasingly evokes the here and now. However, in our increasingly globalized, interconnected, intermixed world, just at this very moment, when we can begin pointing to an emerging, distinct, modern American cuisine, are all 'ethnic' culinary designations, 'American' included, fast becoming meaningless and irrelevant? Is the question 'What kind of cuisine is it?' becoming a relic of the past? What culinary labels will be discarded; what others will be dusted off and refurbished, repurposed? Whatever the answers, successive generations of hungry, curious, creative cooks will continue to emerge, and will find their best positioning between tradition and innovation.

The recipe

Catherine's Wholewheat Fettuccine with Corn, Summer Squash, Chillies, Coriander and Crème Fraiche

Serves 4

Especially good in this summer pasta, adapted in honour of Catherine Brandel's Chez Panisse Café rendition of David Tanis' recipe in *Corn: A Country Garden Cookbook*, is 'bolted' cilantro, the leafy herb also known as coriander or Chinese parsley. Late-summer heat causes the delicate plant to go to seed; in this transformation, the leaves become more fern-like and their characteristic citrusy flavour intensifies. If the plant has produced seed heads, the immature green coriander berries are delicious – coarsely chop a tablespoon's worth and add to the sautéing vegetables.

3 large ears very fresh white or yellow sweet corn, or a combination
4 tablespoons butter, divided
1 medium red onion, finely diced
about ½ teaspoon salt, in all
1 pound assorted small summer squash (courgette), finely diced
1 to 2 serranos or other small, hot green chilli, finely minced

1 pound fresh egg fettuccine, made with a portion of freshly ground wholewheat flour

juice of 1 lime
1 ½ cups loosely packed cup cilantro (coriander) leaves and slender stems, coarsely chopped
Freshly ground black pepper
6 tablespoons crème fraiche

Have ready a large pot of boiling water. Shuck the corn, wipe with a damp towel to remove the silk and cut the kernels off the cobs with a sharp knife into a large bowl. With the back of your knife, scrape out the remaining juice and corn germ from the cobs into the bowl. In a large skillet over a high flame, melt half the butter; when it sizzles, add the onion with a pinch of salt and sauté, stirring constantly, until the onion is almost tender. Add the squash with another big pinch of salt and cook, stirring, another minute. Add the chilli and the corn, including all the corn's juice, and cook the mixture, stirring frequently, for about 2 minutes more, until the corn is heated through.

Meanwhile, salt the boiling water and cook the fettuccine until al dente. Drain, saving a cup of the cooking water, and add the pasta to the vegetables. Add the lime juice, remaining butter, 1 cup of the cilantro and pepper to taste. Gently toss everything together, moistening as necessary with the reserved pasta cooking water. Taste for salt. Divide the pasta and sauce into warmed bowls, top each with a heaping tablespoon of crème fraiche and the remaining cilantro and serve immediately.

Notes

1 John Mariani, *How Italian Food Conquered the World* (New York: St. Martin's Press, 2011).

2 Diana Kennedy, *Nothing Fancy* (San Francisco: North Point Press, 1984).

3 Diana Kennedy, *The Cuisines of Mexico* (New York: Harper and Row, 1972) and *Recipes from the Regional Cooks of Mexico* (New York: Harper and Row, 1978), respectively.

4 Alice Waters, Patricia Curtan and Martine Labro, *Chez Panisse Pasta, Pizza, and Calzone* (New York: Random House, 1984).

5 David Tanis, *Corn: A Country Garden Cookbook* (San Francisco: Collins Publishers, 1995); part of a series by Collins Publishers San Francisco.

6 David Tanis, *A Platter of Figs and Other Recipes* (New York: Artisan, 2008).

7 Judy Rogers, *The Zuni Café Cookbook* (New York: W. W. Norton, 2002).

8 David Chang with Peter Meehan, *Momofuku* (New York: Clarkson Potter, 2009).

13

Café Chairs, Bar Stools and Other Chairs We Sit on When We Eat: Food Consumption and Everyday Urban Life

Henriette Steiner

In Western culture, a meal is typically consumed when sitting not only 'at a table' but also 'on a chair'. Behind this statement lies a long tradition of table manners and design heritage, both of which provide a proper or appropriate setting for the consumption of food both in private and public contexts and bringing together design and architecture with (changing) practices of food preparation and consumption. As we know from our everyday lives, however, eating may take place in many other situations than in neatly organized settings of, say, a formal restaurant or in the private sphere of the home. Food is consumed in many different places: at our work desk, beside a hot dog stand in the street, in a train between two cities or during a picnic in the park. Importantly, each of these situations has its own architectural setting, a tangible place that enables the consumption of food to have a particular structure and meaning – no matter how spontaneous or casual. Most often, this involves some kind of spatial arrangement of tables and chairs, in all possible diverse forms. These furnishings provide the intake of food with a certain degree of decorum. During a meal, the food itself changes status from being a material object in the world of things to entering the body of the individual. They thus give structure to a liminal situation that concerns deeply seated cultural understandings of the relationship between body and world.

But how can we understand these places as sites of not only convention but also tradition and even heritage? This contribution uncovers our latent and often overlooked cultural habits and relationships with food in contemporary urban context. It focuses on the furnished settings we use for eating in cities, thus working through the deep background of architectural and social decorum for consuming food in a contemporary urban environment. It is especially concerned with the design and decorum of the settings that support the making and eating of food in public spaces, such as restaurants, cafés or open-air spaces in the city, but also looks at the domestic realm, which is seen as a place with urban qualities. Rather than dividing 'private' and 'public' spaces into a dichotomous relation, I interpret these two on a continuum where the home is governed by restricted accessibility and social relations over which individuals have a high degree of control, in contrast to a café or an open space in the city. These are seen as comparatively more accessible places and governed by more anonymous social relations. This chapter thus tackles questions of how dividing lines between private and public in the city are negotiated and how they may be seen to be experienced as a set of shifting relations. Part of this conversation will be design and the rootless authenticity of global brands, such as chain coffee shops, as well as tourist restaurants. Are such places nothing more than ersatz renditions of genuine vendors that are located elsewhere (in time and place), or do they instead represent a new form of cosmopolitan authenticity in the twenty-first century?

This study tries to answer these and related questions by means of a piecemeal exploration, taking as a starting point two photographs taken with the camera of an iPhone of chairs on which the author sat during a normal week's activities, and contrasting each of these chairs with the memory of a similar one. This gives rise to two paired situational narratives involving four concrete chairs.[1] The study may thus be seen as a mini field trip into a contemporary urban environment, that is, Copenhagen in Denmark, during a morning in July. Theoretically, it draws on the American philosopher James Dodd's reading of the Czech phenomenological philosopher Jan Patočka concerning the question of how we may understand 'built space', using a phenomenological vocabulary and concepts such as orientation and horizon.[2] But whereas Dodd talks about 'built space' on a philosophical level, this contribution will operationalize the phenomenological vocabulary in relation to concrete settings as well as in relation to the object level. In its anecdote-based, cultural-historical methodology and associative writing style, however, it also is indebted to the approach to the theme of food and culture of the second volume of *The Practice of Everyday Life: Living and Cooking* by the French philosopher Michel de Certeau.[3] But rather than building on a large body of empirical material, it employs an auto-ethnographic approach, exploring two situations of eating in contemporary everyday urban settings and circumventing these through written explorations of daily-life situations in first-person narrative.

FIGURE 13.1 *Faux Arne Jacobsen Ant Chair. Photo by author.*

Breakfast at home and the Ant Chair copy

I eat my breakfast at home: crisp bread with butter, what in the local language is called *knækbrød*. It is the large, round Swedish form of *knækbrød*, bought at an IKEA food shop, I am chewing on while sipping bitter Nescafé with milk. The chair I sit on is one of the millions of near-copies of the Danish architect and designer Arne Jacobsen's 1952 Ant Chair. The spiky legs have a chrome finish. The back is a simpler, rounded version of the more oval and curvy original. It is an upholstered model, covered with textured, black artificial leather. It is quite comfortable, even though the leather gets sticky in hot and humid weather. I am at home but the furniture is not mine. Having just moved back to Copenhagen after a long time abroad, I live in a furnished flat in the inner city. Everyone knows the location where the apartment building is situated, facing, as it is, a canal which is one of the city's top tourist sites. It is a beautiful, discretely classicistic building, dating back to 1770 but significantly altered in 1846 and 1970. This is what I call 'home' – at least for the time being.

The flat is large and full of light. The furniture is solid and rather new, dominated by neutral colours such as white, black, light brown and large, square ochre-coloured rugs with simple geometric patterns. The dining table is large and feels more like a formal conference table at a company than a table meant for cosy family meals. But it is enjoyably multifunctional because of its generous size and the solid materials: chrome legs and white melamine surface. Most of the furniture pieces are reminiscent of famous pieces of Danish design, such as Piet Hein's Superellipse Table or Montana shelves. But just like the Arne Jacobsen-like chair, they are cheaper, mass-produced versions of those originals, probably bought in a mainstream furniture warehouse, and produced abroad. The materials make them practical for daily use, and the fact that they are lookalikes is not always that easy to see. One needs to be aware of the history of Scandinavian design to notice the slight changes to the form, proportions and materials of the furniture. Their presumably different monetary value in comparison to the original design pieces is therefore visible in these details and in the hidden, sometimes somewhat crude, joints and fittings. So, while the quality of the furniture in the flat is generally very high, two of the ant-like chairs broke shortly after we moved in. You could hear the breaking of the plywood beneath the artificial leather at the place where the chair is most narrow: a sharp, crunching sound. The little milky-white pieces of plastic that are meant to create stability between the seat of the chair and the metal legs also tend to slide down the sides of the legs. My nearly toothless toddler sometimes pulls them down, chews on them and gets a finger stuck between the seat and the leg of the chair.

The original Ant Chair had three legs only, and design enthusiasts still buy the three-legged version. The fact that it easily tips over when you sit on it meant that shortly after Jacobsen's death in 1971, a four-legged version, which is now the best-known one, was released to the market. When I was an undergraduate student, I myself purchased a newly manufactured black four-legged Ant Chair – one of the first pieces of furniture I ever bought. I also bought a used wooden-stool version of the original three-legged chair at a sale in a vintage design shop.

Both have the sitting height of the original Ant Chair (44 cm), which, admittedly, is rather low and makes the chair unsuitable as a dining or work chair for a tall person. Even though my furniture is currently stored in a container several thousand kilometres away, sitting on this ant-like chair makes me think of the well-known sound of the squeaks my own stool makes. As if by reflex, I am caught by a sudden gasp of anxiety caused by the memory of the pinching sensation sometimes involved in sitting on the stool and caused by the fact that a previous owner tampered with the stool and inserted a screw with sharp edges into the seat for the sake of stability. The screw needs to be fastened at regular intervals and failing to do so means a high risk that people sitting on the stool end up with holes in their trousers. This may be a slightly too direct reminder of the intimate relation between our bodies and the chairs we sit on, as if glued to them, for what seems to be the majority of our waking life as part of a contemporary Western lifestyle – at a desk in front of the computer, in a car; or, indeed, when consuming food and drinks.[4]

In 1952, the Ant Chair was designed for the canteen of a Danish pharmaceutical company in need of a chair that was stackable, practical and robust. It is Jacobsen's notorious and innovative response to this brief – a chair that was functional and stylish and could be serially produced, following a Bauhaus-inspired Modernist design credo. But the design also draws on an organic formal register with the soft curvatures of the seat and the back, attesting to the principles behind the arguably more humanist Scandinavian variant of architectural Modernism. The Ant Chair may thus be seen as a kind of Scandi-chair-version of the idea of 'Die Wohnung für das Existenzminimum', the minimal dwelling.[5] Jacobsen strove to make a chair in the most minimal yet functional sense for a new democratic post-war era, dominated by peace, production and welfare for all. It may therefore also be seen as an imprint of an idea of what an ideal-typical modern, post–Second World War body may be said to be and thus makes a moral statement about the human condition of the post-war period. The chair is made for a body that only requires the minimal support given by a hard and naked, if friendly, wooden surface. The shape of the human body is mimicked in a polished and carefully crafted if mass-produced form. No comfy upholstery is needed here. And, significantly, it is a chair made for forward-facing body, a body that is involuntarily restrained in the sense that it is unable to move too dynamically (at least on the original three-legged version); the body of a being that is rational, awake, never slumping, never day-dreaming or dozing off. It is a body that only needs a chair, and one chair only: a chair that is movable and stackable.

The Ant Chair thus formalizes any chair's intimate relationship with the body of the person sitting on it and its design is now iconic. But rather than being associated with the human body, its name derives from its similarity to another kind of living creature: ants. Today, and partly due to the millions of copies both of the original Ant Chair and its many near-copies like the one I am sitting on, this name gives rather creepy associations to the behaviour and organization of that insect. Ants make one think of a mass or swarm of individual creatures working towards a common goal seemingly unknown to each of them, or at least unarticulated by them; a semi-militant animal, conjuring up the image of a perfectly ordered and rational society where everybody knows their place. If ants display intelligent or quasi-human forms of organization, as if all the ants of an ant colony were joined as one extended body, it is combined with a total lack of reflection and concern for the individual. To an extent, each ant is reduced to a function, as if part of a machine. Rather ironically, the picture of modern human as a social insect seems rather apt. And since 1952, an army of Ant Chairs has invaded the northern hemisphere, from the original three-legged version in the design museum, to later manufactured four-legged versions in the design café or the room of an (overly) design-conscious student, to the many lookalikes in places like the flat I now live in.

It was that narrow 'neck' of the ant that broke: a narrow point that came into being because of Jacobsen's desire for a minimal use of materials and genius use of the cheap, novel material plywood. But here, this narrow point became a *Sollbruchstelle*, a predetermined breaking point, which was to become the end of the life cycle of these two chairs which were subsequently scrapped by the houseowner.

So, when I sit at 'home', in a flat that will only be 'mine' for a short period of time, on a piece of furniture that I neither own nor desire to own in a location mainly frequented by tourists, the chair reveals itself as being implicated in an entangled web of cultural and historical relations. Sitting on this chair, eating my breakfast, the chair thus simultaneously connects me to something deeply local, a chair made by Denmark's and Copenhagen's most iconic modern designer, but also to wider, even global developments that concern post-war modern Western culture at large, including complicated questions of authenticity and copy – mediated by my own body and this chair, and the basic need to eat and drink.[6]

The situation thus also brings to the foreground of my attention the porous boundaries which exist between outside and inside of a dwelling: The fact that all the products we consume in our everyday life, be it the food we eat or the furniture we sit on while eating, even when we have bought it and call it our 'own', never will completely belong to us. As objects in and of themselves, they are of course implicated in a much larger web of relationships: of materials and production processes that cover a large geographical area; of other people who use, have used or will use this object; and of cultural practices and ideas about design. But we do not need this knowledge to be able to make use of an object in our everyday life. Only when an object such as a chair moves out of the shadowy background of the things we use (ready-to-hand) and make themselves noticed to us, either by breaking, being dysfunctional or making themselves available to strange forms of uses (present-at-hand) or by evoking certain sentiments concerning, for example, taste, values or our personal experience, do we reflect on the presence they have in our daily lives.[7] What is at closest proximity to us–the immediate material environment, or the food that we eat–therefore enters our awareness at a moment that is more acute. Yet, at the same time, this moment also creates as sense of reflective distance. We thus see how in this setting we are embedded in a cultural horizon that links us with others and the *other*, being the world around us, but whose basis is our distance to these others, to the *other* and to ourselves.[8]

Starbucks versus Starstruck – The gaze of the local tourist and the taste of the city

Moving into the city, I drink the second coffee of the day at a sidewalk café: Nice-looking light basket-work type of chairs and wooden foldable tables stand in the shadow beneath large parasols. The chair has armrests and is very comfortable especially since a white cushion on the seat makes it nice and soft. The restaurant is open from early morning till late at night. What it offers changes in the course of the day and with the seasons. The place is not part of a chain as such but is owned by a large consortium that among others owns several cafés and restaurants in different locations in Copenhagen. Large black boards with white letters written on them announce the special offers. I see many tourists here. Here, I take tourists to mean 'not locals' (not many people may be said to be locals in this setting); they may thus be both foreigners and local nationals who live elsewhere in the country or even in the city. Due to its location, the place features on many postcards from Copenhagen, and probably on countless photographs. I am not particularly enticed by the place until I notice the morning offer: coffee and a croissant for a price beneath that which you typically pay just for a cup of coffee elsewhere in the city. The coffee turns out to be decent if a little watery and reminds me of coffee I have had in the United States. After a couple of minutes, a croissant that is baked in the restaurant upon ordering is served on a square white porcelain plate together with a small, individually packed organic butter and a large soft napkin. And so, here I am, alone in a tourist café on the corner of the street where I live, enjoying an unplanned break in the activities of a normal day.

A couple of days previously, I had been sitting at a similar table at a similar time of day at the sidewalk outside a small, new café in a hip part of town, Nørrebro, an inner-city former working-class neighborhood. While the chair, a

FIGURE 13.2 *Comfy café chair. Photo by author.*

foldable wooden chair for outside use, matched the table, it was much less comfortable (with no cushion). The taste of the coffee certainly had been more pungent and refined; the place uses selected beans from a local roastery. Rather than a croissant, I had eaten a more old-fashioned piece of Danish pastry, *thebirkes*, a square pastry folded around a marzipan-base-cream (*remonce*) and covered with blue poppy seeds, served on a retro 1970s glazed earthenware plate. I had paid about twice as much. The summer wind had touched my face, it was a quiet morning, and I watched smart-looking people cycling by, wearing sunglasses. It had looked like a picture from a blog about the world's best travel destinations for the 'urban-cool'. Why had this place – and not the old, famous location that many people think of when you say the word 'Copenhagen' – aroused feelings in me of this being Copenhagen-proper? It was as if not only the coffee had tasted better in this place but my entire sensuous apparatus had felt more open and in tune with the environment around me. It was as if the city itself had a better taste in this location. Or is it, perhaps, more probable that this setting had met my personal taste in a more direct way, attesting to the semantic similarity between taste as having to do with the flavour of food and taste as cultural practice related to style, what the French sociologist Pierre Bourdieu would hold responsible for social distinctions.[9] While the location was distinctly Nørrebro'esque and thus a precise location in Copenhagen, it also had a hint of something undefined and metropolitan, evoking images of places I have visited in Berlin and elsewhere, and therefore an indirect affirmation of my own self-perception as someone with high cultural capital, a cosmopolitan outlook and knowledge of cultural codes.

In a seminal text from 1990, the British sociologist John Urry describes tourism as a cultural phenomenon that is nurtured by its relationship with what is considered home, that is, everyday life and work life.[10] The tourist leaves home to go somewhere that is not home. A certain sense of distance is thus part-and-parcel of what it means to be a tourist, a kind of alienation that contributes to making the tourist open to new sensuous impressions, impressions that are primarily mediated through visual signs or 'sights' in a broad sense. It therefore is a pleasurable alienation much unlike the destructive blasé attitude we know from Georg Simmel's sociological writing on the modern metropolis of the early twentieth century.[11] At the same time, the tourist will bring with him or her many of the routines of the everyday, and many tourist shops make a business out of alleviating the sense of estrangement of the travel destination by offering food, goods or settings through which the tourist will feel a heightened degree of at-homeness (when seen in relation to the general situation of estrangement). In combination, these different layers or levels of what creates a sense of 'presence', a complex interplay between proximity and distance (in both cases of something known and of something different), will attune the tourist to the surroundings and direct his or her body and gaze in certain ways and with the help of cultural intermediaries (the guide, guide book, the camera, etc.).[12] When I sit in a tourist café, which happens to be a local café to me in the sense that it is close to my home, we may conclude that I am simultaneously inevitably part of this culture, and its supposed opposite.

As we know, tourism is a huge economic factor in contemporary urban economies, and the battle over the money of the tourist is to a high degree played out over food.[13] People also often travel to challenge their taste buds, and since everyone obviously needs to eat at regular intervals during the day, they buy food at the foreign location. Bringing all food from home is only possible or common in very special scenarios, for example, a camping trip. Therefore, this function of unestrangement due to the soothing experience of being able to consume familiar food in an unfamiliar setting may be brought about when local places offer consumer goods that are specifically taken from the home setting of particular groups of tourists. But it most often is done by catering for a particular global style in direct opposition to a sense of an authentic local style, like serving Coca-Cola, or, as is the case here, by offering US-style coffee and French-style pastry. These are alimentary products that belong to everyone and nobody, a bit like the food you often will find in airports. It therefore also is a kind of food that may not necessarily be seen as being in opposition to the place where it is served. In and of itself, ordering a Coca-Cola or buying bottled water obviously does not make me a tourist. We thus enter a complicated and ambiguous territory of cultural practices where the general mood of a place or setting as well as the cultural horizon that governs our interpretation of it is significant for the choices we make about food, but also how we understand – and even taste – within a specific situation.

On the level of vision, Urry identifies four types of gazes through which the tourist will typically mediate the visual impression of the surroundings: the *collective* gaze, the *romantic* gaze, the *environmental* gaze and that of the *post-tourist*. This makes for a complex picture that can be used to interpret the different ways in which tourism takes part in modern mass culture's consumption of goods, food, culture (high and low alike) and places. The so-called collective gaze concerns mass-tourism, where the individual wants to *see* what every other tourist *sees* and be a part of the visual culture of tourism by visiting famous tourist sights. Thereby, the tourist has 'been there', 'seen it, too', and finally has a picture taken next to the site to document the event. In the case in question, I am involuntarily caught in this kind of culture when I sit down to have coffee and a croissant at the next street corner. Despite the proximity of the café to residential buildings, its main economic rationale is not local residents but tourists and other visitors who come to this place because of the sight-value of the old canal and the architectural setting around it. My rather distant attitude to this setting means that my attunement to the situation and my gaze, insofar as it can at all be said to be a tourist gaze, may be seen as in line with what Urry calls the *environmental* tourist gaze. This should be seen as a morally inflicted gaze feeding on indignation – someone noticing the pollution on the beach or being appalled by the high-rise concrete block-tower hotel in a picturesque setting. Or, as in this case, the environmental tourist gaze perceives the other tourists, and the tourist culture by which they are surrounded, as a kind of *socio-architectural* pollution, tainting an in-principle, more authentic and 'real' urban place. Or, perhaps I am rather a *post-tourist*, one who goes against the mainstream commercialized forms of tourist consumerism (but who may also be drawn to it and use it to nurture a form of pastiche when making unexpected choices).

For the post-tourist, a raised awareness about the flatness, or, in-authenticity, of a tourist café is so evident that it creates a different form of estrangement – I react by feeling out of place and with ironic astonishment upon receiving the nice croissant and the coffee I do not want to like. In contrast, my visit to the Nørrebro café, which specifically cultivated a feeling of authenticity and of being local (despite the fact that local coffee roasters and gourmet retro pastries are a rather new thing in this setting, and that cafés like this one seem to pop up everywhere in the city at the moment, making it not all that unique), ironically allowed me to filter the situation through something like what Urry calls the *romantic* gaze of the tourist. This is constituted by an attunement to the sensuous enjoyment of the present and of being present 'here and now', an experience of something unique. And in this case, it sedimented feelings in me of belonging, of being 'local', perhaps even of being 'at home'. But of course, I am no tourist in Nørrebro or in Copenhagen. And though I have exited my dwelling in this city, consuming food and drinks in the cafés of the city is part of my everyday-life routine. It therefore should not be surprising that the exterior spaces of the city may evoke feelings of at-home-ness.

Yet, the distinction between tourist and local is a complicated one. I am not simply involuntarily caught up in residual practises of tourist consumerism of high modernity in the first café, while simultaneously maintaining critical reflective distance and living out the pastiche of a late-modern urban dweller, and, to make things even more complicated, being caught by a belief in and longing for something more authentic in the city, of which I find an approximation in the other café. We thus need to dig deeper than the level of visuality to which Urry's conceptual apparatus is so strongly committed in order to understand the complex interplay between interpretation and appropriation of an architectural setting governing the cases in question.

To do this, another approach could be to take a starting point in the aphoristic book *Einbahnstrasse*, in which the German-Jewish cultural theorist and critic Walther Benjamin writes that the way the city is read is determined by a set of both individual and collective myths.[14] This also reminds us of another famous writer on urban culture, the French philosopher Roland Barthes, who has described such myth in relation to the Eiffel Tower, a monument which is often described in a quasi-mythopoetic language as being organically connected to the city of Paris, and central to defining what we consider Paris to be. In fact, the intimate relation between the Eiffel Tower and the city of Paris may be experienced as so overwhelming that it gives rise to post-touristic sentiments. Barthes initiates his text by referencing the French author Guy de Maupassant, who used to eat lunch in the Eiffel Tower since, to him, this marked out the only place in Paris where he was not forced to constantly see the tower.[15] But even if the very reason for travelling to something foreign rests on a bodily encounter with the architectural culture of that *other* which we know from such quasi-mythic narratives and visual representations, a city like Copenhagen is in itself a wild mixture of both a general horizon of European cosmopolitan culture and highly place-specific symbols formed by spatial and architectural practices that are particular to this place. Even place myths that are further fuelled by the tourist industry's endless repetition of what is 'unique' and 'authentic' are thus marked by such (potentially productive) fundamental ambiguities.

But perhaps even such place myths may contribute to structuring the locals' knowledge about themselves and their lifeworld. To even *see* the beauty or uniqueness that attracts tourists to a site in the first place, and which constitutes a stimulation of the sensuous apparatus of the tourist in a way that stands in opposition to everyday life and which makes it seem extraordinary, is a form of destabilization of the common order of things. The fact that the encounter with a new place hinges on preverbal form of experience, moreover, makes it even more relevant to think about the role of material culture, be it architecture, furniture or food, in the tourist experience. Similarly, however, even to *see* the invasion of a place by a 'flattening' form of global culture, and by acting out particular forms of aesthetic reflection in order to set oneself apart or have an ironic distance to that culture, feeds the self-understanding and aesthetic sensibility both of the tourist and of the local.

In conclusion, it may be possible to say that reading situations of everyday urban life as a form of touristic practice, mediating between different aspects of the ideal-typical gazes of the tourist, makes it sensible to, like Urry, talk about a certain degree of touristification of everyday urban life.[16] To some degree, in contemporary urban culture, we are already caught in the dualism between commercialized but also deeply rooted cosmopolitan practices of European modern culture, such as drinking coffee at a sidewalk café, and their different degrees of 'inauthenticity'. This is a duality that may produce strong responses, spanning from hedonistic enjoyment to sensations of alienation and resistance. And, moreover, this is placed against a longing for being *rooted*, to exist as a *genuine local* who belongs and is attached to the city; in other words, to be at home in the city, to experience the city through an emotional register based on degrees of proximity.

And yet, it is important to emphasize, as Dodd argues, that in the phenomenological vocabulary, the kinds of phenomena that most emphasize our connection with others through the material environment – expressly a city – exist precisely because of the fact that they and the city are always there as a distant horizon.[17] Or, we might say that, as a horizon, a central condition of urban life has distance as a main constitutive factor. Similarly, as I have argued elsewhere, this should be understood through cultural phenomena that build on distance, an example being anonymity.[18] For it is a fact that all we are able to do is simply *get on with* daily life in the city. Since in modern urban culture it is difficult to rid ourselves of our double role as both citizens and consumers, we constantly see and consume the things that are *in* the city (food, objects, places, etc.) and thereby inevitably take part in producing the collective myths about that city.[19] But we also should remain aware of the things that are *of* the city, the things and phenomena that produce the general condition of urbanity and those that make it possible for us to be attuned to that general horizon for praxis that the city is.[20] And this is a condition which we may only begin to subject to interpretation if we recognize that it holds an inherent tension between proximity and distance, a tension that lies deep down in the way specifically urban phenomena are culturally instituted.

Concluding the Story: *Dinér transportable* and *Le Déjeuner sur l'herbe*

Carolyn Steel, the author of *Hungry City*, has scrutinized the fraught relationship between urban life and food production. More particularly, she has extended this observation to consider how the traditional notion of hinterland is being confronted – literally uprooted – in unprecedented ways by the growth of cities. As she writes, while the urbanized part of the world is expanding and cities may thus be seen to be set to dominate the future, 'living in them presents a dilemma, since their food must come from elsewhere: a place we persist in calling "the countryside", although the images conjured by the term bear little relation to the realities of modern food production'.[21] When we eat in the city, we thus immediately nurture images of nature and culture, both inner and outer, in a way that parallels how the intertwined relation that exists between images of authenticity and inauthenticity was discussed above. Such issues also are emphasized when we regard situations of eating in the city that draw on natural imagery in a more direct way, such as when we take our lunch as a picnic in the park, or even the sensation that is created if it starts raining when we sit at a sidewalk café. Such situations may also be investigated with the kind of associative writing method practiced in this study. At the same time, it is possible to consider how other forms of eating would allow us to place questions concerning the consumption of food and architecture in a way that would help us unravel our ideas of food in relation to a perceived nature/culture dualism. For instance, when we eat while on the move, such as when we are passengers in a train between two cities, we are drawn to consider also the experience of driving through that landscape.

Similarly, we may use other forms of cultural material, such as paintings or literary texts, to support our investigation. For example, questions of culture and nature are central to Eduard Manet's famous painting *Le Déjeuner sur l'herbe* (Luncheon on the Grass) from 1863. Here, a painting of a picnic in the park by a group of well-dressed gentlemen who sit next to a nude allows us to begin to think about the complexities of nature, culture and modern life; about what we *see*, what we want to *see* and how we *see* it. The situation-a luncheon, and the place of that act of eating, on the grass-as a cultural act is emphasized by the almost unreal, studio-like light and the rough contours of the painted trees, making them reminiscent of a stage-set. This is underscored by the dream-like appearance of a woman in the background of the painting. She stands in a kind of clearing in the forest scene, in a pool of water, and is dressed in a thin, white frock, which she holds with one hand while bending forward, her hand sliding into water or mist at the ground. Her curvaceous body shape, dark, done-up hair and mysterious smile as she looks towards the ground make her look like a Classical statue. Only very few visual markers separate the realism of the painting from its mythopoetic features, and we should not be surprised that it is a representation which continues to provoke aesthetic reflection, wonder, curiosity and even cultural uproar, as when it was banned from the French salon.

Yet, importantly, the outlined scenes of everyday urban life in this chapter and the richness of interpretation they offer emphasize that in each situation of eating a particular architectural setting makes for a tangible place which enables the consumption of food to have a particular structure and meaning. This is, crucially, a situation that grounds us in that human and urban culture in which we instinctively take part, regardless of the moment's degree of (self)-reflection – just as is the case when it comes to the countless numbers of coffee I have had, whether sitting on an Ant Chair (original or copy) or in a café in the city.

Notes

1   This choice of topic and methodologies is indebted to multiple discussions I have had with Ignaz Strebel, sitting at a variety of office and café chairs at the ETH Hönggerberg Campus in Zurich. I also would like to thank Signe Bøggild for her comments and suggestions.

2   James Dodd, 'Jan Patočka and Built Space', in *Husserl's Ideen*, eds. Lester Embree and Thomas Nenon (Vienna, New York: Springer, 2013), 283–294.

3   Most often, the first volume of this study, *The Practice of Everyday Life*, with the original French subtitle *Arts de Faire*, is more well known in an urban studies context. The second volume was a collaboration: Michel de Certeau,

Luce Girard and Pierre Mayol, *The Practice of Everyday Life, Vol. 2: Living and Cooking*, trans. by Timothy J. Tomasik (1980, repr., Minneapolis: University of Minnesota Press, 1998.

4 For a cultural history of 'sitting', see Hajo Eickhoff, *Himmelsthron und Schaukelstuhl* (Munich: Carl Hanser, 1993).

5 See Carsten Thau and Kjeld Vindum, *Arne Jacobsen* (Aarhus: The Danish Architectural Press, 2002).

6 From 1954 to 1957, the exhibition *Design in Scandinavia* travelled the United States and Canada and was seen by more than half a million people, many of whom were already beginning to create a narrative of a golden age of Scandinavian Design. Today, a vintage collector's item, which is seen as more authentic and more directly born out of its age, will more often than not be more expensive than a newly produced piece.

7 This discussion references the Heideggarian terminology of 'vorhandensein' and 'zuhandensein' as described in his main philosophical treatise *Sein und Zeit* from 1927. See Martin Heidegger, *Sein und Zeit* (1927, repr., Tubingen: Max Niemeyer Verlag, 2001). The discussion of the possible use of Heidegger's philosophy in an architecture and design context is extensive and difficult. In the present context, the essay 'The Thing' is a good starting point. I have discussed these terms in relation to urban studies and concepts such as context, situation and setting in the closing chapter of my book, *Emergence of a Modern City – Golden Age Copenhagen 1800–1850* (Farnham: Ashgate, 2014).

8 See the discussion of the concepts of horizon and distance in Dodd, 'Jan Patočka and Built Space'.

9 See Pierre Bourdieu, *La distinction: critique sociale du jugement* (Paris: Edition de Minuit, 1979).

10 See John Urry, *The Tourist Gaze* (London: Sage, 1990).

11 Georg Simmel, 'Die Grosstädte und das Geistesleben', *Die Grossstadt. Vorträge und Aufsätze zur Städteausstellung. Jahrbuch der Gehe-Stiftung Dresden*, vol. 9, ed. T. Petermann (Dredsen: Petermann, 1903), 185–206.

12 See Arlie Hochschild, 'The Commercial Spirit of Intimate Life and the Abduction of Feminism: Signs from Womens Advice Books', *Theory, Culture and Society* 11, (London: Sage, 1994), 1–24, 22. I would like to thank Anna Ilsøe for first alerting me to this topic and corpus of sociological writing on tourism by now many years ago.

13 Today, NOMA, allegedly one of the best restaurants in the world, is located in Copenhagen. In a sense, this 'food temple' with its concept of authentic yet avant-garde New Nordic food can be said to be one of the biggest Danish design successes of the young twenty-first century.

14 Walter Benjamin, *Ensrettet gade*, trans. by Dorthe Jørgensen (Aarhus: Forlaget Modtryk, 1993), 80.

15 Roland Barthes, 'La Tour Eiffel (1964)', in *Oeuvres complètes* (Paris: Seuil, 1993), 1379–1402 (1388).

16 John Urry, *Consuming Places* (London: Routledge, 2000), 148–149.

17 Dodd, 'Jan Patočka and Built Space', 290.

18 Steiner, *Emergence of a Modern City*, 151–158. Please also see
        my forthcoming article (in Danish) 'Hvad Michel de Certeaus blinde
        vandringsmand så i New York - Tanker om byens (u)målbare orden', in
        Periskop Tidsskrift - Forum for Kunsthistorisk Debat.

19 Ulf Hannerz, *Exploring the City – Inquiries toward an Urban Anthropology*
        (New York: Columbia University Press, 1990).

20 See also Peter Carl, 'Type, Field, Culture, Praxis', *Architectural Design*, 81.1
        (2011): 38–45 (43–44).

21 Carolyn Steel, *Hungry Cities: How Food Shapes Our Lives*, 2nd ed. (London:
        Random House, 2008).

Bibliography

Barthes, Roland. 'La Tour Eiffel (1964)'. In *Oeuvres Completes*, 1379–1402. Paris:
     Seuil, 1993.

Benjamin, Walter. *Ensrettet gade.* Translated by Dorthe Jørgensen, Aarhus:
     Forlaget Modtryk, 1993.

Bourdieu, Pierre. *La distinction: critique sociale du jugement.* Paris: Edition de
     Minuit, 1979.

Carl, Peter. 'Type, Field, Culture, Praxis'. *Architectural Design* 81(1) (2011): 38–45.

de Certeau, Michel, Luce Girard and Pierre Mayol. *The Practice of Everyday Life
     vol. 2: Living and Cooking.* Translated by Timothy J. Tomasik. 1980. Reprint,
     Minneapolis: University of Minnesota Press, 1998.

Dodd, James.'Jan Patočka and Built Space'. In *Husserl's Ideen*, edited by Lester
     Embree and Thomas Nenon, 283–294. Vienna, New York: Springer, 2013.

Eickhoff, Hajo. *Himmelsthron und Schaukelstuhl.* Munich: Carl Hanser, 1993.

Hannerz, Ulf. *Exploring the City – Inquiries toward an Urban Anthropology.* New
     York: Columbia University Press, 1990.

Heidegger, Martin. *Sein und Zeit.* 1927. Reprint, Tübingen: Max Niemeyer Verlag,
     2001.

Hochschild, Arlie. 'The Commercial Spirit of Intimate Life and the Abduction of
     Feminism: Signs from Women's Advice Books'. *Theory, Culture and Society*
     11.2 (1994): 1–24.

Simmel, Georg. 'Die Grosst.dte und das Geistesleben'. In *Die Grossstadt.
     Vorträge und Aufsätze zur Städteausstellung. Jahrbuch der Gehe-Stiftung
     Dresden*, edited by T. Petermann vol. 9, 185–206. Dredsen: Petermann, 1903.

Steel, Carolyn. *Hungry City – How Food Shapes Our Lives.* London: Random
     House, 2008.

Steiner, Henriette. *Emergence of a Modern City – Golden Age Copenhagen
     1800–1850*, Farnham: Ashgate, 2014.

Steiner, Henriette. 'Hvad Michel de Certeaus blinde vandringsmand så i New
     York – Tanker om byens (u)målbare orden'. *Periskop Tidsskrift – Forum for
     Kunsthistorisk Debat* (forthcoming, 2016).

Thau, Carsten and Kjeld Vindum. *Arne Jacobsen.* Aarhus: The Danish
     Architectural Press, 2002.

Urry, John. *Consuming Places.* London: Routledge, 2000.

Urry, John. *The Tourist Gaze.* London: Sage, 1990.

14

Celebrating the *Festa dell'Uva*: Invented Traditions, Popular Culture and Urban Spectacle in Fascist Rome

Ruth W. Lo

On 28 September 1930, the Italian fascist regime launched its very first annual *Festa dell'Uva* (Grape Festival), a large nationwide campaign that required citizens to celebrate the Italian fruit and to augment the consumption of grapes. Relying heavily on folklore and exalting the virtues of rural life, the regime invented a tradition by modifying and then relaunching an agrarian feast that would become an entirely fascist event. The regime skilfully utilized its many organizations and media outlets to promote grapes, not merely as a native food item but also as a vehicle to fulfil its other political agendas by using alimentation to penetrate a visceral and quotidian aspect of life. As such, grapes became a multivalent object, and the Grape Festival – like many other fascist public rituals – was a symbolic, manufactured representation of fascist politics.[1]

In order to build a unified national identity, the regime deployed folklores and regional customs to validate the cultural experience of the Grape Festival. The organizers seamlessly engineered popular traditions into the event, making them highly visible on ornate floats, temporary kiosks and exhibitions on the salutary properties of the fruit and of viticulture. Awards for best presentation and display offered further incentives for active, and often competitive, participation. All the while, Fascism's gentle indoctrination worked steadily, thus rendering the Grape Festival a powerful tool in selling not only the fruit but also the authentic experiences of Italian culture. Deliberately stripping grapes of their associations to Christianity, the regime made the Grape Festival entirely fascist, even becoming a part of what Emilio Gentile calls the 'fascist civic religion'.[2]

Another way in which the Grape Festival was so effective in engaging citizens was the staging of a comprehensive urban spectacle that rendered its presence in the city difficult to ignore. While the Grape Festival took place all over Italy, as mandated by the regime, nowhere were the events more elaborately orchestrated and meaningful than the ones in Rome. It was here, in the urban landscape of the Italian capital, where the celebrations of the Grape Festival negotiated seemingly opposite poles: regional and national, pastoral and urban, pagan and Christian, ancient and modern. The regime conceived of this one-day event – ephemeral yet annually repetitive – as an unproblematic synthesis that could reconcile these tensions in Italy's process of modernization.

The two organizing fascist commissions, the Opera Nazionale del Dopolavoro and the Federazione dei Commercianti di Roma, selected a constellation of sites throughout the city where these complex relationships were juxtaposed and ostensibly mediated by the Grape Festival. The event and the city developed a symbiotic relationship in celebration of a national cause. Though seemingly focused on what the regime constructed to be an ideal 'Italian fruit', the Grape Festival was also an opportunity to showcase fascist Rome, which was undergoing significant urban changes planned by Mussolini. While some buildings and streetscapes became backdrops, others were expressly enlisted by the regime to authenticate the Grape Festival and to legitimize a specifically fascist historical continuum that linked the *ventennio* directly to the glories of ancient Rome.[3] The city's architecture and streetscape contextualized this tightly choreographed fascist event, and the Grape Festival's parades and pageantry elevated these sites and the streets of Rome from their everyday banality into places charged with layered historical and political symbolism. As the festival moved through the city, it created audiences – pedestrians-turned-temporary viewer-participants – that imbued the streets with meaning beyond their quotidian purposes.

This chapter analyses the ways in which the fascist regime authenticated the invented tradition of the Grape Festival by engaging the architecture and urbanism of Rome to augment a sense of nationalism. An examination of the Grape Festival in the national press and media, many of them controlled by the State, reveals the ways in which the event used Rome's built environment to manufacture a fascist historical narrative. The organizers utilized the Grape Festival to mediate the regional–national relationship by transforming the city into a microcosm of Latium. The different events unfolding on the day also created a temporary urban network by linking together key sites that supported various types of regime propaganda. Reminding the public of the fascist ethos rooted in ruralism, the Grape Festival used the bucolic setting of Villa Borghese to evoke pastoral ambience in an urban environment. The procession routes through Rome reflected the challenges that the State posed to the Church, suggesting to its citizens civic worship as an alternative to Christian devotion. At Trajan's Market, where the main exposition and selling of grapes were staged, the architecture became a framing device – quite literally in a documentary newsreel – for Fascism's dexterous negotiations of the ancient and the modern. I analyse the Grape Festival's mitigation of opposing poles in the first years of its inception, prior to Mussolini's decision to invade Ethiopia in 1935. After this time, much of Italian politics and agricultural policies changed, and it would be difficult to explicate them in detail with the rest of the materials presented here. This case study looks at the Grape Festival celebrations in Rome as they engaged the city's architecture and urban fabric through an assessment of issues related to fascist politics, folklore, agriculture and religion.

(Re)inventing traditions

In a memorandum dated 22 July 1930 sent to Mussolini, the undersecretary of agriculture Arturo Marescalchi asked for permission to establish a *Giornata dell'Uva* (Day of Grapes) to take place on 28 September.[4] He cited that several Italian cities have had 'splendid outcomes' in the past years with a day dedicated to grapes. Reminding Mussolini that this proposal was a response to the Duce's own concerns about the viticulture sector in Italy, Marescalchi suggested to join forces with the Farmers' Federation and Merchants' Federation. The fascist official asked specifically to engage artisans and to capitalize on the contemporary zeal for folklore to ensure the success of a Day of Grapes.

Marescalchi's letter to Mussolini was an appeal to a larger trend in Italy at this time that used folklore to manufacture a sense of nationalism. Towards the end of the 1920s, the fascist regime began to aggressively pursue ethnographic studies of Italian traditions and popular culture. Several important factors motivated this obsession with 'folklore' – a foreign term that caused some controversy but remained widely in use at the time.[5] The onset of Modernism, which was changing many aspects of Italian life, stimulated the rising anxiety of party officials concerned with the negative effects of the modernization process. The regime embraced folk culture – believing it to be more virtuous – as a way to overcome the degradation and alienation of urbanization.

A return to traditions was especially useful in promoting Fascism's idea of ruralism rooted in agricultural production and an agrestic way of life. Mussolini firmly believed that an orientation to the rural and provincial instead of the metropolitan and international helped to capture the real essence of *italianità*.[6] This autochthonous approach also exploited the slippage between the double meanings of *paese*, which may refer either to the national or the provincial country. The emphasis on regional attributes may seem contrary to the national project of centralization, but party officials recognized that comprehensive ethnographic surveys of Italian regions served to underscore the diversity and cultural richness of the nation as a whole.[7]

Under Fascism, regional distinctiveness was further worked into Mussolini's idea of *romanità*, which the regime used widely and in various forms to legitimize its cultural and political projects. The concept of *romanità*, translated variously as 'Romanness' or 'Romanity', was central to the regime's self-representation by connecting itself directly with the Roman past to authenticate and aggrandize its existence in a historical context. While the use of *romanità* may appear to render the regime backward-looking, it was in fact a strategy that Fascism employed for modernity. As Joshua Arthurs argues, *romanità* was 'a coherent language with which to articulate aspirations for the contemporary world'.[8] This approach is what scholars Diane Ghirardo and D. Medina Lasansky term 'telescoping', whereby the dominant narrative validates a specific view of history while it excludes accounts that do not fit the favoured model.[9] In the case of Fascism, the regime used *romanità* as a politically charged rhetorical tool to draw connections between the fascist present and the Roman past, underscoring continuity and authenticity of many aspects of Italian culture. The concept was especially useful for the regime in Rome as it sought to foster a sense of shared history specific to this place. Like the idea of regionalism for nationalism, *romanità* was conceived to be in the service of the grander *italianità* as part of the state-building process.

Fascism's use of *romanità* in defining a collective sense of identity based on its chosen history, especially in the invented Grape Festival, was also tied to the regime's use of folklore. In order to establish direct links between the fascist present and the Roman past, the regime made its people the connection, where 'all felt there was a common bedrock of culture, an Italian race or stock'.[10] As such, the study of the different cultures of the same people – or 'folklore', the umbrella term deployed at the time – became indispensable to the regime's creation of an 'imagined community'.[11] The fascist fervour for folklore manifested in its invention of traditions, an influential concept first analysed by Eric Hobsbawm and Terence Ranger.[12] The authors use the term 'invented tradition' to refer to a set of ritual or symbolic practices that 'normally attempt to establish continuity with a suitable historic past', by presenting them as constant and invariant as a response to the changes beget by modernity.[13] These traditions not only include those invented ex-novo but also, more broadly, ones that modified existing traditions and recast them as preserving historical continuity.

The regime understood that a Day of Grapes had vast potential beyond economic benefit if it were packaged as a reinvented tradition. By the end of July 1930, Mussolini had approved Marescalchi's original proposal but changed the name of the event from *Giornata dell'Uva* to *Festa dell'Uva*.[14] The jettisoning of *giornata* (day) in favour of *festa* (feast, festival, or celebration) connotes an important semantic change. *Festa* marks a special occasion that is in its nature extraordinary, that which is exceptional to the everyday. *Giornata*, on the other hand, does not carry the same linguistic valence. The marking of atypical time thus enhances the meaning of *festa*: (1) as a deliberate temporal break from work and the usual fascist-organized leisure; and 2) as repeated action with the pronouncement of the first, second, third and so-forth celebration.[15] Indeed, *festa* suggests ritual – its system of prescribed procedure has been and shall be repeated – for the production of collective memory, but in the case of the Grape Festival, it was no longer underpinned by Christianity and instead replaced by Fascism. *Festa* also draws much closer connections to folklore, thus conveniently acquiring historical legitimacy for the invented tradition. The framing of the Grape Festival, instead of the Day of Grapes, as a celebratory event masked its more serious commercial and political objectives. It would also become one of a series of traditional festivals that the fascist regime invented or, in its own language, reprised.

The fascist rhetorical strategy surrounding the Grape Festival and many others promoted and popularized at this time never actually used the word 'invention'. This is not surprising, especially considering the regime's attempt to reclaim these festivals as long-standing traditions that previous political administrations had carelessly overlooked. The official words in reference to the festivals almost always carried the prefix *ri* (or 're' in English): *risveglio* (reawakening), *rinascita* (rebirth), *rinnovamento* (renovation or renewal), *rifiorare* (to bloom again), *ripreso* (recovered), *ripresa* (reclaimed or resumed), *ritorno* (return), *riportato* (returned or brought back), *rimessa in voga* (restored or put back in style) and so forth. The concept of reclaiming something, the fascist idea of *bonifica* – whether it be of land, customs or people – as Ruth Ben-Ghiat points out, 'was central to many discourses of fascist modernity' that sought to renew or regenerate Italian society and culture.[16] Indeed, organizers of regime-sanctioned festivals often saw their roles as re-establishing links to previously important historical periods in their respective localities for nation building. This was particularly visible in Tuscany, where many towns repackaged Medieval-style events and claimed historical ownership of local traditions.[17]

The Grape Festival, however, presented a more complex scenario than these local events, because it had to set up historical connections on a national level while simultaneously grounding them in regional traditions. The rhetoric surrounding the Grape Festival in the capital thus relied heavily on the concept of *romanità*, wherein ancient Roman eating habits, religions, myths and territorial possessions all played a part in legitimizing the invented tradition for the nation as a whole. While the Festival used *romanità* to support the idea of a nation unified by its production of grapes, it also had to be truly local in practice. The regime mandated regional centres or towns to hold their own celebrations on the nationally designated day, and that highlighted achievements in viticulture in their immediate areas and invoked their own traditions. In other words, the national Grape Festival was broken up into – or rather, composed of – smaller local Grape Festivals. The idea was that the *piccole patrie* (small fatherlands) made up the *Patria grande* (big Fatherland).[18] The concurrent celebrations in cities across Italy rendered the Grape Festival an unequivocal manifestation of the complicated local–national relationship under Fascism.

To shape the national spirit through the Grape Festival, the regime entrusted the planning of Rome's celebrations to two organizations: The Opera Nazionale del Dopolavoro (OND) and the Federazione dei Commercianti di Roma (The National Recreational Club; and Merchants' Federation of Rome). The OND, the fascist leisure organization, arranged the floats and parades throughout the city, ostensibly displaying the incorporation of folklore and regional customs in them. The Merchants' Federation of Rome was responsible for the exhibition and commercial aspects of grapes at Trajan's Market to boost sales of the fruit. This architectural setting conveniently allowed the regime to deploy *romanità* to connect modern with ancient Rome. Both organizations had unparalleled opportunities in Rome to perpetuate the regime's politics by capitalizing on the city's existing environment for the Grape Festival: it strategically staged celebrations at symbolic sites that reflected Fascism's various political visions and its version of history.

Temporary network: Urban diffusion and the Grape Festival in Rome

To navigate the complex national–regional relationship in Rome, the OND had to ensure that the event would first fully penetrate the public's consciousness by making the Grape Festival omnipresent to the city's residents during the days of celebration. In order to achieve this, the OND staged a variety of events – ranging from exhibitions, parades, tableaux, kiosks and store window decorations – spread throughout the city centre. By doing so, it created a temporary but vast network with the Grape Festival's spectacles and processions that altered the urban experience.

Whereas most cities and regional centres had to rely on provisional settings and ephemeral architecture to intimate the long history of grapes in Italy, Rome's diverse urban landscape and plentiful Roman ruins provided the requisite backdrop for the Grape Festival (Figure 14.1). In the sylvan gardens

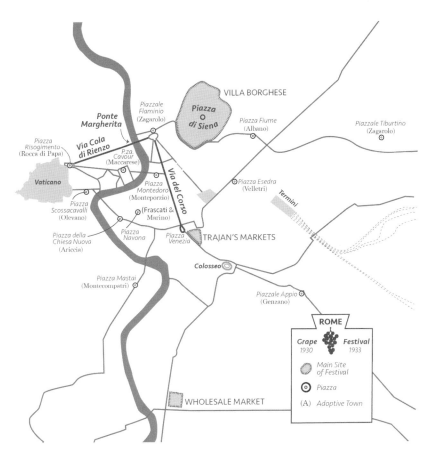

FIGURE 14.1 *Main sites and parade routes of the Grape Festival in Rome, 1930–1933. Diagram courtesy of Samantha L. Martin-McAuliffe.*

of Villa Borghese, the floats circled Piazza di Siena, where the citizens admired them and the judges decided on awards. As the newspaper *Il Popolo di Roma* described, 'Piazza di Siena, with its striking amphitheater in the splendid nature of Rome's most beautiful park, in a delightful setting with lush pines, could not have been a more perfect place for this ritual. The beautiful scenery actually harmonizes very well with this rustic celebration.'[19] On the other side of Rome, Trajan's Market housed the exhibition on viticulture, and it was also the central vending point of the fruit to the public. Choosing this site not only allowed the organizers to emphasize the connection between fascist and ancient Rome, it also brought the public to an area in the city that the regime was working diligently to liberate from its undesirable surroundings.[20]

Outside of the designated celebration venues, the OND also ensured that the Grape Festival was present throughout the city in order to mark the importance of the event to the national cause. The OND encouraged shop owners to decorate store windows by holding a citywide competition for the best storefront display involving a grape theme.[21] With the promise of medals and certificates as rewards, the OND offered incentives to help augment the visibility of the Grape Festival in Rome. The city also festooned the streets with ephemeral grape decorations, especially along the parade route of the floats. Grape vines – actual and facsimile – draped the balconies and facades of buildings along the way. A L'Unione Cinematografica Educativa (LUCE) newsreel from 1933 panned across a street and zoomed in on balloons tied together to form an arch with a grape cluster hanging from it.[22] While Rome appeared unmistakably metropolitan, the OND used these ephemeral elements to bring, however fleetingly, the feel of the countryside into the city centre.

Further enriching this temporary urban network were the kiosks that the OND set up in various piazzas across Rome. In addition to the ten stalls at Piazza di Siena in Villa Borghese, the OND entrusted the city's major piazzas to individual towns to sell their own grape products. In 1931, for example, Piazza Navona was assigned to Frascati and Marino, Piazza Esedra to Velletri, Piazza della Chiesa Nuova to Ariccia, Piazza Fiume to Albano, Piazza Cavour to the Società Bonifica Maccarese and so forth.[23] Allowing Latian towns to claim Roman piazzas as their own was a strategic way of addressing the utility of particular regions in service of the State. Like the concept of regionalism for nationalism, the Grape Festival in Rome represented the idea of municipalism for regionalism, whereby local uniqueness was highlighted to demonstrate the diversity and richness that made up the collective. During the Grape Festival, the OND effectively transformed Rome into a microcosmic metaphor for the region of Latium, which also stood in for the nation of Italy as a whole.

Other elements of the Grape Festival's temporary network were less conspicuously on display for the spectacle consumers but nonetheless contributed to the celebration's urban diffusion. An example was Rome's wholesale market, the *mercati generali*, which received, stocked and distributed all grapes to be sold and exhibited in the city (Figure 14.2). This newly built complex located in the industrial Ostiense neighbourhood was not a venue for the public's direct participation in the celebration, but the press rigorously documented it and emphasized its centrality to the Grape Festival. Photographs of important fascist officials inspecting cartons of grapes stacked neatly under vine-covered pavilions appeared in newspapers year after year. For the first Grape Festival in 1930, *Il Popolo di Roma* featured two photographs of the wholesale market side by side: on the left was an image of the fruit crates and the fascist youth *balilla* organizing them, and on the right was a photograph of Marescalchi and Rome's governor, Francesco Boncompagni Ludovisi, eating clusters of grapes.[24] The press had made clear

FIGURE 14.2 *Preparations for the Grape Festival at the wholesale market, 1930. Photo courtesy of Archivio LUCE.*

that the market was indispensable to the Grape Festival, and indeed, it was integral to the event and regime politics.

Despite its location on the periphery of Rome, the wholesale market was symbolically important to the Grape Festival, the city and the nation. Its function as a distribution centre for the Grape Festival was representative of the kind of centralization that the fascist regime attempted to achieve in Rome, capital of the Latium region and of Italy. All grapes from the Latian towns for the festival had to come to the wholesale market first to be collectively examined and stored, as well as displayed for the media. This created a process of gathering the different grapes in the region in one central location in Rome, then reintroducing them into the different piazzas and exhibitions as specialties particular to individual towns. This practice at the wholesale market exposed the intricacies of the municipal–regional– national relationship at work during the Grape Festival. By centralizing the handling of the grape stock, the OND was also able to keep careful records of how much grape was consumed, which provided a measure of success for the event. Even though it was not a principal celebration site, the wholesale market was nonetheless an essential part of the Grape Festival's diffused urban network.

Pastoral cosmopolitanism: Simulacrum and allegories at the Villa Borghese

On the opposite side of Rome from the wholesale market, the OND staged large-scale events at Villa Borghese, a pseudo-natural environment where floats convened for public display and competed for prizes. To create a fleeting simulacrum of the country in the city, the OND used an exaggerated imbrication of Roman, Italian, local and national narratives to further the regime's *ruralesimo* (ruralism) and alimentary autarchy campaigns.[25] Elaborate floats with costumed participants illustrated metaphors of Roman mythology, the importance of folklore, the strength of regionalism for nationalism, the unbridled promotion of fascist achievements, the nation's agricultural goals and an idealization of country living.

The way in which the regime legitimized its selection of Villa Borghese as a venue for the Grape Festival was another example of its masterful construction of a fascist historical narrative. Even though Villa Borghese was a central site for the well-known harvest festivals called the *ottobrate* in eighteenth- and nineteenth-century Rome, fascist organizers disregarded this direct and historically recent lineage. The Borghese gardens, as writers and artists represented, featured prominently in the autumnal harvest, when the prince would open the grounds to the public as a gesture of his magnanimity and paternalistic good will in the hopes of strengthening fealty. The historical proximity and similarity of the festivities at the Borghese *ottobrate* were the most obvious antecedents to the fascist Grape Festival, but the regime elected to ignore this connection. The chosen fascist historical narrative focused instead on allusions to ancient Roman history and pagan rituals by highlighting the '*gioiosa bellezza*' of the fecund Italian land that had sustained its people for millennia.[26]

The regime's ardent interest in *romanità* provided one explanation as to why it telescoped to antiquity and gave less emphasis to, or altogether ignored, the in-between periods to simplify the story and to fortify the chosen historical link. Its blatant disregard for the *ottobrate* history could also be attributed to the ways in which writers and artists depicted them. In many of the genre paintings of the *ottobrate*, for example, artists illustrated scenes of debauchery and bacchanalia.[27] While the regime glorified the figure of Bacchus and used him liberally as one of the symbols of the Grape Festival, it condemned excessive drinking and the indulgent behaviours often represented in the paintings of the *ottobrate*. The regime's description of ancient Romans and their relationship with grapes, on the other hand, centred on their healthy ingestion of the fruit and moderate imbibing habits; practices informed by their knowledge of the grape's salutary properties.

FIGURE 14.3 *A float featuring the head of Bacchus during the parade at Piazza di Siena in Villa Borghese, 1936. Photo courtesy of Archivio LUCE.*

The denial of the *ottobrate* tradition at the Villa Borghese was representative of Fascism's overall approach to the Grape Festival, whereby it manipulated history and memory in order to suppress what it deemed problematic and to activate the constructive. Edward Said points out that 'memory is not necessarily authentic, but rather useful' to the creation of a national narrative and a unified identity.[28] This observation rings particularly true to the OND's Grape Festival as it represented an array of the regime's key political agendas. The 'useful memory' was manifested ostensibly via the convoluted displays on the floats that paraded first in Villa Borghese and then through the streets of Rome. History of the ancient civilizations on the Italian peninsula enriched with Roman myths, and regional folklores combined with the idealization of country life, all mixed indiscriminately in the service of contemporary politics (Figure 14.3).

The floats on exhibit within the bucolic settings of the Villa Borghese were the perfect props for OND's mission of education through entertainment. They offered yet another opportunity to express the fascist concept of localism and regionalism for nationalism, as individual municipalities perpetuated the idea of distinct cultures coming together in the regional capital to celebrate a national holiday. Therefore, the OND wanted, as a 1931 article in *Il Messaggero* stated, 'more than just an exhibition of colorful floats and costumes, but rather, lessons on the past to inform the present – to convey a certainty for the future of our agriculture, the greatest wealth of Italy'.[29] The newspaper continued to describe the best 'symbolic floats', as they were called, organized by the Società Bonifica Maccarese (Land Reclamation Society of Maccarese).[30] The society presented a highly allegorical group of floats that recounted the birth of Maccarese, which was a small part of an ambitiously large land reclamation project throughout Italy under Fascism.[31] The Maccarese floats, 'to which the jury rightfully assigned the first prize', told a story not only of significance to local history but also of great national importance as it was an integral part of the fascist history that the regime was aggressively making.[32] The presentation of the floats and the media attention on them were deeply political: they were tools for the regime to boast its achievements of the *bonifiche*, or reclamation projects, especially in the Pontine Marshes, an area south of Rome in the Latium region.

The Grape Festival was, in many ways, conceived as a tremendous opportunity for the regime to showcase its agricultural feats and to propagandize the virtues of ruralism. Another newspaper article from 1932 highlighted the first grapes grown in the *Agro Pontino*, formerly marshlands, that were exhibited at Piazza di Siena at the Grape Festival. 'This year, for the first time', the article read, 'marvelous grape clusters, products of the redeemed land of the Agro Pontino, have appeared'. Undersecretary Marescalchi, being so struck by the beauty of these grapes grown on fascist soil, demanded to meet the farmer. Upon learning that the grape did not have a name yet, Marescalchi suggested to call it '*l'uva littoria*', after the fascist new town founded in June 1932.[33] Like the Maccarese floats, the *uva littoria* brought the Latian countryside into the city of Rome, connecting fascist earth with the fascist regional and national capital. The spotlight on the land reclamation projects during the Grape Festival affirmed the regime's worship of mother earth (*terra madre*) as part of the larger fascist adulation of the fatherland (*Patria*) that was intended to eclipse the devotion to Christianity.

Urban spectacle: Processions and the fascist religion in the city

Amidst the panoply of allegories and symbols on the Grape Festival floats at the Villa Borghese, references to Christianity, however, were largely absent. Whereas many traditional festivals reprised by the OND were based on religious celebrations of saint's days, holy processions or relics, the fascist Grape Festival was devoid of Christian connections. The OND's national Grape Festival made references only to Roman deities and pagan rituals in order to further suggest that the contemporary Grape Festival derived from ancient traditions. Floats with Bacchus figures and participants in Roman costumes circled the Piazza di Siena arena in Villa Borghese before parading into the streets of Rome.

Fascism's intentional disregard of Christianity in the Grape Festival was not ambivalence towards it, but rather an indication of its contentious relationship with the Catholic Church. Many aspects of the Grape Festival demonstrated an affront to the Church's authority, as both Mussolini's government and the Vatican vied for the power of influence in Rome. A major point of contention was Fascism's expropriation of the Church's ritual time, which seriously attenuated the temporal control that the latter had on Romans. The regime planned for the Grape Festival to take place on Sunday, a direct challenge to the Church's mandate of attending mass and observing the day of rest. The regime also approved of stores – general merchandise, food and clothing – to be open on the day of the Grape Festival, even encouraging this practice by holding contests for the best storefronts and window displays decorated with grapes.[34] To create an all-immersive atmosphere for the Grape Festival in the city that aggrandized fascist politics and achievements, it was necessary to render invisible the Church's influence especially as many traditional Italian festivals had Christian origins. While direct references to Christianity were absent on the floats, the Grape Festival parades nonetheless resembled religious processions. The pageantry, in this case, paid tribute not to Christianity but to the 'fascist civic religion'.[35]

Coursing through the festooned streets were floats emblazoned with politically self-referential signs that commanded the attention and demanded the reverence of the crowds. Photographs by the Istituto LUCE, commissioned by the regime, featured floats replete with OND and fascist symbols marching through congested streets thronged with spectators.[36] Slogans and titles, such as 'DUX' and 'OND', adorned the floats, as well as giant fasces entirely draped in grape clusters (Figure 14.4). These larger-than-life representations rendered the Grape Festival unmistakably fascist, and they elicited from the citizens the kind of devotion traditionally reserved for religious rites. As Herbert W. Schneider and Shepard B. Clough suggested in their 1929 sociological study, the fascist regime invented itself as the centre of a neo-pagan religion through imitations of pre-Christian festivals and rituals.[37]

The use of Rome's urban landscape by the Grape Festival further revealed the mounting conflict between the fascist regime and the Vatican in the 1930s, which was especially visible in the planning of the parade route. During the first three years of the event (1930–32), the floats marched down the Via del Corso, the primary route for religious and Carnival processions in preceding centuries. Known simply as *Il Corso*, this thoroughfare had served as the city's main parade route since the fifteenth century. During

Una suggestiva scena della Festa dell' Uva, svoltasi per volere del Duce, il 28 settembre, in tutte le città d'Italia.

FIGURE 14.4 *A float with giant fasces draped in grapes featured on the cover of* Gente Nostra, *5 October 1930.*

the fascist period, military and political manifestations often marched on the Corso, beginning or ending at Piazza Venezia, where Mussolini's office was located in front of a large gathering place for rallies. It seemed logical, then, that the Grape Festival also paraded the floats from Villa Borghese through the Via del Corso before finally dissolving them in Piazza Venezia.[38] This route allowed the floats to travel down some of the busiest parts of the city centre, and it also brought the crowd right into the heart of fascist excavations of Roman ruins, including that of Trajan's Market, a major site for the Grape Festival.

Starting from 1933, however, the floats took an entirely different route after they left Villa Borghese and went towards the Vatican. The parade began by heading down Via Ferdinando di Savoia, crossing the Ponte Margherita to Piazza della Libertà and then moving down Via Cola di Rienzo before finally ending in Piazza del Risorgimento adjacent to Vatican City for the award ceremony.[39] Neither official correspondence nor the press addressed this radical route change, but contemporary news events pointed to mounting discords between the Church and State that may have prompted the organizers to bring the Grape Festival close to the Vatican Walls as symbolic challenge of religious authority in Rome.

A major crisis culminated in 1931 following hostile encounters between the fascist blackshirts and Catholic Action constituents, necessitating the involvement of Mussolini and Pope Pius XI. The Pope issued the encyclical *Non abbiamo bisogno* ('We do not need') that condemned the belligerence of Mussolini's regime and Fascism's cultivation of 'a real pagan worship of the State'.[40] The Vatican and the fascist regime eventually signed the reconciliatory September Accords of 1931, and Mussolini made an official visit to Pius XI in February 1932, but tensions continued to lurk beneath superficial harmony.[41] The Grape Festival was an example of Fascism's implicit antagonism to Catholicism, as it constituted precisely the kind of paganism that the Pope denounced. Its emulation of ancient Roman rites, veneration of the *terra madre*, aggrandizement of the state and the complete disregard of the grape's symbolism in the Christian Eucharist all contributed to establishing an unmistakably fascist event. Seemingly an innocuous celebration of an Italian fruit, the Grape Festival was in reality a challenge to the Church's influence. As its parade route changed in 1933 to head towards the Vatican and to adjourn right outside its walls, the Grape Festival was a nonviolent, but by no means passive, confrontation with the Church.

One of the ways in which the OND and the regime fashioned an authentically fascist image of the Grape Festival was through the visual documentation of the event that not only reinforced the political self but also erased traces of Christianity. The Istituto LUCE, charged by the regime with the task of photographing the Grape Festival, documented the new route more abundantly than it did the previous processions. Many photographs were taken on the Via Cola di Rienzo, a principal avenue that connected the Piazza del Popolo and the Vatican. In the aerial views of the street, however, the Vatican remained invisible to the viewer. Instead, these carefully composed images featured floats with fascist symbols passing in front of the Mercato dell'Unità, a covered neighbourhood market constructed during the Fascist Era in 1928

FIGURE 14.5 *Floats passing in front of the Mercato dell'Unità towards the Vatican, 1933. Photo courtesy of Archivio LUCE.*

(Figure 14.5). Capitalizing on the market building typology to construct a food-centric narrative for the Grape Festival, the fascists replaced the imposing Saint Peter's Basilica with the Mercato dell'Unità in the photographic representations of the neighbourhood immediately surrounding the Vatican. The exclusion of the Church's presence in these visual documents – commissioned by the regime and published widely in newspapers and official periodicals – was a proclamation that the Grape Festival and the city of Rome were both unquestionably fascist, and thus, to be understood as authentically Italian.

Enterprising archaeology: *Romanità* and commercialism at Trajan's market

While the OND organized the majority of events for the Grape Festival – celebrations at Villa Borghese, parades through the city and grape kiosks in the piazzas – the Merchants' Federation of Rome managed the activities at Trajan's Market. In this structure dating to the second century AD, the Merchants' Federation organized the selling of the autarchic fruit through the clever interweaving of history, education and commercialism for the economic success of the nation. The organizers deliberately chose this ancient site as a venue for the Grape Festival because it was recently excavated in 1928 and restored to its assumed Roman configuration. Under the direction of the archaeologist Corrado Ricci, the structure was rebuilt to resemble a shopping complex, the function that regime officials believed it served in antiquity.[42] Employing the fascist concept of *romanità*, the Merchants' Federation transformed the reconstructed ruin into an ideal setting for the Grape Festival, exploiting, in particular, its supposed history of commerce. Once again, the fascists deployed the rhetoric of historical continuity, from ancient to fascist Rome, to build a conceit of authenticity that would sell both the event and the product.

The selection of Trajan's Market as a main celebration site for the national Grape Festival in Rome was also linked to the larger urban transformations in its immediate surrounding. The area of the imperial forums was of great historical and political significance to the regime, as Mussolini sought to solidify his link to Augustus and the Roman Empire through archaeological propaganda. Workers began to perform *sventramento*, the 'disembowelment', in 1925 to liberate the ancient ruins from what the fascists considered to be the undesirable contexts that had obstructed their glory for many centuries. To achieve this, the regime eradicated entire neighbourhoods and displaced thousands of inhabitants. This massive undertaking was to create a principal avenue, the thirty-metre-wide Via dell'Impero, that would connect the Colosseum to Piazza Venezia and be flanked by the newly exposed Roman ruins-turned-monuments on both sides. Despite the fact that work along the Via dell'Impero had not concluded by the inauguration of the first national Grape Festival in 1930, the regime had nonetheless selected Trajan's Market as a venue. Undoubtedly, this decision was to make visible, through the food celebration, both the Roman structure and the regime's urban planning initiatives around it.

Trajan's Market hosted the *Mostra dell'uva*, or Grape Exhibition, that educated the public on the cultural, moral, nutritional and economic values that the regime attributed to the fruit. The exhibit showcased local grape varieties and viniculture by highlighting the regime's numerous efforts in advancing grape production. However, the displays made clear the distinction between the *uve da tavola* (table grapes) and the *uve da vino* (wine grapes), as fascist propaganda cautioned against the dangers of alcoholism and encouraged instead the purchasing and consumption of table grapes.[43]

Indeed, the Grape Festival had everything to do with the commercialism of grapes. In Marescalchi's original letter to Mussolini, he suggested a Day of Grapes primarily to stimulate the sell of the fruit in excess. Citing the exact amount of grapes sold in regional centres where such a local celebration was held previously, Marescalchi persuaded Mussolini that a national festival would boost the sales of the fruit.[44] Marescalchi also saw an opportunity in the

Grape Festival to revive failing artisanal practices throughout the country. He noted that presentation of the fruit would be important to attract buyers, thus he proposed to commission the wicker artisans of the Piave River region – who he claimed were in need of financial assistance – to make the baskets.[45]

The Merchants' Federation promptly engaged the Piave basket makers for the first Grape Festival in its effort to demonstrate the inextricable link between artisanal craft, folklore and commerce. The artisans made 'rustic looking baskets decorated with the town colors that reflected the origins of the grapes'.[46] Buyers could only acquire the baskets if they purchased the larger two-kilogram size, since half- and one-kilogram packages were sold only in paper. To ascertain that the Grape Festival was an unmistakably fascist event, the paper bags and basket linings were stamped with a logo of the *puttino vendemmiatore*, a grape-picking putto, surrounded by a fasces on each side. In the days leading up to the Grape Festival, newspapers reprinted the design by the artist Giovanni Duprè, a drawing approved by Minister Acerbo and Undersecretary Marescalchi, to build anticipation for the event and legitimize the commercialism of the fruit.[47] Tricolour ribbons representing the Italian flag also embellished the baskets and bags, reminding buyers that their grape purchase was a show of support for the national cause. Taking this even further, the organizers devised a way of distinguishing those who bought grapes by adding a vine leaf to the packages, so the buyers could thread it through a buttonhole or wear it with a pin as 'proof of having contributed to the Festival'.[48] The Merchants' Federation thus engineered the acquisition of grapes to be a consummate act of patriotism: not only did the buyer intend on eating a healthy Italian fruit; he or she also supported traditional craft, made a contribution to the economy and participated actively in a folkloric festival. These were all causes that the regime actively supported and promoted through its various organizations, especially the OND.

Further enhancing the selling of grapes during the Grape Festival was the resourceful combination of commercialism and *romanità* at Trajan's Market with the use of tableaux vivants. The architectural setting, as stated, was chosen specifically to provide an atmosphere that suggested the derivation of the contemporary folkloric celebration from a 'delightfully imperial rite'.[49] To render the environment even more convincing, as the press reported, 'some of the exhibitors had the idea of putting on Roman costumes to better harmonize the exhibition with the building'.[50] Newspapers and regime-published journals were replete with photographs of vendors dressed in Roman tunics and stoles in the *tabernae*, shops reconstructed by the fascists, at Trajan's Market. Photographs published in newspapers showed tableaux of vendors wearing Roman costumes holding grape clusters. In one instance, the subjects were framed by the entrance of a *taberna*, and in another, costumed vendors were featured on a terrace of Trajan's Market (Figure 14.6).[51]

FIGURE 14.6 *Vendors on the terrace of Trajan's Market. Photo from* Il Tevere, *29 September 1930.*

The Classical-themed tableaux at Trajan's Market intermixed with folkloric scenes to promote the selling of grapes and to underscore an authentically Italian experience fortified by the bonds of history and local culture. Next to the above-mentioned photograph of the *taberna* in *La Tribuna*, a photograph showed Minister Acerbo and other festival organizers posing solemnly amidst a group of young women dressed in regional costumes. This scene presented the other narrative of the Grape Festival, one that focused on Italian traditional culture rather than on the Roman historical connections. Both accounts served the Grape Festival's goals, and the organizers used both strategies repeatedly to sell the event through constructed tropes.

At Trajan's Market, the Merchants' Federation also organized a film projection to reinforce the authenticity of Italian grapes as it related to the Italian land and the fascist celebration of the Grape Festival. According to contemporary newspapers, the Istituto LUCE produced documentary clips illustrating peasant life and grape harvests throughout Italy to be shown inside the ruins.[52] These vignettes served as testimony of the authenticity of the Italian grapes as they were planted, tended and harvested by Italian farmers on Italian soil. The role of the Istituto LUCE at Trajan's Market was thus doubly important to the fascist mission: it not only had the task of documenting the Grape Festival celebrations; it also had to present the regime's propagandistic message unobtrusively and as part of the exhibition to the attendees. Indeed, Mussolini envisioned film to be both a cultural and political agency in mass indoctrination, and he even proclaimed that cinema was '*l'arma più forte*' (the most powerful weapon) of the state's *bonifica* campaigns.[53] While festival-goers watched the propagandistic clips at Trajan's Market, they themselves were being filmed by LUCE as part of future newsreels that would boast the success of the fascist Grape Festival. These were likely to be shown in movie theatres prior to feature films.

One of these film assemblages from the first Grape Festival in 1930, for example, demonstrated the careful framing and splicing of clips that the Istituto LUCE crafted to convey a fascist narrative.[54] The three-part film opened with a scene at the wholesale market with cartons of grapes neatly stacked by the fascist *balilla*. While merchants weighed the grapes, fascist officials arrived to examine the stock and to sample the fruit. The second part cut to a scene at a retail kiosk richly decorated with grape clusters and vines under a glass pavilion; the scene ended swiftly with the crowd purchasing bags of grapes. The final, and longest, part of the film showed the 'exhibit and selling of table grapes to the public' at Trajan's Market, and it underlined the immense size of this ancient structure. What followed were a series of views inside Trajan's Market and the Grape Festival activities. While depicting the structure's interior, the camera strategically framed views of the surrounding monuments through the building's openings. These included the Roman forums and the Altar of the Fatherland, a clear emphasis on national instead of religious worship.[55] Tracking shots featuring the architecture of Trajan's Market adorned with Grape Festival decorations preceded close-ups of tableaux vivants of actors in Roman costumes eating grapes in the *tabernae*. The camera then cut to fascist officials surrounded by women in regional costumes carrying baskets of grapes, and it zoomed out again to end with an aerial view of the busy venue.

Conclusion

The deliberate framing and portrayal of the Grape Festival in contemporary media underscored the regime's painstaking efforts to utilize the invented tradition to construct a narrative and history that wove together many aspects of Fascism, ranging from its agricultural policies to urban planning initiatives in Rome. The fascists did not seek to create an account that was unilinear or historically veracious, but rather, authentic, in the sense that the Grape Festival would serve as a rhetorical tool for conveying what was supposed to be genuinely Italian. The staged authenticity was intended for national, and especially local, consumption, and not for foreign or touristic purposes. The regime aimed to achieve two main goals with the theatrical displays performed throughout the city: (1) to improve the commercialism of Italian agricultural economy, and (2) to foster a sense of nationalism through regionalism. These goals were successfully executed through the regime's inventive integration of selective history into Rome's architecture and urban landscape.

The Grape Festival was paradigmatic of Fascism's reinvention of a tradition as it deployed folklores and rituals to accentuate the uniqueness of regional customs to strengthen national cohesion. While there were nineteenth-century precedents to this model of nationalism, Fascism institutionalized the practice in Italy by making a distinction between the political and spiritual values of regionalism. The fascist reinvention of festivals and folklores was not the fantastical designs of nostalgic officials or the tourism board, but rather, the plans of enterprising bureaucrats who understood the many ways to capitalize on grapes for the national economy and the consensus-building process. The embrace of popular traditions was a strategic way of assimilating the lower social classes into the State, especially as Fascism saw the potential of political influence on the peasant masses in the *Mezzogiorno*.[56] The Grape Festival created a temporary semblance of egalitarianism, while in reality, its rituals and symbols further subjugated the individual to the dominating structure. Yet, the regime's careful orchestration of the Grape Festival should not be considered entirely hegemonic, since many people participated without necessarily subscribing to its political symbolism. It was clear, however, that the Grape Festival made tangible the authority of the fascist regime and emphatically not that of the Catholic Church.

The tensions between the Church and State most visibly manifested through the Grape Festival's engagement with Rome's physical space. By selecting Trajan's Market and the wholesale market as venues, the organizers devised a continuous history between ancient and fascist Rome. The use of Villa Borghese further reinforced the values that the regime placed on its ruralism project. In all of these narratives, Fascism aimed to render the Church invisible by redirecting religious worship to the State. The 1933 change in the parade route from the Via del Corso towards the Vatican was representative of Fascism's explicit challenge to the Church following violent confrontations. Contemporary media outlets – many of which were controlled by the State – recorded floats emblazoned with fascist symbols marching down Via Cola di Rienzo against a backdrop that featured fascist accomplishments in architecture and urbanism. State-commissioned photographers turned their backs to the Church and avoided giving viewers even a glimpse of the recognizable dome of Saint Peter's Basilica in the distance.

The Grape Festival's spatial engagement with Rome continued to change as Italian politics evolved in the 1930s. After Italy's invasion of Ethiopia in 1935, the float decorations began to incorporate elements that reflected Fascism's

FIGURE 14.7 *The Maccarese float, 1936. Photo courtesy of Archivio LUCE.*

colonial ambitions. The 1936 Grape Festival took place just months after Mussolini declared an Italian Empire on 9 May 1936 and made direct references to Italy's military campaigns in Africa. The Maccarese float, for example, was composed of a fasces and disembodied African heads made of paper mache that resembled grapes (Figure 14.7). The organizers also added the 'recently liberated' Basilica of Maxentius as a venue, where a stone tablet map showing Fascism's new empire was to be mounted on 28 October 1936.[57]

The Grape Festival in Rome continued until 1942, when the Second World War severely hampered the staging of the celebrations in the city. However, various forms of grape harvest events still take place in smaller towns throughout Italy today. Many of them, like Marino, Greve, Impruneta, Lu and Cupramontana, had a long tradition of celebrating the grape harvest even before the fascist institution of the national Grape Festival, due to the centrality of oenology to the local economy.[58] Yet, while there is no longer a large-scale national Grape Festival, these provincial celebrations borrow elements from the fascist reinvention of a tradition and perpetuate the historical narratives and myths developed in the 1930s. This practice is consistent with other popular 'historical' events in Italy today, like the Sienese *palio*, which the fascist regime made quintessentially Italian by relying on, and not a rejection of, regional distinctiveness. In the case of the Grape Festival in Rome, the fascists constructed an authenticity rooted in *romanità* by aggrandizing the city's Roman past in the service of *italianità*.

The specificity of place – that of Rome – was rendered palpable by the Grape Festival's physical movement through the fascist urban landscape and the requisite stops at a constellation of meaningful sites. The Grape Festival's ephemeral engagement with the city therefore facilitated the weaving together of an inventive, but authentic, fascist narrative of history.

Notes

1 Other examples of fascist public ritual celebrations are numerous and include those for the March on Rome, cult of motherhood and the 'Day of Faith' whereby Mussolini asked Italian housewives to donate their wedding rings to the state. For a presentation and analysis of some of these rituals, see Mabel Berezin, 'The Festival State: Celebration and Commemoration in Fascist Italy', *Journal of Modern European History* 4.1 (March 2006): 60–74.

2 Emilio Gentile, *The Struggle for Modernity: Nationalism, Futurism, and Fascism* (Westport, CT: Praeger, 2003), 120. See also Emilio Gentile, *The Sacralization of Politics in Fascist Italy*, trans. Keith Botsford (Cambridge, MA and London: Harvard University Press, 1996).

3 The Italian term *ventennio* refers to the approximately twenty years of fascist governance, beginning on 30 October 1922, when Mussolini assumed power, and ending on 25 July 1943.

4 Archivio Centrale dello Stato (ACS), Presidenza del Consiglio dei Ministri (PCM), 1930, *busta* 14/2, *fascicolo* 11898: 'Appunto per S.E. il Capo del governo' from il Sottosegretario di stato per l'agricoltura e per le foreste Marescalchi to il Capo del governo Mussolini, 22 July 1930.

5 On the controversy surrounding the use of 'folklore' in the Italian language and the various decrees issued by the fascist government regarding this, see: William E. Simeone, 'Fascists and Folklorists in Italy', *The Journal of American Folklore* 91.359 (January–March 1978): 551.

6 *Italianità*, or Italianness, is the spirit that Fascism aimed to achieve after Unification, and especially during the *ventennio*, to establish a national identity.

7 See Stefano Cavazza, *Piccole patrie: Feste popolari tra regione e nazione durante il fascismo* (Bologna: Il Mulino, 1997) and Stefano Cavazza, 'Tradizione regionale e riesumazioni demologiche durante il fascismo', *Studi Storici*, 34.2/3 *Storia russa e storia sovietica nella 'perestrojka'* (April–September 1993): 625–655.

8 Joshua Arthurs, *Excavating Modernity: The Roman Past in Fascist Italy* (Ithaca and London: Cornell University Press, 2012), 2.

9 Diane Ghirardo, 'City and Theater: The Rhetoric of Fascist Architecture', *Stanford Italian Review* 8.1–2 (1989): 184, and D. Medina Lasansky, 'Urban Editing, Historic Preservation, and Political Rhetoric: The Fascist Redesign of San Gimignano', *Journal of the Society of Architectural Historians* 63, 3 (September 2004): 347.

10 Stefano Cavazza, 'Regionalism in Italy: A Critique', in *Region and State in Nineteenth-Century Europe: Nation-Building, Regional Identities and*

Separatism, eds. Joost Augusteijn and Eric Storm (Houndmills, Basingstoke, Hampshire, UK: Palgrave Macmillan, 2012), 83.

11 The phrase 'imagined community' is a concept presented by Benedict Anderson in his book *Imagined Communities: Reflections on the Origin and the Spread of Nationalism* (London and New York: Verso, 1983). He believes that a nation is actually a socially constructed community rather than an actual community based on physical togetherness.

12 On the concept of 'invented traditions', see Eric Hobsbawm, 'Introduction: Inventing Traditions', in *The Invention of Tradition*, eds. Eric Hobsbawm and Terence Ranger (Cambridge and New York: Cambridge University Press, 1983), 1–14.

13 Ibid., 1.

14 ACS, PCM, 1930, *busta* 14/2: 'Appunto per S.E. il Capo del governo' from Presidenza del consiglio dei ministri to il Capo del governo Mussolini, August 1930.

15 The fascist regime had a tradition of solipsistic time-marking. The official fascist calendar began in October 1922 after the March on Rome, which marked the first year of the *Era Fascista* (usually abbreviated as E.F., followed by the Roman numeral of the year). The regime designated 1930 as the first year of the Grape Festival and counted subsequent years as the second, third and so on, even though some Italian towns had pre-existing grape harvest celebrations.

16 Ruth Ben-Ghiat, *Fascist Modernities: Italy, 1922–1945* (Berkeley and Los Angeles: University of California Press, 2001), 4.

17 For examples of fascist reimagining, see D. Medina Lasansky, *The Renaissance Perfected: Architecture, Spectacle, and Tourism in Fascist Italy* (University Park, PA: Pennsylvania State University Press, 2004), 63–73; D. Medina Lasansky, 'Tableau and Memory: The Fascist Revival of the Medieval/Renaissance Festival in Italy', *European Legacy* 4.1 (1999), a special issue entitled *Post-Modern Fascism*, with guest editor Richard Bosworth: 26–53; and D. Medina Lasansky, 'Political Allegories: Redesigning Siena's *Palio* and Patron Saint during the Fascist Regime', in *Early Modern Visual Allegories: Embodying Meaning*, eds. Cristelle Baskins and Lisa Rosenthal (Aldershot, UK; Burlington, VT: Ashgate, 2007), 109–134.

18 See 'Preface' of the fascist propaganda pamphlet by Amy Bernardy, *Rinascita Regionale* (Rome: Tipografia del Littorio, 1930), 5.

19 'La grandiosa celebrazione della festa dell'uva in tutta Italia', *Il popolo di Roma*, Cronaca di Roma, 30 September 1930.

20 On the fascist reorganization of Rome and its treatment of archaeological ruins in the city, see, for example, Arthurs, *Excavating Modernity*; Borden W. Painter, Jr., *Mussolini's Rome: Rebuilding the Eternal City* (New York: Palgrave Macmillan, 2005); and Paul Baxa, *Roads and Ruins: The Symbolic Landscape of Fascist Rome* (Toronto: University of Toronto Press, 2010).

21 'Il pieno successo della Festa dell'uva', *Il popolo d'Italia*, 30 September 1930.

22 Istituto LUCE, *Roma: Il trionfo della festa dell'uva. Il pittoresco corteo dei carri allegorici*, Giornale LUCE B0351, 1933.

23 'Nella serena giocondità del vendemmiale', *Il Messaggero*, La II festa nazionale dell'uva, 27 September 1931.

24 The *balilla* were school-grade boys belonging to the fascist Opera Nazionale Balilla youth organization. They were very involved in the Grape Festival celebrations throughout Italy. Roma celebra oggi la festa dell'uva. Il grandioso corteo vendemmiale per le vie dell'Urbe', Il Popolo di Roma, Cronaca di Roma, 26 September 1930.

25 While Fascism's promotion of ruralism may appear contradictory to large-scale urbanism (especially in Rome), the regime actually promoted the two projects simultaneously for different social, economic and geographical contexts throughout Italy.

26 Exultations of Italian soil were plentiful in regime propaganda and contemporary newspapers. This phrase comes from the article: 'La celebrazione della Festa dell'Uva: Esposizioni nei negozi e ai Mercati Trajanei: Il grande corteo a Piazza di Siena', *Il Messaggero*, 26 September 1931.

27 Artists of the *ottobrate* genre paintings included Bartolomeo Pinelli and Antoine-Jean-Baptiste Thomas, and examples of their works are reproduced in *L'Ottobrata: Una Festa Romana*, ed. Giovanna Bonasegale (Rome: Fratelli Palombi Editori, 1990).

28 Edward Said, 'Invention, Memory, and Place', in *Landscape and Power*, 2nd edition, ed. W. J. T. Mitchell (Chicago and London: University of Chicago Press, 2002), 245.

29 'Promesse della terra feconda nella gioia dei grappoli d'oro', *Il Messaggero*, 29 September 1931.

30 Ibid.

31 The land reclamation projects in Italy, especially in the Pontine Marshes of Latium, were some of the largest architecture and urban schemes that the fascist regime endeavoured. For studies on the projects and the building of New Towns in Latium, see Diane Ghirardo, *Building New Communities: New Deal America and Fascist Italy* (Princeton: Princeton University Press, 1989); and Federico Caprotti, *Mussolini's Cities: Internal Colonialism in Italy, 1930–1939* (Youngstown, NY: Cambria Press, 2007).

32 'Promesse della terra feconda nella gioia dei grappoli d'oro'.

33 'Il corteo folkloristico a Piazza di Siena', *Il Messaggero*, Cronaca di Roma, 27 September 1932.

34 In the notes seeking Mussolini's approval of the Grape Festival, the programme stated that 'the Prefects should authorize, even in cities where a rest day is observed on Sunday, those stores that wish to remain open for the sale of grapes on the morning of 28 September'. ACS, PCM, 1930, *busta* 14/2: 'Appunto per S.E. il Capo del governo' from Presidenza del consiglio dei ministri to il Capo del governo Mussolini, August 1930. Newspaper articles, such as the 'Roma celebrerà domenica prossima la festa vendemmiale', *Il Tevere*, 25 September 1930, also stated that stores of different types would stay open on the Sunday of the Grape Festival to sell grapes. In *Il Messaggero*'s 'Promessa della terra feconda nella gioia dei grappoli d'oro', the article stated that grape exhibits in clothing stores were especially well attended. Prizes for stores with the best grape displays received gold medals and special certificates.

35 Gentile argues that Fascism borrowed its rituals from Catholicism, resulting in a new political religion. See Gentile, *The Sacralization of Politics in Fascist*

Italy. Pope Pius XI condemned Fascism's religiosity in a 1931 encyclical titled *Non abbiamo bisogno.*

36 Mussolini established the Istituto LUCE (L'Unione Cinematografica Educativa) in 1925 as the state's official newsreel and photo documentary agency.

37 Schneider and Clough give examples of fascist pagan-like festivals, including the burning of debts in October 1927. See Herbert W. Schneider and Shepard B. Clough, *Making Fascists* (Chicago: University of Chicago Press, 1929).

38 From 1930 to 1932, the floats paraded in and around Villa Borghese towards Piazza Venezia. The first parade in 1930 followed this route: Villa Borghese, Piazza del Popolo, Corso Umberto, Via del Corso, Piazza Venezia. Contemporary newspapers recounted the parade route. See, for example, 'La celebrazione della "Festa dell'Uva" nelle manifestazioni folkloristiche di ieri', *La Tribuna*, 30 September 1930.

39 'Domenica avrà luogo la IV Festa dell'uva', *Il Messaggero*, 12 October 1933.

40 The text of the encyclical *Non abbiamo bisogno* can be found in Eucardio Momigliano, ed. *Tutte le encicliche dei sommi pontefici* (Milan: Dall'Oglio, 1959). On the conflict between fascist blackshirts and Catholic Action, see, for example, John F. Pollard, *The Vatican and Italian Fascism, 1929–32: A Study in Conflict* (New York: Cambridge University Press, 1985).

41 Mussolini's visit to Pope Pius XI occurred on the third anniversary of the signing of the Lateran Pact that took place on 11 February 1929.

42 Scholars today continue to debate the function of Trajan's Market in antiquity. While many claim that the complex was devoted to food trade and government activities, others argue that it housed government offices and was not for commercial activities at all.

43 The regime made a clear distinction between moderated and excessive drinking in its propaganda on wines and grapes. For example, a pamphlet on the 1932 national Grape Festival celebrated in Matera repeatedly emphasized repeatedly the negative effects of alcoholism, citing that drunkenness 'degenerates and kills humanity with the terrible plague of alcoholism'. Guido Spera, *La festa dell'Uva – Perchè?* (Cattedra Ambulante di Agricoltura, 1932).

44 ACS, PCM, 1930, *busta* 14/2, *fascicolo* 11898: 'Appunto per S.E. il Capo del governo' from il Sottosegretario di stato per l'agricoltura e per le foreste Marescalchi to il Capo del governo Mussolini, 22 July 1930.

45 Ibid.

46 'La grandiosa celebrazione della festa dell'uva in tutta Italia'.

47 'La festa dell'uva nelle diverse forme di propaganda', *La Tribuna*, Cronaca di Roma, 20 September 1930.

48 Ibid.

49 'Roma celebrerà domani la sua Sagra vendemmiale', *Il Tevere*, 27 September 1930.

50 'La celebrazione della 'Festa dell'uva' nelle manifestazioni folkloristiche di ieri'.

51 Ibid.

52 'La celebrazione della Festa dell'uva', *Il Messaggero*, 26 September 1931.

53 Mussolini's dictum can be seen in a frame of the LUCE newsreel on the construction of the new Istituto LUCE complex from 11 November 1937. Istituto LUCE, *Mussolini visita il cantiere per la costruzione del nuovo edificio dell'Istituto Nazionale LUCE*, film, Giornale LUCE, B1199, 1937.

54 Istituto LUCE, *La giornata dell'Uva ai Mercati Traianei di Roma*, Giornale LUCE, A0664, 1930.

55 The Altare della Patria is also known as the National Monument to Victor Emmanuel II.

56 See, for example, Arrigo Serpieri, 'Il fascismo e i ceti rurali', *Gerarchia* 4.1 (January 1924), 9.

57 Originally the regime inaugurated four stone tablets depicting maps alongside the Basilica of Maxentius facing the new Via dell'Impero on 21 April 1934. The four maps provide a narrative linking the early days of the Roman Empire to its greatest territorial possession under Trajan. A fifth tablet was added following Mussolini's incursions into Africa and his declaration of an Italian Empire.

58 Some of the local grape festivals are documented in: Francesca Giovannini, *La festa dell'uva di Firenze e dell'Impruneta: Storia di una 'tradizione inventata'* (Florence: Florence Art Edizioni, 2009); Carlo Baldini, *La Festa dell'Uva a Greve in Chianti* (Sancasciano: Tipografia M.B., 1994); Michele Filippo Fontefrancesco, 'Inventare la festa: la Sagra dell'Uva di Lu', *Bollettino dell'Atlante Linguistico Italiano* III Serie, no. 32 (2008): 169–186.

Bibliography

Anderson, B. *Imagined Communities: Reflections on the Origin and the Spread of Nationalism*. London and New York: Verso, 1983.

Arthurs, J. *Excavating Modernity: The Roman Past in Fascist Italy*. Ithaca and London: Cornell University Press, 2012.

Baldini, C. *La Festa dell'Uva a Greve in Chianti*. Sancasciano: Tipografia M.B., 1994.

Baxa, P. *Roads and Ruins: The Symbolic Landscape of Fascist Rome*. Toronto: University of Toronto Press, 2010.

Ben-Ghiat, R. *Fascist Modernities: Italy, 1922–1945*. Berkeley and Los Angeles: University of California Press, 2001.

Berezin, M. 'The Festival State: Celebration and Commemoration in Fascist Italy'. *Journal of Modern European History* 4.1 (March 2006): 60–74.

Bernardy, A. *Rinascita Regionale*. Rome: Tipografia del Littorio, 1930.

Bonasegale, G., ed. *L'Ottobrata: Una Festa Romana*. Rome: Fratelli Palombi Editori, 1990.

Caprotti, F. *Mussolini's Cities: Internal Colonialism in Italy, 1930–1939*. Youngstown, NY: Cambria Press, 2007.

Cavazza, S. 'Tradizione regionale e riesumazioni demologiche durante il fascismo'. *Studi Storici* 34, no. 2/3 (April-September 1993) 625–55. *Storia russa e storia sovietica nella 'perestrojka'*.

Cavazza, S. *Piccole patrie: Feste popolari tra regione e nazione durante il fascismo*. Bologna: Il Mulino, 1997.

Cavazza, S. 'Regionalism in Italy: A Critique'. In *Region and State in Nineteenth-Century Europe: Nation-Building, Regional Identities and Separatism*, edited by Joost Augusteijn and Eric Storm, 69–89. Houndmills, Basingstoke, Hampshire, UK: Palgrave Macmillan, 2012.

Fontefrancesco, M. F. 'Inventare la festa: la Sagra dell'Uva di Lu'. *Bollettino dell'Atlante Linguistico Italiano* III Serie no. 32 (2008): 169–86.

Gentile, E. *The Sacralization of Politics in Fascist Italy.* Translated by Keith Botsford. Cambridge, MA and London: Harvard University Press, 1996.

Gentile, E. *The Struggle for Modernity: Nationalism, Futurism, and Fascism.* Westport, CT: Praeger, 2003.

Ghirardo, D. *Building New Communities: New Deal America and Fascist Italy.* Princeton: Princeton University Press, 1989.

Ghirardo, D. 'City and Theater: The Rhetoric of Fascist Architecture'. *Stanford Italian Review* 8: 1–2 (1989): 165–93.

Giovannini, F. *La festa dell'uva di Firenze e dell'Impruneta: Storia di una 'tradizione inventata'*. Florence: Florence Art Edizioni, 2009.

Hobsbawm, E. 'Introduction: Inventing Traditions'. In *The Invention of Tradition*, edited by Eric Hobsbawm, and Terence Renger, 1–14. Cambridge and New York: Cambridge University Press, 1983.

Lasansky, D. M. 'Tableau and Memory: The Fascist Revival of the Medieval/Renaissance Festival in Italy'. *European Legacy* 4.1 (1999): 26–53, a special issue entitled *Post-Modern Fascism*, with guest editor Richard Bosworth.

Lasansky, D. M. *The Renaissance Perfected: Architecture, Spectacle, and Tourism in Fascist Italy.* University Park, PA: Pennsylvania State University Press, 2004.

Lasansky, D. M. 'Urban Editing, Historic Preservation, and Political Rhetoric: The Fascist Redesign of San Gimignano'. *Journal of the Society of Architectural Historians* 63.3 (September 2004): 320–53.

Lasansky, D. M. 'Political Allegories: Redesigning Siena's *Palio* and Patron Saint during the Fascist Regime'. In *Early Modern Visual Allegories: Embodying Meaning*, edited by Cristelle Baskins and Lisa Rosenthal, 109–34. Aldershot, UK; Burlington, VT: Ashgate, 2007.

Momigliano, E., ed. *Tutte le encicliche dei sommi pontefici*. Milan: Dall'Oglio 1959.

Painter, B. W. *Mussolini's Rome: Rebuilding the Eternal City.* New York: Palgrave Macmillan, 2005.

Pollard, J. F. *The Vatican and Italian Fascism, 1929–32: A Study in Conflict.* New York: Cambridge University Press, 1985.

Said, E. 'Invention, Memory, and Place'. In *Landscape and Power*, edited by W. J. T. Mitchell. 2nd ed. Chicago and London: University of Chicago Press 2002.

Schneider, H. W. and Shepard B. Clough. *Making Fascists.* Chicago: University of Chicago Press 1929.

Serpieri, A. 'Il fascismo e i ceti rurali'. *Gerarchia* 4.1 (January 1924).

Simeone, W. E. 'Fascists and Folklorists in Italy'. *The Journal of American Folklore* 91.359 (January–March 1978): 543–57.

Spera, G. *La festa dell'Uva – Perchè?* Cattedra Ambulante di Agricoltura, 1932.

Index

Note: Locators followed by the letter 'n' refer to notes.